"Karen Swallow Prior is among the most helpful Christian literary critics writing today. In *The Evangelical Imagination*, she introduces us to the creative works and metaphors that have formed the priorities of American evangelicalism and the ways that these have malformed the movement. Her call for the reformation of evangelicalism is a call to repent, to allow new metaphors and analogies to drive us to more faithfully read and put into practice the Scriptures. Prior offers an insightful work of love that aids a holy transformation of our imaginations."

—**Tish Harrison Warren**, Anglican priest and author
of *Liturgy of the Ordinary* and *Prayer in the Night*

"*The Evangelical Imagination* is a marvelous book—thoughtful, elegantly written, literate, and timely. Karen Swallow Prior understands the essential role of the imagination in the search for truth. An evangelical herself, Prior has done a masterful job of identifying the unstated assumptions that have shaped evangelical Christianity. In doing so, she is performing a profoundly important service: separating Christ from Christian culture, including some of the most deforming aspects of Christian culture. American evangelicalism is in crisis; *The Evangelical Imagination* helps us to understand why and what needs to be done to make it an instrument of grace in a world that desperately needs it."

—**Peter Wehner**, contributing writer, the *New York Times*
and *The Atlantic*

"Karen Swallow Prior wants evangelicals to think carefully about how they think, particularly to understand how much we as evangelicals take for granted in the metaphors we use, the assumptions we make, and the conventions we follow. The book brings together the history of evangelicalism, Prior's expertise in Victorian literature, and sensitive analysis of the present moment into an indictment of the 'evangelical imagination,' but an indictment with hope because of evangelical engagement with the gospel."

—**Mark Noll**, author of *A History of Christianity
in the United States and Canada*

"Christians know that we should love the Lord with all our heart, soul, mind, and strength. But what about loving him with all our imagination? In this important new book Karen Swallow Prior argues that the imagination is a vital and neglected area of discipleship for today's church. She attacks the cultural cholesterol of ideas like improvement and sentimentality that sclerotize the evangelical imagination, and she invites us to enjoy a more healthy and biblical imaginative life. This is a crucial book for anyone who wants to bring every faculty—including the imagination—under the lordship of Christ."

—**Christopher Watkin**, Monash University;
author of *Biblical Critical Theory*

"If you think you've read everything on evangelical culture, think twice: *The Evangelical Imagination* will blow your mind! As well as encourage your heart to desire what is beautiful again. Prior's writing is sharp, substantive, and engaging. You will be quoting her to friends and sharing her insights with your family as you struggle to remember the false paradigms you used to live under. With her deep knowledge of the past three hundred years of history, literature, and philosophy, Prior unmasks our assumptions about evangelical culture and shows us both the good and the bad of our inherited social imaginary. You need this book to remind you why you love the evangelical church and to inspire you to be an active culture maker for the kingdom."

—**Jessica Hooten Wilson**, author of *The Scandal of Holiness*
and *Reading for the Love of God*

"If 'examination is an act of love,' as Karen Swallow Prior rightly asserts, then this important book is a loving examination of many of the received ideas, metaphors, and stories that evangelicals have inherited and that inform their worldview. Prior's examination of this history, this underlying imagination, in light of Scripture and the deepest truths of faith, offers contemporary Christians a chance for self-awareness, renewal, and hope. The insights offered in this book are not always comfortable, but they are just that kind of truth which the gospel promises 'will make us free,' free to move through culture to Christ, rather than letting our culture obscure or diminish him."

—**Malcolm Guite**, author of *Lifting the Veil: Imagination
and the Kingdom of God*

The Evangelical Imagination

The
Evangelical
Imagination

How Stories, Images, and Metaphors
Created a Culture in Crisis

Karen Swallow Prior

BrazosPress

a division of Baker Publishing Group
Grand Rapids, Michigan

Published by Brazos Press
a division of Baker Publishing Group
www.brazospress.com

Printed in the United States of America

Library of Congress Cataloging-in-Publication Data
Names: Prior, Karen Swallow, author.
Title: The evangelical imagination : how stories, images, and metaphors created a
    culture in crisis / Karen Swallow Prior.
Description: Grand Rapids, Michigan : Brazos Press, a division of Baker
    Publishing Group, [2023] | Includes bibliographical references.
Identifiers: LCCN 2023002055 | ISBN 9781587435751 (cloth) | ISBN
    9781493441914 (ebook) | ISBN 9781493441921 (pdf)
Subjects: LCSH: Evangelicalism—United States. | Christianity and culture—
    United States.
Classification: LCC BR1642.U5 P75 2023 | DDC 277.308/3—dc23/
    eng/20230314
LC record available at https://lccn.loc.gov/2023002055

Baker Publishing Group publications use paper produced from sustainable forestry
practices and post-consumer waste whenever possible.

23   24   25   26   27   28   29   7   6   5   4   3   2   1

To Jane Doe 2, whose courage, strength, integrity, grace, and love embody the way of Jesus

CONTENTS

INTRODUCTION

Victorians, Evangelicals, and the Invitation

Imagine, if you will, that you are in my classroom. We are studying Victorian literature, a subject I teach often, whether within the context of a general education survey class (the kind every college student is required to take) or an upper-level course filled with English majors.

The Victorian age (as well as the literature it produced) is named after Queen Victoria, who reigned in Great Britain from 1837 to 1901. The period's beginning is often marked at 1830, as this was the year the nation's first Reform Bill was introduced, setting off a series of social and political reforms that would define the age—from expansion of voting rights to increased protections for laborers. It was a heady age marked by rapid change, optimism, prosperity, and progress—all undergirded by the evangelical faith that had grown increasingly influential throughout the previous century.

In this imaginary class, we are reading a variety of literary genres, including essays, novels, poetry, and drama. We will read writers such as Alfred, Lord Tennyson, Charles Dickens, John Ruskin, George Eliot, Charlotte Brontë, Matthew

Arnold, Christina Rossetti, Gerard Manley Hopkins, Robert Louis Stevenson, Oscar Wilde, George Bernard Shaw, Rudyard Kipling, Thomas Hardy, and many others. (Some of these writers, and others, will appear in the pages that follow.)

If you are an evangelical Christian (as most of my students are), you will probably begin to notice something over the course of our study together. You will notice a pattern emerging from all this Victorian literature. You will see in both the texts and their surrounding historical contexts qualities strangely similar to many of the defining characteristics of modern American evangelical culture. And by seeing in that literature many of the values and beliefs prominent within American evangelicalism today, you might find yourself wondering whether some of the ideas that characterize today's evangelical culture are *Christian* as much as they are *Victorian*.

It is this recurring question that raised the idea for this book, one that explores the origins and continuing power of some of the primary images, metaphors, and stories of the evangelical movement that began around three hundred years ago. The Victorian period sits right in the middle of this story. Most scholars agree that evangelicals, who emerged a century before, created much of the ethos that defined the Victorian age and, as I hope to show in the pages that follow, this ethos defines much of evangelicalism today. As historian Timothy Larsen, who writes frequently on both Victorians and evangelicals, observes, "Almost all of the issues that we are wrestling with today that have salience for us the Victorians had a version of that conversation that is still ongoing."[1]

Yet, in my own context—in the classroom and out, inside the church walls and outside of them—I've found that there is not enough of this conversation happening. Instead, the religious beliefs and cultural currents that birthed the evangelical movement in the eighteenth century and manifested as political and social values in the centuries that followed exist now as unexamined assumptions swirling within the evangelical imagination.

If evangelicalism is a house, then these unexamined assumptions are its floor joists, wall studs, beams, and rafters—holding everything together but unseen, covered over by tile, paint, paper, and ceilings. What we don't see, we don't think about. Until something goes wrong and something needs replacement. Or restoration. Or reform.

> If evangelicalism is a house, then these unexamined assumptions are its floor joists, wall studs, beams, and rafters—holding everything together but unseen, covered over by tile, paint, paper, and ceilings.

The evangelical house is badly in need of repair. We must confess, with Augustine, about ourselves and our movement, "My soul's house is too meager for you to visit. It is falling down; rebuild it. Inside are things that would disgust you to see: I confess this, and I know it. But who's going to clean it?"[2]

The crisis facing American evangelicalism today—manifest in increasing division, decreasing church membership and attendance, mounting revelations of abuse and cover-up of abuse, and an ongoing reckoning with our racist past and present—is one in which the decorative layers that have long adorned the evangelical house are being peeled away. Now we can see, some of us for the first time, the foundational parts of its structure. Some of these parts are solid. Some are rotten. Some can be salvaged. Some ought not to be saved.

Many have said that what has been exposed within the evangelical movement in recent days, months, and years is apocalyptic.

It is.

The biblical meaning of the Greek word translated into English as "apocalypse" is simply an *uncovering* or *revelation*. We often associate apocalypse with the end of the world because of the vision given in the book of Revelation about future days. We also make this association because some moments of revelation in human, church, or personal history do seem like the end of the world. There are times when this particular historical moment—which has included crises in the church, the first global pandemic in a century, and deep political polarization—seems to portend the end of the world. But perhaps it's only, as the rock group R.E.M. put it, "the end of the world as we know it." And maybe that's fine.

Many truths that have been hidden are being brought to light. Many deeds that have been covered up are being uncovered. Many assumptions that have been unexamined are being brought to the surface and scrutinized in order that we may consider whether they are rooted in eternal truths or merely in human traditions. In the process, Jesus is revealing more of himself. As he said to his Father in Matthew 11:25, "You have hidden these things from the wise and learned, and revealed them to little children." It is significant that the word translated as "revealed" in this verse is the Greek word for "apocalypse."

Some of what is hidden from us is spiritual reality, divine truths that can be revealed to us only through God's divine power.

But some of what is hidden remains so because of our own limited human nature, along with our habits, practices, and traditions. Human beings and, cumulatively, human cultures develop language, stories, metaphors, images, ideas, and imaginations that shed light on some corners of reality only to cast shadows in other places. Every good story offers a slice of reality. Every true metaphor illuminates certain likenesses. Every beautiful image has a frame. Each of these reveals something but also leaves something out. We see through a glass darkly, as Paul reminds us (1 Cor. 13:12).

There is no limit to the things that fill the evangelical imagination. And there is, of course, no *one* evangelical imagination. There are dozens more subjects I could have chosen to cover in this book beyond those in the chapters that follow. And there are hundreds more examples of each of these I could have included. But these are the ones that I know—the images, metaphors, and stories that I have pondered, taught, examined, or questioned, and seen others do the same.

I must also note that I am not a historian. I am not a theologian. I am not a philosopher. I am an English professor. I am a reader and writer who cares about the way imagination shapes our world and each of us. And I am an evangelical, one who has been formed by the surrounding culture—and cultures—just like everyone else. I am not attempting in these pages to outline a historical linearity, a doctrinal critique, or any *post hoc ergo propter hoc* claims. I know that correlation is not causation. The human imagination is not so neat as any of these.

In a way, what follows in these pages is simply my testimony. It is a picture of the evangelical imagination as I have found it over the course of years of researching, studying, reading, worshiping, and living and grappling with my own imagination—what fills it and fuels it.

The stories, metaphors, and images I identify in these pages as influential within evangelical social imaginaries are not strictly evangelical, of course. Nor are they uniquely Christian. They are certainly not exhaustive. They are simply part of the larger culture that has made evangelical culture—and that evangelicalism has made—for good and ill.

As you read about the images, metaphors, and stories I have chosen to illuminate as forming part of the evangelical imagination, as you consider with me how these things have brought good and how they have been distorted or abused, I hope you will look for other ones around you. Let them be evocations. Let them invite your own examination. Examination is an act of love.[3] Look for the images, metaphors, and stories that fill your own imagination, your community's social imaginary, and your own cultural experience.

Weigh them against the eternal Word of God.

Weigh them against the truth, justice, and mercy to which he calls all his people.

Weigh them against what Dante calls "the Love which moves the sun and the other stars."[4]

I make this invitation without asking you to close your eyes or raise your hand. In fact, keep them open. Look. See. Go forward, down the aisle, to the altar. Walk in confidence that God's foundation is true, the walls of the house he has built are strong, the steeple is upright, and all the windows will allow the light to stream in, now and for all generations to come.

1

Made in His Image

Imagination, Imaginaries,
and Evangelicalisms

Many of us associate imagination with children's playtime, creative problem-solving, and hobbits.
Imagination might seem to be merely a fun but optional exercise, enjoyable but indulgent. We also tend to think of it as an individual ability or gift. "Use your imagination," we say. Or "She's really imaginative," we might observe about someone else curiously. Most of us aren't likely to think of imagination as something arising from our communal experience and exerting tremendous influence on our social lives, let alone our religious beliefs and practices. But the power of the imagination is large, pervasive, and overwhelming. Imagination entails much more than our individual fancies and visions, and its hold on us reaches far beyond the limits of our own minds. The imagination shapes us and our world more than any other human power or ability. Communities, societies, movements, and, yes, religions are formed and fueled by the power of the imagination.

Evangelicals are no exception. Now, this is not to suggest that the Holy Scriptures or confessional creeds or cloud of great witnesses are figments of our imagination. By no means. Rather, the evangelical imagination—like any imagination at the heart of any culture—has been forming a particular kind of people, and those people have been helping to form the world for hundreds of years.

> Communities, societies, movements, and, yes, religions are formed and fueled by the power of the imagination.

But what is the evangelical imagination?

First, we must consider the imagination itself. At its most literal level, the word "imagination" refers to the mind's process of making an image: the act of imaging. In this way, imagination is simple. At this level, it is also very much an individual, solitary behavior.

Yet, much surrounds this image-making activity that includes far more than an individual making an image independently in one's own mind. The images our minds make are drawn from the objects we perceive, just as the phenomena we perceive through our bodies come through the senses. As Owen Barfield explains, there's "no such thing as an unseen rainbow."[1] What we perceive depends on what makes up our surroundings. It also depends on what we are paying attention to. What we pay attention to derives from a host of experiences, associations, emotions, thoughts, practices, and habits. Do you have the habit of looking up when you walk? Then you will notice things above and around you. Or do you watch your feet to make sure you don't stumble? Then you might be more likely to spot a four-leaf clover. Do you have the habit of staring at your phone as you go through your day? Then you will notice far less of the physical things around you. Just as our dreams are filled with the things that fill our days, so too is our imagination formed by the things we perceive. Reality as we understand it is what registers. (And some of us have to see, hear, or read something half a dozen times before it registers!)

Barfield notes that we don't perceive anything solely through the sense organs but with our "whole human being," the being that makes meaning of what we perceive. He explains,

> Thus, I may say, loosely, that I "hear a thrush singing." But in strict truth all that I ever merely "hear"—all that I ever hear simply by virtue of having ears—is *sound*. When I "hear a thrush singing," I am hearing, not with my ears alone, but with all sorts of other things like mental habits, memory, imagination, feeling and (to the extent at least that the act of attention involves it) will.[2]

Metaphors Are Life

The ability of the human mind to imagine—to make images that have meaning—reflects the marvelous fact that we are made in the image of God. We are the product of his imagination in a very literal—as well as metaphorical—sense. The ability to imagine is a reminder of the one in whose image we are made. One of the greatest philosophers on the imagination, Samuel Taylor Coleridge, characterizes the imaginative act as "a repetition in the finite mind of the eternal act of creation in the infinite I AM."[3] Indeed, even the incarnation—God in the image of human flesh—is a work of God's imagination, for Christ is "the image of the invisible God" (Col. 1:15). We who are made in God's image, from his imagination, reflect our Creator's image through our acts of imagination. Imagination engages our whole humanity: physical, emotional, intellectual, and spiritual. This truth is the starting point of any right understanding of the imagination, including its role, power, and significance.

Imagination is such a simple concept in some ways. Yet our ideas about the workings and wonders of the imagination have a long and complicated history.

Like all human abilities, imagination has been idolized and debased—and held in every valuation in between. At times, imagination has been understood as merely a brain function, while at other times it has been treated as mystical or even magical. Indeed, from the creation and fall told in Genesis, to the prohibition against graven images given in the second commandment, to the myth of Prometheus, the powers associated with the imagination were in ancient times often linked to human transgressions into powers reserved for the divine. Some of this mythology about the imagination carries over into today in the way we imagine artists to be mad geniuses or especially sensitive (or even weak) souls.

Painted in the broadest strokes, the history of how we imagine imagination consists of two parts. First, imagination was understood, generally, as a mirror, then later as a lamp (this pair of metaphors being made famous by literary critic M. H. Abrams's treatment of imaginative literature in a book titled *The Mirror and the Lamp*). Imagination as a mirror is manifest in the classical tradition, where imagination and its associated activities are understood primarily in terms of imitation or mimesis. For Plato, the idealist whose ideas were and continue to be influential, imitation is by its very nature inferior at best and dangerous at worst. Plato sees imitation as but a shadow of true reality, an illusory shadow having the power to lead us away from what is real if we mistake imitation for its source.

Plato's student Aristotle, however, disagreed with his teacher and argued powerfully in *Poetics* in favor of the value of the imitative arts. Aristotle saw in imitation both the pleasure of learning and the opportunity to practice through art the habits that lead to virtue.

But a radical shift in the way we think about imagination occurred in the modern age—not coincidentally, right around the time the evangelical movement began. With the Enlightenment, imagination came under closer examination, as did other human faculties and abilities. At the height of the Enlightenment, the imagination became an object of fascination for writers and philosophers, reaching its peak in published texts coincidentally (or not) right around 1776. Even the term "imagination" rose to its highest prominence in the eighteenth century, as a search on Google's Ngram Viewer shows.[4] It might seem ironic that the age so closely linked to science, rationalism, and reason also brought the idea of imagination to the fore. But reason and imagination are by no means as opposed as they are commonly thought to be. What they share is in fact central to the ethos of human invention that is at the heart of the Enlightenment and the modern age it birthed. After all, the scientific revolution and all its discoveries were the fruit of the powers of the human mind. What the Enlightenment, the birth of the evangelical movement, and a changed understanding of the imagination share is their new emphasis on individual experience and the authority of that experience.

Beginning in the eighteenth century, the varieties of individual intellectual experience and authority became a source of fascination and study as philosophers, poets, and critics developed particular interests in nuanced categories of intellectual abilities such as wit, fancy, judgment, and imagination. Imagination began to be seen as capable of far more than mere imitation. Imagination came to be understood as a faculty responsible for invention and creativity. This view took flight in the Romantic age in the following century, and imagination has never looked the same since. Furthermore, novelty—as a phenomenon and as a value in and of itself—also gained traction in the emerging modern age (we'll explore that in greater depth in chap. 5). Thus, the imagination's ability to create and invent new (or seemingly new) things—rather than to merely imitate something already in existence—became a source of growing fascination.

As imagination became increasingly understood as a phenomenon connected to perception, it came to be conceived of more as a subjective experience (based on personal, sensory, emotional sensation) than an objective one (based on the mind's ability to replicate an object outside itself). Imagination moved from being viewed as mechanistic to organic, from intellectual to sensory—not, of course, that any of these functions are entirely separate from the other; indeed, even these terms, being metaphorical to some degree, are also imaginary.

Because perception is the ground of imagination, the new philosophical field of aesthetics, which also arose in the eighteenth century, was closely tied to emerging ideas about imagination. Aesthetics—the philosophical study of beauty—is directly connected to sensory perception and therefore to subjective, bodily experience. The word "aesthetic," which means "sensuous cognition," first appeared in 1735. At the time, it was related not only to art and beauty but to all ways in which we experience "felt cognition."[5]

> While the objective world in all its entirety exists all around us, our imagination draws only from what we perceive. And we primarily perceive what we attend to.

While the objective world in all its entirety exists all around us, our imagination draws only from what we perceive. And we primarily perceive what we attend to. Just consider the way we can hear what someone is saying while we are texting someone else on our phone but moments later have no recollection of what they said. Or think of the way we might pass the same scene every day on our commute to work yet never notice it until something out of the routine draws our attention to it. This way of understanding the relationship between the objective world and our subjective experience—which constitutes the field of philosophy called phenomenology—now informs the way we think about both aesthetic experience and the imagination.

Perceiving Is Believing

In *Imagining the Kingdom,* James K. A. Smith describes imagination as "a kind of faculty by which we navigate and make sense of our world, but in ways and on a register that flies below the radar of conscious reflection, and specifically in ways that are fundamentally aesthetic in nature."[6] Smith further explains,

> Much of our action is not the fruit of conscious deliberation; instead, much of what we do grows out of our passional orientation to the world—affected by all the ways we've been primed to perceive the world. In short, our action emerges from how we *imagine* the world. And that shaping of our character is, to a great extent, the effect of stories that have captivated us, that have sunk into our bones—stories that "picture" what we think life is about, what constitutes "the good life." We live into the stories we've absorbed; we become characters in the drama that has captivated us. Thus, much of our action is acting out a kind of script that has unconsciously captured our imaginations.[7]

In this way, Smith says, "perception is already an evaluation."[8] Again, we perceive what we pay attention to.[9] This is why Coleridge describes imagination as the "prime agent of all human perception."[10] Imagination serves as a bridge between objective and subjective human experience. We act based on what we imagine about the objective, external world, yet we also imagine based on what we perceive and receive from the world. As C. S. Lewis famously observed, "We are half-hearted creatures, fooling about with drink and sex and ambition when infinite joy is offered us, like an ignorant child who wants to go on making mud pies in a slum because he cannot imagine what is meant by the offer of a holiday at the sea. We are far too easily pleased."[11] In other words, we cannot desire what we cannot imagine. (We certainly can't name that desire, anyway.) If we are to envision an expression of the Christian faith within our culture that is as true to Christ as can be, then we must imagine beyond the realities of our culture that limit our sight.

This meaning-making function of the imagination connects it to religion. While imagination helps us make meaning, our religion (even our rejection of it) is the ultimate arbiter of all the meanings we make. In creating "images out of the chaotic influx of our sense perceptions," imagination constitutes "our fundamental mode of insertion in the world" and thus "has deep religious implications."[12] For example, we might believe as a matter of religious doctrine that all human beings are made in the image of God. But how we imagine that belief inserting itself in the world—or how we ourselves insert that belief in the world—will reflect (or perhaps not reflect) that doctrinal teaching. Thus, the "function of imagination is such that it never merely copies the world or translates perceptions; it is a constantly active and creative faculty that shapes the world we perceive and that uses our hopes, fears, and other emotions in that shaping."[13]

Human beings are, as Douglas Hedley writes in *The Iconic Imagination*, "deeply symbolic" creatures. "We are body and spirit, and the imagination is the unifying field of this duality rather than its dissolution."[14] While some think of imagination as a flight from reality, what Hedley is saying here is that imagination is the bridge between the physical and spiritual worlds. The imagination is not only "a mediating power" but no less than "the 'locus' of revelation,"[15] not only spiritual revelation but the revelation of all that is encompassed by the Logos or ultimate reality named in John 1:1. Even the logic of a correct mathematical formula, for example, has no meaning apart from what the imagination reveals to be that meaning.

Clearly, imagination is not merely making an image. The images we make are drawn from what we attend to, and what we attend to are the things that already have meaning for us—and create more meaning too. The images we make arise from and make meaning out of our lives. It is impossible, then, to separate the role that our religious belief has in directing our perceptions and meaning-making from the role our perceptions and meaning-making have in directing our theological understanding.

The Imagination and the Social Imaginary

These theological implications of the imagination are both individual and cultural.

As examined above, imagination as a reflection of God's image in all human beings is suggestive for how we treat the work of our own and others' individual imaginations. Our own individual imaginations create dreams for the future, plans for our next vacation, conjectures about the meeting our boss asked to have tomorrow, and countless works of music, poetry, and art.

Collectively, the works of our imaginations reflect and create cultures. Sculptures uphold standards of beauty. Love songs shape our views of romantic love. Movies give us images of sexual encounters that establish new norms and expectations. "Poets," as Percy Bysshe Shelley famously wrote in 1821, "are the unacknowledged legislators of the world."[16]

While the work of imagination contributes to the making of a culture, a culture in turn provides individuals with a precognitive framework—a framework that includes unconscious, unarticulated, and unstated underlying assumptions—that directs, shapes, and forms our thoughts and desires and imaginations in ways we don't necessarily recognize. Again, think of the unseen parts that form the structure of a house. Philosopher Charles Taylor calls these frameworks "social imaginaries." In his early work *Modern Social Imaginaries*, Taylor defines the social imaginary as a culture's shared pool of "images, stories, and legends" that shape one's social existence and expectations and "the deeper normative notions and images that underlie these expectations."[17] The social imaginary forms a "common understanding that enables us to carry out the collective practices that make up our social life." This "understanding is both factual and normative; that is, we have a sense of how things usually go, but this is interwoven with an idea of how they ought to go."[18] Put another way, our social imaginary is both descriptive and prescriptive. It makes a particular practice possible, and, in turn, "it is the practice that largely carries the understanding" forward.[19] Our practices, Taylor says, both reflect and maintain "self-conceptions" and "modes of understanding."[20]

A culture is composed of both the ingredients we know and recognize—material artifacts, social and political relationships and institutions, and ideas and beliefs—and the unexpressed assumptions and attitudes that make up the social imaginaries therein. The autonomy and agency that the modern age has taught us to believe in (part of our social imaginary) fools us into ignoring the fact that we are shaped by the culture in which we exist in ways that can be difficult, if not impossible, to recognize.

Nearly a century ago, Virginia Woolf perceived this problem as she wrestled with the art of representing a life through memoir and biography: "Consider what immense forces society brings to play upon each of us, how that society changes from decade to decade; and also from class to class," she wrote, pointing out the need to examine the "invisible presences" in our lives. "I see myself as a fish in a stream; deflected; held in place; but cannot describe the stream."[21]

This concept has been more recently expressed in a 2005 commencement speech given by writer David Foster Wallace:

> There are these two young fish swimming along, and they happen to meet an older fish swimming the other way, who nods at them and says, "Morning, boys. How's the water?" And the two young fish swim on for a bit, and then eventually one of them looks over at the other and goes, "What the hell is water?"[22]

Yet, human beings are not goldfish. The water we live in is language—*logos*. When the images we make from our imaginations emerge in our minds from the precognitive state, they accumulate meaning through language. Thus, while a certain distinction between image and word is helpful and important to maintain and understand, we must also consider the way in which both our individual imaginations and our social imaginaries are shaped by language. (In the beginning was the Word, after all.)

In *Metaphors We Live By*, George Lakoff and Mark Johnson make an argument similar to Charles Taylor's when they describe what they call our "conceptual system":

> The concepts that govern our thoughts are not just matters of the intellect. They also govern our everyday functioning, down to the most mundane details. Our concepts structure what we perceive, how we get around in the world, and how we relate to people. Our conceptual system thus plays a central role in defining our everyday realities.[23]

As with Taylor's social imaginary, Lakoff and Johnson explain that our conceptual system "is not something we are aware of."[24]

But one way they propose that we goldfish can see the water we are swimming in, to invoke Wallace's metaphor, is to examine language. While the most literal understanding of the imagination centers on image making, language is inseparable from the working of the human imagination. Language allows humans to make connections that exceed the merely instinctual level of a mouse and a lever or Pavlov and his dogs. This is where metaphor comes in. Lakoff and Johnson claim that "most of our ordinary conceptual system is metaphorical in nature."[25] If the word "metaphor" brings unpleasant flashbacks to college literature classes, fear not. Metaphors, though they can be rich, complicated, and profound, are also simple and part of our everyday thinking. A metaphor, simply put, is a similitude, the seeing of one thing in terms of another. "You are a mist," James 4:14 says, "that appears for a little while and then vanishes." "The LORD is my shepherd," Psalm 23:1 proclaims. We know instantly what these metaphors are saying. And we know, too, that they are not to be understood literally. Metaphors are so prevalent that it's easy, like the goldfish in the water, not to see them. "The essence of metaphor is understanding and experiencing one kind of thing in terms of another," explain Lakoff and Johnson,[26] and "metaphoric reasoning" is the means by which human beings make sense out of experience.[27] Lakoff and Johnson show that the orientational metaphors that pervade our language express the way our spatial experience grounds all experience. As they point out, we *fall* asleep, we wake *up*, we *rise* early, we *fall* ill, we take *over*, we *decline* an offer, we *incline* our hearts, we stay on *top* of the situation, we feel *down*, we cheer *up*.[28] Other categories of common metaphors used to process human experience, Lakoff and Johnson show, include containment metaphors (by which concepts are understood to be *in* or *out*), visual metaphors (*"See* what I mean?"), and entity and substance metaphors (in which abstract concepts are expressed in terms of quantity), as well as personification, metonymy, and countless other figures of speech.[29]

The Myth of the Machine

Even science—what we consider to be the most objective field of knowledge—is built on metaphors that create myths, which in turn orient our attention and shape our thinking, according to philosopher Mary Midgley in her book *The Myths We Live By.* It is important to recognize that myths are not "lies" or "detached stories." Rather, myths "are imaginative patterns, networks of powerful symbols that suggest particular ways of interpreting the world." Such symbols are "an integral part of our thought structure," Midgley explains, offering as an example the imagery and metaphors related to machinery that have determined the way science has been approached since the seventeenth century. It's notable that the English word "science" derives from a Latin root meaning "knowledge." The fact that we at some point in the development of the English language repurposed a word that once referred to *all* kinds of knowledge to designate the specific field of *scientific knowledge* demonstrates the supreme role we have given to science. As Midgley says, "The way in which we imagine the world determines what we think important in it, what we select for our attention among the welter of facts that constantly flood in upon us." Our "official, literal thoughts and descriptions" emerge out of the thought structure built by symbols and imagery, not the other way around.[30]

An everyday example of how this Enlightenment-era machine metaphor persists comes from a friend who has a daughter with Down syndrome. My friend heard someone observe that a classmate was "low-functioning" in comparison to my friend's child. This well-intentioned comment made my friend realize that talking about any person's abilities in terms of "functions" is dehumanizing because it serves "to compare them to a machine." When we use language such as "functioning" to describe human beings, my friend wrote, "we play into the dehumanizing rhetoric of modernity."[31] We treat ourselves, as Abraham Joshua Heschel writes, as if we were "created in the likeness of a machine rather than in the likeness of God."[32]

This hiddenness of the metaphorical nature of language contributes to a phenomenon that linguists call "hypocognition." Hypocognition describes experiences and concepts that have little or no representation in words (whether in a particular language or within a culture) and therefore remain under-recognized, unarticulated, and even unseen. They fly under the radar, so to speak. Hypocognition involves not only concepts that are "accepted but unexamined" but also those that obscure what is left out. In short, hypocognition refers to the "unknown unknowns."[33]

I want to pause here to emphasize this concept of hypocognition, because it is essential to this book. To examine previously unexamined assumptions is to acknowledge not only that there are things we don't know—aspects of reality yet hidden to us—but also that there are things we don't even know that we don't know.

> To examine previously unexamined assumptions is to acknowledge not only that there are things we don't know—aspects of reality yet hidden to us—but also that there are things we don't even know that we don't know.

Reality as we conceptualize it is shaped by the habits of our language, which includes the things we have words for and the things we don't have words for.[34] This is where categories and labels, so ubiquitous in the modern age and helpful in many ways, also leave out aspects of *reality* that the *terms* leave out. But this is also why the language of metaphor is so helpful: because metaphor—along with symbol, analogy, and all kinds of figurative language—points to connections and similarities without closing borders. (This is why reading literary works— which use language in figurative ways—develops the ability to see unexamined assumptions. It's similar to the way an experienced builder can spot with a glance a hidden structural flaw that has gone unnoticed by an inhabitant for years.)

Philosopher and activist Cornel West offers another description of the social imaginary, one also rooted in language. What West calls "the structure of modern discourse" consists, he writes, of "the controlling metaphors, notions, categories, and norms that shape the predominant conceptions of truth and knowledge in the modern West." He says that these elements of modern discourse "are circumscribed and determined by three historical processes: the scientific revolution, the Cartesian transformation of philosophy, and the classical revival."[35] In other words, the very things that have formed what Taylor calls "a secular age." These elements that comprise the structure of our thinking, West argues, "produce and prohibit, develop and delimit, specific conceptions of truth and knowledge, beauty and character, so that certain ideas are rendered incomprehensible and unintelligible."[36] Like a door, language, along with the structures it builds, lets some things in and leaves some things out.

What does all this have to do with the role of imagination in evangelicalism?

First, I hope to have shown—ever so briefly—just how central imagination is to all of us every day. Imagination encompasses far, far more than creative works of art or ingenious inventions, the sorts of things with which we tend to associate the term "imagination." Imagination is central to the way we think, the way we go through our days, and even the way we believe and enact those beliefs. If we think about imagination as, in its essence, the way our minds form images, it's important to recognize that the materials from which these images are made are not entirely of our own choosing. For example, I can imagine what my travel next week will be like in a way that someone living two hundred years ago could not have imagined. In addition to my cognitive thoughts about this travel will come various precognitive feelings, impressions, and (for me anyway) anxieties. (It took me a long time to realize that being sick to my stomach days before a trip was because of the trip! My body reacts in ways my mind doesn't always recognize.) We are born into communities and societies that have their own languages, practices, values, beliefs, associations, metaphors, and stories. We inherit all of these structures, and they provide molds that help to shape the way we think (and feel) about our experiences. This molding often exists without our even being aware of it—at the precognitive level. A conceptual system is like a field that has been prepared (or not) to receive and grow certain seeds. We can think of a conceptual system, or a social imaginary, as a kind of perceptual ground that has been made more fertile for some impressions and images than others. It's fruitful to reflect, too, on how the Bible prepares our perceptual ground by using language (inspired by God) in ways that invite from us heightened perception and imaginative response, preparing our perceptual ground for the reception of its truth.

Second, to be an evangelical is to inherit social imaginaries that have been developing for as long as evangelicalism has existed as a coherent movement. That movement, in turn, participates in the longer history of the modern age. Of course, I must define what I mean by "evangelical."

What Is an "Evangelical"?

As a result of the 2016 election, the term "evangelical" for many has taken on a new—and to some, unshakable—association with American politics. But the evangelical movement is much older than 2016 (it originated in the early eighteenth century), and it began, and continues, far outside the borders of America. One researcher estimated that in 2020, there were 660 million evangelicals around the world, 93 million of whom are in the United States.[37] In short, evangelicalism is a movement that is nearly three hundred years old with a global presence that dwarfs that in America.

The movement that would later be called "evangelical" began in England in the early decades of the eighteenth century.[38] It's crucial to understand that evangelicalism arose within a context of a complacent, cultural Christianity in a country in which Christianity had been for a couple of centuries the official religion, with an established state church. Within this deadened traditionalism—perhaps a replay of the dead traditionalism of the earlier church that had brought about the Reformation—some recognized the need for a spiritual awakening both within individuals and within the church. Two of the most prominent of these leaders were John Wesley (1703–1791) and George Whitefield (1714–1770), who brought about tremendous revival in England and America. Refusing to adhere to the cold traditionalism of the Church of England, warmed by what came to be called a "religion of the heart," Wesley and Whitefield took their preaching to the open air when refused by the church. Masses of people heard, and the evangelical movement was born (see fig. 1).

Because the movement, also called the Evangelical Revival, was not limited to any church or denomination (and indeed was scorned by many of them), evangelicalism was never unified or defined by particular doctrinal distinctives but rather constituted a spirit that Christians across denominations could accept or reject. (Eventually, it birthed denominations reflective of its emphases.) The most widely accepted definition of "evangelical" is given by historian David Bebbington, one accepted by the National Association of Evangelicals, and commonly called the Bebbington quadrilateral:

- Conversionism: the belief that lives need to be transformed through a "born-again" experience and a lifelong process of following Jesus
- Activism: the expression and demonstration of the gospel in missionary and social reform efforts
- Biblicism: a high regard for and obedience to the Bible as the ultimate authority
- Crucicentrism: a stress on the sacrifice of Jesus Christ on the cross as making possible the redemption of humanity[39]

These characteristics described by Bebbington apply equally to politically liberal and politically conservative Christians, to those for whom "social reform" means the abolition of the slave trade or the abolition of abortion or the death penalty.

The National Association of Evangelicals expresses these points in less technical language, often used by researchers and pollsters:

- The Bible is the highest authority for what I believe.
- It is very important for me personally to encourage non-Christians to trust Jesus Christ as their Savior.
- Jesus Christ's death on the cross is the only sacrifice that could remove the penalty of my sin.
- Only those who trust in Jesus Christ alone as their Savior receive God's free gift of eternal salvation.[40]

Because Bebbington begins his analysis of evangelicalism with its roots in Great Britain, his definition is Anglocentric in a way that is not reflective of global evangelicalism today. In the *Cambridge Companion to Evangelical Theology*, Timothy Larsen offers an alternate definition, one that better accommodates the growth of the evangelical movement around the world. Larsen defines an evangelical as:

1. an orthodox Protestant
2. who stands in the tradition of the global Christian networks arising from the eighteenth-century revival movements associated with John Wesley and George Whitefield;
3. who has a preeminent place for the Bible in her or his Christian life as the divinely inspired, final authority in matters of faith and practice;
4. who stresses reconciliation with God through the atoning work of Jesus Christ on the cross;
5. and who stresses the work of the Holy Spirit in the life of an individual to bring about conversion and an ongoing life of fellowship with God and service to God and others, including the duty of all believers to participate in the task of proclaiming the gospel to all people.[41]

Larsen argues that because some pre-Reformation figures in church history could easily fit Bebbington's definition and because evangelicalism is a distinctly Protestant movement that clearly arose from the revivals mentioned in the second point, his first characteristic needs to be part of the definition. Larsen further explains that he considers conversionism central to Bebbington's definition as part of the work of the Holy Spirit expressed in his fifth characteristic.

John Stackhouse counters these definitions by offering an interesting alternative, arguing that evangelicalism is essentially a style within larger Christianity. "Christianity in the modern era" can be seen in "three main styles: a conscientious maintenance of the past, a determined freedom toward the present and future, and a way between the two." Evangelicalism is the "third way" within Protestantism, between conservatism and liberalism. Although rooted in both tradition and the "text at the heart of that tradition," Stackhouse explains, "evangelicals feel free to appropriate the tradition selectively in terms of what they see to be the core of Christianity and then innovate as necessary in order to fulfill their mission."[42]

Of course, most people who belong to evangelical churches don't define themselves according to these academic definitions. Most laypeople aren't even aware of them, including those surveyed by pollsters outside voting booths. In general, however, these definitions, though broad, set evangelicals apart from Catholics, most traditional mainline denominations, and any traditions that elevate personal experience or revelation above Scripture. And all of these definitions form the foundation of the evangelical house, whether seen or not.

A Rose by Any Other Name

Because of the way in which the word "evangelical" has become connected with partisan politics in recent years, some are questioning whether the label has reached the end of its usefulness in the church, while others are choosing to reject the label altogether.

Writing about a recent dustup over the definition of evangelical and who might rightly (or wrongly) be described as one, one Christian historian draws on Benedict Anderson's *Imagined Communities* in observing that evangelicalism is "an imagined religious community." There are, she argues, "many evangelicalisms," and they are "imagined" in the sense that it "has always been a dynamic, fluid movement, or series of movements, imagined and maintained through networks, alliances and authority structures, each drawing and enforcing the boundaries of 'evangelicalism' for varying purposes."[43] Who or what an evangelical is differs if that question is being asked by a church historian, a pastor, a politician, a pollster, or the marketing director of a book publisher.

Of course, most labels are imaginary, as elastic as language itself. Labels are tools that are both helpful and limiting. Whether or not one goes by the label "evangelical," or whether the label goes by the wayside at some point, there still exists a group of Christians here in America and around the globe, within various denominations, who believe Christ is their personal Savior, the Bible is God's authoritative Word, Christianity can change lives, and that message is worth sharing. We have a history that cannot be rewritten. But that history can be better understood in the present as we write the future.

While there are many approaches and angles to consider in understanding that history, one that has not been examined often or closely enough is the evangelical imagination. By this, I really mean the evangelical social imaginaries, the collective pool of ideas, images, and values that have filled our books, our thoughts, our sermons, our songs, our blog posts, and our imaginations and have thereby created an evangelical culture.

American evangelicalism in particular is shaped by a social imaginary that reflects the longer history of the movement as well as more recent history. As Willie James Jennings demonstrates so thoroughly in *The Christian Imagination*, "The deeper reality of theology and theological identity" is "hidden beneath" our history.[44]

Evangelicalism, like America, is a product of the modern age, in addition to being a movement of the Spirit. It is, perhaps, a paradox that this "religion of the heart" was born from the age of reason. Indeed, it reflected the spirit of the modern age, which, like evangelicalism itself, emphasized the "new and improved," individual experience, the authority of the written word, and the promise of progress. Early in the twentieth century, the American evangelical movement gained traction as a sort of middle way that emerged between the fundamentalist/liberal split. The term "evangelical" reached peak usage in the middle of the eighteenth century before steadily declining until it was resurrected about a century later in America.[45] The retrieval of the term is largely owing to the rise of Billy Graham and his decision to adopt the term as a way of distinguishing his "big tent" Protestantism from the increasingly separatist fundamentalists.[46] In the midst of these controversies, evangelicals staked out a spot within American Christendom that claimed adherence to the traditional orthodoxy that liberal Christians increasingly rejected while attempting to eschew the anti-intellectualism that characterized the fundamentalist movement. Events in the early and mid-twentieth century resulted in a division between Christians who identified as fundamentalists and those who, eschewing both fundamentalism and mainline liberalism, began increasingly to call themselves evangelicals.

Apostles of Imagination

In *Apostles of Reason*, Molly Worthen examines the history of ideas, particularly those around authority, which have formed American evangelicalism as we know it today. She sees as central to evangelical existence the tensions inherent in a movement emphasizing individual, subjective experience while being based on the external, objective authority of God and his Word. By Worthen's account, evangelicalism is characterized by competing claims of authority. Evangelicals "are the children of estranged parents—Pietism and Enlightenment—but behave like orphans," she writes. "This confusion over authority is both their greatest affliction and their most potent source of vitality."[47] One fruit of this confusion is a "fraught relationship between reason and imagination."[48] She writes, "If American evangelicals do not share a single mind, they do share an imagination."[49] Rather than speak of an "evangelical mind," as many historians and critics are wont to do, Worthen suggests it "may be wiser to speak instead of an 'evangelical imagination.'" She explains,

> In every individual, the imagination is the faculty of mind that absorbs ideas and sensations as fuel to conjure something new. It is a tool for stepping outside oneself or plunging into egocentric delusion. But we might also speak of the imagination that a community shares, no matter how furious its internal quarrels: a sphere of discourse and dreaming framed by abiding questions about how humans know themselves, their world, and their God.[50]

The ingredients of the modern imagination and the evangelical imagination may not be universal or eternal, but they are pervasive and formative. The elements of the social imaginaries of the evangelical movement explored in the chapters that follow are not exhaustive, but they are representative and, to my thinking, central to what has formed the evangelical imagination for three hundred years.

> The ingredients of the modern imagination and the evangelical imagination may not be universal or eternal, but they are pervasive and formative.

Of course, the images and ideas found within the evangelical social imaginary don't necessarily belong to evangelicalism alone. Some, in fact, are part of the larger modern social imaginary and have become part of the evangelical imagination because evangelicalism is, as later chapters will show, a product of modernity. Because I am writing within the current evangelical context, some of these ideas may be as representative of America as they are of evangelicalism. The fact is that twenty-first-century American evangelicalism can hardly be separated from either the modern age or the American Dream. As Jennings says in *The Christian Imagination*, "Christianity in the Western world lives and moves within a diseased social imagination."[51] It is not simply that Christianity and evangelicalism are infected by other ideologies and identities—it's also that too often we don't recognize their undue influence on our beliefs, narratives, images, traditions, and institutions.

Wherever our evangelical imaginations are informed and formed by modernity, Romanticism, Victorianism, or any *-ism* other than the tenets of our faith, the disease will fester. A central goal of this book is to help tease out the elements of the evangelical social imaginary in such a way that those elements that are truly Christian can be better distinguished from those that are merely cultural. This also means that it is hardly possible, as noted above, to talk about evangelicalism rather than evangelicalisms. This now-global movement is not contained by the qualities and characteristics of a George Whitefield, John Wesley, Jonathan Edwards, or any of its other founders and leaders.

This is not to say that all that is cultural is bad—or good. Human beings exist in culture, and that is by God's design. (Otherwise, he would have had us skip this part of human existence before he brings the new heaven and the new earth.) Nor are these images and ideas necessarily consistent with one another. In fact, they may contradict not only each other but even, at times, more clearly biblical ideas. But this is the nature of a conceptual system. The precognitive notions that populate our imagination come from various sources and take various expressions. The social imaginary or conceptual system is similar to what we might encounter during a commercial break on television. During those two minutes, we might see ads for fresh pizza, the latest model sports car, a financial investment firm, and bikini-clad women enjoying a Caribbean cruise. There is no logic to tie together these tantalizations (except that they indeed aim to tantalize). They even work against one another, inasmuch as pizza works against the bikini body depicted, and expensive cars deplete finances. But all of the images seep into the viewer's imagination, leaving the mind, consciously or unconsciously, to work them out. Thus, our very desires are ordered—if not produced—by the power of our imaginations and the social imaginary that is our context.

As James K. A. Smith explains, "It is because I imagine the world (and my place in it) in certain ways that I am oriented by fundamental loves and longings. . . . My longings are not simply 'chosen' by me; they are not self-generated 'decisions.' . . . We don't choose desires; they are *birthed* in us."[52] The social imaginary primes us even before we make any decision on our own. Gaining our bearings requires us to first recognize that we have been oriented—much the way that the one who is "it" is blindfolded, spun around, and left flailing. Only when the blindfold is removed will we see what direction we are facing, and only then can we decide which turns to take as we move forward.

The metaphors, images, and stories we live by orient us. To recognize these metaphors, images, and stories—and to understand their power as part of the imagination we share—is to remove the blindfold and to see.

2

Awakening

Mumford, MLK, Hurston, Hughes, and Other Poets

On a warm, dreamy August day several years ago, I stood with my niece in a crowd of people assembled on a grassy expanse fronting an ocean inlet. The arched summer sky was robin's egg blue and curved gracefully down to meet the inky waters stretched before us, sky and water disappearing into one another like a crease in the universe. In front of us, on the shore, loomed a stage where a succession of loud, boisterous bands played, hour after hour. It was a perfect day.

Evening came, and finally, too, the headline band we'd all been waiting for. By the time they played one of their last—most beloved—songs, all had darkened around us save the lights from the stage and the occasional cigarette lit by someone in the crowd. On their final chorus of this song, the band lowered the sound. We in the audience could hear only ourselves as our voices rose above those of the band members, lifting upward and outward into the darkness, singing, pleading, "Awake, my soul!"

Many in the crowd held up their cell phones like prayer candles lit to an unknown god as we sang on. Some belted the words out. Some swayed silently along. All—drunken college boys, cutoff-clad teenage girls, aging hippies, and cool aunts alike[1]—were, in singing these words, whether we realized it or not, praying.

Praying as we sang for an awakening of our souls.

Awakening as a Universal Symbol

While the lyrics of the song by Mumford and Sons we chanted that evening are overtly Christian and even evangelical, the idea of awakening is universal. It is so foundational to the human psyche, so common across all times, cultures, and religions, so archetypal, that it is considered a universal or cosmic symbol. After all, we all sleep and we all wake—just as we all live and we all die.

But the metaphor of awakening has a central place within the evangelical imagination. To better understand that place, it is helpful to consider its long hold within the human imagination as a universal symbol.

Symbols are a kind of metaphor. Like all symbols, awakening invokes a range of concepts, all related: awareness, knowledge, enlightenment, and illumination, to name a few. The symbol of awakening appears in different contexts, too, each related to aspects of our essential humanity. These include sexual awakening, moral awakening, and, of course, spiritual or religious awakening, the ultimate concern of this chapter. At its most powerful, the metaphor of awakening can suggest the stirring of all these desires because we—creatures made in the image of a creative, moral spirit who is the I AM—are all of these things. To be fully awakened is to desire what we were created to be.

In this way, awakening is related to desire, the form of love philosophers call "eros." Eros (from which we get the word "erotic") refers to the passionate human desires that create and affirm life. While today we associate the word "erotic" primarily with sexual desire, erotic love, traditionally understood, encompasses much more. For Plato, in particular, eros often refers to the desires awakened by beauty. Perhaps no one captures this understanding of beauty better than Augustine as he confesses his long blindness to its power:

> I took too long to fall in love with you, beauty so ancient and so new. I took too long to fall in love with you! But there you were, inside, and I was outside—and there I searched for you, and into those shapely things you made, my misshapen self went sliding. You were with me, but I wasn't with you. Those things, which wouldn't exist unless they existed in you, held me back, far from you. You called and shouted and shattered my deafness. You flashed, you shone, and you put my blindness to flight. You smelled sweet, and I drew breath, and now I pant for you. I tasted you, and now I'm starving and parched; you touched me, and I burst into flame with desire for your peace.[2]

Our attraction to beauty is ultimately life-giving because this desire—this hunger and thirst—leads us to the true, eternal source of all Beauty,[3] who is also the source of the True and the Good.

Such an awakening—to beauty, sex, and life—is portrayed achingly in Zora Neale Hurston's novel *Their Eyes Were Watching God* in a scene early in the life of the novel's central character, Janie. Upon receiving her first kiss, given over the gatepost outside her grandmother's house, Janie later realizes that "her conscious life had commenced at Nanny's gate."[4] On the surface, this "conscious life" seems merely to be a sexual awakening. But as the narrative goes on, we see how this sexual awakening becomes, in fact, an awakening of Janie's soul to greater, transcendent awareness and desire. Here is what led up to that scene of the birth of Janie's "conscious life" on a vibrant spring afternoon:

> Janie had spent most of the day under a blossoming pear tree in the back-yard. She had been spending every minute that she could steal from her chores under that tree for the last three days. That was to say, ever since the first tiny bloom had opened. It had called her to come and gaze on a mystery. From barren brown stems to glistening leaf-buds; from the leaf-buds to snowy virginity of bloom. It stirred her tremendously. How? Why? It was like a flute song forgotten in another existence and remembered again. What? How? Why? This singing she heard that had nothing to do with her ears. The rose of the world was breathing out smell. It followed her through all her waking moments and caressed her in her sleep. It connected itself with other vaguely felt matters that had struck her outside observation and buried themselves in her flesh. Now they emerged and quested about her consciousness.[5]

As Janie lies under the pear tree (note the symbolism suggested in her doing so for three days) and watches a bee enter a blossom, she sees in this act "a picture of marriage."[6] Desire blooms within her for the first time, not only for sexual union but for love and a place in the world:

> She was sixteen. She had glossy leaves and bursting buds and she wanted to struggle with life but it seemed to elude her. Where were the singing bees for her?

Searching her small world marked by the stoop, the gate, and the road, and finding no ready answer, Janie is left

> looking, waiting, breathing short with impatience. Waiting for the world to be made.[7]

Here—under the pear tree, another type of the tree of life—is a picture of the awakening of eros, a desire for life and life abundant. A desire for the bees who will sing for her.

We who are awake all desire the bees to sing for us.

"Death's Second Self"

These ideas of awakening/life and sleep/death are tightly interwoven and often appear together in religion, myth, art, and literature.[8] The image of awakening implies sleep, of course. And sleep has long been seen as a picture or image of death. In sleep, we are dead to the waking world. In sleep, our dreams take on a life of their own, drawn from our waking life, yet other than this too. As with so many other enduring images, poets have expressed these metaphorical connections well.

> In sleep, our dreams take on a life of their own, drawn from our waking life, yet other than this too.

Shakespeare perfectly and memorably captures the link between death and sleep in just half a line from sonnet 73 when he describes sleep as "death's second self, that seals up all in rest."[9] The word "rest" does double duty here, evoking both the "rest" of sleep and of death.

Shakespeare's famous soliloquy from *Hamlet* expounds on this relationship even more as Hamlet ponders the lure death holds amid a life ridden with pain and weighs whether he should commit self-murder:

> To die, to sleep—
> No more—and by a sleep to say we end
> The heartache, and the thousand natural shocks
> That flesh is heir to—'tis a consummation
> Devoutly to be wish'd. To die, to sleep—
> To sleep—perchance to dream. Ay, there's the rub!

> For in that sleep of death what dreams may come,
> When we have shuffled off this mortal coil,
> Must give us pause—there's the respect
> That makes calamity of so long life.[10]

Hamlet surmises that just as dreams come after sleep, so too must life come after death. As he toys with the temptation to end his life, however, he considers that death, that "undiscover'd country," might bring unknown ills even worse than those we know in life. He thus chooses wakefulness (life) over sleep (death).

A couple of centuries after Shakespeare, poet John Donne (a more devout Christian than Shakespeare's Hamlet) portrays in the image of death something far more promising:

> Death, be not proud, though some have called thee
> Mighty and dreadful, for thou are not so;
> For those whom thou think'st thou dost overthrow
> Die not, poor Death, nor yet canst thou kill me.
> From rest and sleep, which but thy pictures be,
> Much pleasure; then from thee much more must
>   flow,
> And soonest our best men with thee do go,
> Rest of their bones, and soul's delivery.
> Thou'art slave to fate, chance, kings, and desperate
>   men,
> And dost with poison, war, and sickness dwell,
> And poppy or charms can make us sleep as well
> And better than thy stroke; why swell'st thou then?
> One short sleep past, we wake eternally,
> And death shall be no more; Death, thou shalt die.[11]

A metaphysical poet, Donne uses earthly, material metaphors to address spiritual, eternal ideas—in this case, personifying death. The culminating paradox with which the poem closes declares, profoundly, that the death of death is an eternal awakening. To gain one's life, one must lose it. To awaken, one must sleep. Writing from within a Christian framework, Donne knew that to die is to live. In *Confessions*, Augustine famously puts it this way: "In yourself you rouse us, giving us delight in glorifying you, because you made us with yourself as our goal, and our heart is restless until it rests in you."[12] As Paul writes in Philippians 1:21, "To live is Christ and to die is gain."

To Sleep, Perchance to Dream

In between rest or sleep and awakening come dreams. The dream as a metaphor for the precursor to awakening is everywhere. Thus, many narratives of spiritual enlightenment or conversion are set within a dream. And Christian history is replete with dream narratives. Indeed, Christian art and literature had depicted dreaming for centuries before the Great Awakening.

One famous dream in early Christian history is recorded in Bede's *Ecclesiastical History*. It is the account of Caedmon, a seventh-century English cattle herder. One night, the after-dinner entertainment turned to songwriting, and Caedmon, who was illiterate, left the party and went to bed in the cow barn. That night, an angel appeared and told him to sing a song. Protesting that he was unable to sing, the angel told him to sing about creation. And miraculously, the story goes, Caedmon composed a song, the first recorded hymn in English.

Following this miracle, Caedmon was invited to reside in the monastery at Whitby. There, as a monk, he wrote more such songs of worship over the rest of his life. It was in monasteries like the one where Caedmon lived where these kinds of English texts—both ecclesiastical and imaginative—were preserved. With these texts, Christianity grew and spread. And it started, so the story goes, with a dream.

As fabulous as it is, Caedmon's story is told as fact, not fiction. In premodern times, the categories of fiction and nonfiction hardly mattered. The truths revealed in a dream vision were true even if the story in which they appeared was not.

One imaginative work that revealed Christian truth early in English history, a work that is among the earliest extant works of Christian literature, exemplifies the genre of the dream vision. *The Dream of the Rood*, an Anglo-Saxon poem that dates back at least to the eighth century, depicts an unnamed narrator who is approached in a dream by the rood of Christ ("rood" is the Old English word for "rod," or "cross"), who tells the dreamer the story—from the rood's unique perspective—of Christ's crucifixion. The rood's story is one of complete identification with Christ. Within the narrative, both the rood and Christ receive the nails and are lifted up, then taken down together. The dreamer awakes, embraces the story of salvation told to him by the rood, and goes forth to share the story with others. Such identification with Christ occurs through the imagination. Dreams are one form of imagination.

Within the larger Christian literary tradition, dream visions leading to spiritual awakenings include Boethius's *On the Consolation of Philosophy*, Dante's *The Divine Comedy*, William Langland's *Piers Plowman*, and John Bunyan's *The Pilgrim's Progress*.

Nothing but a Dreamer: Before There Was Supertramp, There Was John Bunyan

Bunyan's role in the evangelical imagination is so substantial that his work will appear several times throughout this book. On the surface, it would seem that Bunyan's significance—

both in church history generally and in the evangelical movement in particular—owes mainly to his role as a minister who was imprisoned for his faith as a Dissenter, one of the many Protestant believers who separated from the Church of England in conscientious disagreement with its doctrines and practices. But such men are plentiful within the annals of church history. I would argue that it is the impact of his literary art—the works of his imagination—that has given Bunyan an outsized (and worthy) influence within the evangelical movement that emerged not long after his death.

The Pilgrim's Progress is one of the world's most known, most loved, and most published works. Its place in church history has never waned in all the centuries that have followed its first publication in 1678. For a long time, it was second only to the Bible in terms of copies published. While most Christians know it (or some version of it, for there are many), they may not necessarily realize just how influential this work was, not only in advancing Puritan theology but in shaping the modern evangelical imagination.

Interestingly (and significantly), the central conceit of the story is the dream vision. The tale is "delivered under the similitude of a dream," as the original subtitle of *The Pilgrim's Progress* states (see fig. 2). This literary device of the dream vision is explicit in the work's famous opening line: "As I walked through the wilderness of this world, I lighted on a certain place where was a Den, and I laid me down in that place to sleep: and, as I slept, I dreamed a dream."[13] Of course, it is the reader whom the tale hopes to awaken. Centuries after *The Pilgrim's Progress* first appeared, the Methodist Episcopal Church's *Probationer's Companion* of 1893 included a study guide of the story in its handbook for new members. The guide describes *The Pilgrim's Progress* as a portrayal of the "Christian life from awakening to glorification," it being "profitable for all who are trying to walk in 'the way.'"[14]

The metaphor of awakening so crucial to the evangelical movement's beginnings appears, not surprisingly, in the Bible: "Awake, O sleeper, and arise from the dead, and Christ will shine on you," exhorts the apostle Paul in Ephesians 5:14 (ESV). This verse echoes the poetic lines of Isaiah 60:1:

> Arise, shine, for your light has come,
> and the glory of the LORD rises upon you.

Thus, while awakening is a universal metaphor, the way the Bible speaks of it gives a particular resonance and applicability for evangelical Christianity. Awakening is understood as release from the grip of spiritual death. In 1 Corinthians 15:20, for example, death is likened to sleep: "But Christ has indeed been raised from the dead, the firstfruits of those who have fallen asleep." Romans 13:11 also invokes this metaphor: "The hour has already come for you to wake up from your slumber, because our salvation is nearer now than when we first believed." Partly because of passages such as these, early Christians imagined not only salvation but also the second coming of Christ in terms of an awakening, "an event in the near future which would be a final awakening from the nightmare of history."[15]

> While awakening is a universal metaphor, the way the Bible speaks of it gives a particular resonance and applicability for evangelical Christianity.

The Great Awakenings

Whether in the Bible, in ancient myth, in modern psychology, or in common parlance, the metaphor of awakening suggests some moment of illumination or enlightenment that leads to change. Though the metaphor of awakening is not distinctively evangelical, or even distinctively Christian, it has been central to the evangelical imagination since the movement's beginnings. This fact is expressed no more obviously than in the name given to the series of revivals in America known as the Great Awakenings. The First Great Awakening was foreseen in the inchoate visions of human equality and progress that eventually came to be called the American Dream. Both the dream and the awakening are more than mere facts of history. They are the outworking of a collective imagination.

The historical conditions that led to the spiritual sleep that would be shaken awake by the first evangelicals will be discussed in more detail in the next chapter. It is enough here to simply point out that the church in both England and America—which had centuries before birthed some of the most devout Christian believers in modern history—had fallen back asleep. The metaphor of awakening is used both for new converts and for those who had fallen asleep in their faith but had been "roused to new vigilance."[16]

In America, in particular, the generations that followed the Puritan settlers—those PKs (Puritans' Kids)—grew complacent in the faith. The religious fervor that had brought the settlers to the New World had died down so much that by the latter half of the seventeenth century, some of the congregational churches in Puritan New England changed their membership rules to accommodate those who had been baptized as infants (as had been the practice in England) but had not given evidence of their conversion by offering their conversion testimony. This Half-Way Covenant (as it was called by those who opposed it) returned, to some degree, the nominal Christianity that had given rise to Puritanism in the first place (and to their eventual settlement in the New World), creating the conditions for a renewed spiritual hunger. Later historians in the nineteenth century would come to apply the term "Great Awakenings" to a series of American revivals that began in the 1730s and 1740s. The appearance of the term "awakening" rose steadily in printed literature and reached its peak around 1910,[17] an indication of the hold the idea had in the larger social imaginary.

As early as 1674, protoevangelical Samuel Torrey invoked the idea in *An Exhortation unto Reformation*, where he offers an "awakening watchword" to those disposed "to sleep, by indulging themselves unto carnal rest and ease, shutting their eyes against all awakening discoveries, and stopping their ears against all awakening voices."[18] Through the publication of his 1737 sermon "The Nature and Necessity of Our New Birth in Christ Jesus," George Whitefield (whose role will be detailed more in the next chapter) helped crystallize the metaphor of awakening within the movement. For Whitefield and other early evangelicals, awakening referred to "spiritual excitement and inquisitiveness, especially among those who had not yet experienced conversion."[19] Becoming awake was the first step to conversion—and salvation. It presupposes a kind of slumber.

The Awakening Conscience

But it was in the middle of the nineteenth century—in England, where the evangelical movement began—that a striking example caused the metaphor of awakening to take an even greater hold within the social imaginary of a culture greatly shaped by evangelicalism. From the 1830s into the mid-1850s, key Victorian art and texts depicted passionate Christian feeling through the trope of awakening.[20] The prominence of this emphasis on awakening is vividly exemplified by a famous work by painter William Holman Hunt. Hunt was one of the founders of a group of artists and poets known as the Pre-Raphaelites, who combined attention to realistic detail with the older medieval period's emphasis on spirituality. Around the time when Hunt's religious belief was becoming more evangelical, he produced a painting called *The Awakening Conscience* (1853; see fig. 3). Because of the way the picture tells a story, the painting is part of a genre called narrative paintings.

At the center of the painting is a woman who is just beginning to rise from where she had been seated in the lap of a gentleman wearing distinguished whiskers and an amused look. Various details communicate that the woman is a mistress to this man (including the lack of a wedding band on her finger). What is most immediately noticeable, however, is the expression of recognition, even revelation, on her illuminated face. The Tate Museum, where the painting is displayed, offers a detailed reading of the painting and its many symbolic features. This description points out that the woman's gaze is directed to the lush growth outside, which can be seen reflected in the mirror. The injured bird lying in the clutches of a cat on the carpet symbolizes the woman, broken by her sin. Similarly, the twisted skein of yarn lying on the floor suggests the tangled web of immorality that has captured the woman. The suggestion that the woman is a prostitute or mistress is reinforced by the man's glove, also on the carpet, where it has been carelessly tossed, foreshadowing the usual "fate of a cast-off mistress." Even the painting's frame, which was also designed by Hunt, has symbols: "The bells and marigolds stand for warning and sorrow, the star is a sign of spiritual revelation."[21]

> Within evangelicalism the idea of spiritual awakening is often barely distinguishable from moral awakening.

As *The Awakening Conscience* shows, within evangelicalism the idea of spiritual awakening is often barely distinguishable from moral awakening. One can just as easily precede the other. The trap of an immoral lifestyle can awaken a spiritual hunger. So, too, can a spiritual awakening open once-blind eyes to sin. The conscience itself is a concept that evokes both spiritual and moral responsibility.

Yet, *The Awakening Conscience* also serves to illustrate a tendency—perhaps a human tendency as much as an evangelical one—to fetishize the conviction of other people's consciences. The painting portrays the moral awakening, not of the kind of person most likely to view or display the work, but of someone from another class of people. In fact, when it was exhibited to the world at the Royal Academy in 1854, *The Awakening Conscience* was criticized for pandering to the choir: exhibitions were attended by members of the upper and middle classes, not by kept women (although perhaps those audiences may have included a philanderer or two).[22] If Hunt hoped to teach a lesson to the prostitute class, that lesson would not reach them through the painting. But it did serve to affirm the previously held beliefs and values of those most likely to see the painting.

From Awakened to Woke

The life of nineteenth-century evangelical John Newton illustrates the way these two sorts of awakenings—moral and spiritual—can be mutually reinforcing. By his own accounting, Newton lived a dissipated life from the time of his youth before eventually becoming involved in the slave industry. Newton experienced his first spiritual awakening when a storm at sea caused him to fear for his life and turn to God. Yet, it was some time later, after experiencing a moral awakening, that Newton—once blind to it—could see the inhumanity and sin of the slave trade. Only after this, long after his conversion, did he finally and fully surrender his life to God. He later described this complete awakening in the beloved, well-known hymn "Amazing Grace," declaring, "I once was ... blind but now I see."

Individual conscience as we understand it today is a modern idea but one significantly shaped by Christianity. The concept of conscience that early Christianity inherited from the classical world was based on community or public opinion, according to Paul Strohm in his history of conscience. Christianity developed an understanding of conscience that emphasized conscience as inner, individual, and personal. Yet, this newer understanding carried with it the older one rooted in "public expectation," Strohm explains. Thus, from the start, "Christian conscience would always potentially serve two masters: its possessor or subject, on the one hand, and the doctrinal or theological views of its ecclesiastical sponsor, on the other."[23]

This tension helps explain how consciences can be dulled, conflicted, and even deformed by a culture or its social imaginary. Our consciences are pulled at from without and within, by the Word, the Holy Spirit, and the fallen world. Thus the need for awakenings.

> **Our consciences are pulled at from without and within, by the Word, the Holy Spirit, and the fallen world. Thus the need for awakenings.**

Scholars characterize awakenings in general as extended times of revitalization in which values and beliefs undergo deep examination and change.[24] In contemporary culture, we often speak of pricking or awakening the conscience, whether in matters of personal, individual sin or of social, systemic wrongs.

This description applies well to the contemporary vernacular term "woke." The modern context of the term "woke" is illuminating for all who desire to understand or evoke the power of the metaphor of awakening in any of its forms. Because wokeness has become a flashpoint within certain corners of the evangelical world in recent years, it's especially important for evangelicals not just to know but also to embrace our shared history with this powerful metaphor. As a metaphor, being woke is simply another expression of the universal symbol of awakening that appears across time and cultures, and it is one of the originating metaphors that gave rise to the evangelical movement.

The term "woke" centers on the idea of "consciousness 'waking up' to a new reality or activist framework," according to journalist Aja Romano.[25] Consciousness has for African Americans (who first used and popularized the term "woke") always been a "double-consciousness," a term used by W. E. B. Du Bois in *The Souls of Black Folk*. For the Black person, America is "a world which yields him no true self-consciousness, but only lets him see himself through the revelation of the other world" by "looking at one's self through the eyes of others."[26] Such awareness is a kind of awakening.

In her article, Romano documents how "woke" and the fuller phrase from which it comes, "stay woke," date back at least to the 1930s, when they appeared in songs protesting the legal injustices perpetrated on a group of Black teenagers charged with raping two white women. In 2014, both terms—"woke" and "stay woke"—were catapulted back into the American lexicon through the power of social media in the aftermath of the death of Michael Brown at the hands of police, and soon the words came to signify one's recognition of the reality of systemic racism. It didn't take long, however, for those asleep to systemic racism to plunder the metaphor, weaponizing the term "woke" either by claiming that those using it were performing or virtue signaling or by hurling it against them as an insult or accusation.[27]

To destroy a metaphor is to destroy more than a word. It is to destroy a likeness seen and articulated by those made in God's likeness. To allow a metaphor to dull is to dull, too, the perceptions that allow us to make, recognize, and weigh connections. Dulled perceptions create false intuitions, and flawed imaginations construct a distorted sense of reality.

I'm reminded of a powerful statement written by a young Black writer, Dante Stewart, who for a long time was immersed in majority-white evangelical churches, schools, and culture. As Stewart began to discover the works of Black Christians and to see that their voices, experiences, and ideas were not welcomed by their white brothers and sisters, he came to see that he, too, was not truly welcome—in the totality of who he was—in these spaces. In recounting this painful realization, Stewart offers a keen observation about the shortcomings of the evangelical imagination:

> If the white folk I worshipped and went to school with and had dinner with had the imagination to see C. S. Lewis's Aslan in *The Lion, the Witch, and the Wardrobe* as Jesus, then I knew there should have been no problem when Black folk said Jesus was Black and Jesus loved Black people and Jesus wanted to see Black people free. Just as they found meaning in the symbol of Aslan's representation of love, I found meaning in the symbol of Jesus's solidarity with Blackness. But, sadly, I found out that many could see the symbol of divine goodness and love in an animal before they could ever see the symbol of divine goodness and love in Blackness.[28]

More important than this failure of imagination, however, is the way the white Christians Stewart knew "never really understood the connection between the Black bodies being lynched and the body of Jesus being lynched."[29]

Metaphors are hard.

To discover similarities, to find connections once unseen, comprises some of the holiest work we can do as human beings, for it is a work of reconciliation. But this truth also entails the obverse: making wrong connections can be as dangerous as attaching the wrong cable clamp to the wrong battery terminal.

Any social imaginary reflects both what is real and what is not, both what is in the waking world and what is a product of our dreams, wishes, and illusions. So how do we distinguish between false connections and true? How do we distinguish between illusion and reality, between what is just a dream and what is a real awakening?

This is exactly what C. S. Lewis addressed in a famous essay from *The Weight of Glory*, which contains one of his most beloved lines. The context for this line, the part that is far less quoted, finds Lewis wrestling with the attempt to distinguish between his dream state and his state of awakening. "The waking world is judged more real because it can thus contain the dreaming world; the dreaming world is judged less real because it cannot contain the waking one," Lewis writes. The same is true, he says, of the scientific world and the theological one. Since the Enlightenment, the Western world tends to think the scientific world is the "real" one. But Lewis counters this claim, saying, "I am certain that in passing from the scientific points of view to the theological, I have passed from dream to waking." He continues with that famous line, "I believe in Christianity as I believe that the Sun has risen, not only because I see it, but because by it I see everything else."[30]

We must take an account of and study not only our dreams but the images, metaphors, and stories that fill our dreams and our waking lives too. Such study doesn't require reading scholarly books or taking classes (although that's always an option). Sometimes the most fruitful study is simply listening to the experiences of others, enlarging our perspective, not replacing subjective experience for objective truth, but rather seeking to understand how Jesus, the Logos at the center of all creation, accommodates all human experience. Only when that same Logos is our center can our experiences be rightly ordered and understood—whether those experiences emerge from the waking world or the dreaming one.

While the Christian and evangelical traditions are filled with imagery of dreams and dream visions that lead to spiritual flourishing, such experiences are not universal. Alluding to Proverbs 13:12—"Hope deferred makes the heart sick, but a desire fulfilled is a tree of life" (ESV)—Harlem Renaissance poet Langston Hughes asks in the opening line of one poem, "What happens to a dream deferred?" After presenting a number of likely, gloomy answers using powerful images, the poem hints that one possible answer is that the dream explodes.[31] The "dream," of course, alludes to the American Dream, one withheld for too long from too many Americans. The ambiguity of the word "explode," with which the poem ends, offers the suggestion not only of violence and death but also of life-giving energy and creativity, the sort of thing that results in an explosion of arts seen in the Harlem Renaissance. Or the sort of vision that gives birth to the dream expressed by Martin Luther King Jr. in his iconic speech, "I Have a Dream," offering a fuller vision for the American Dream.

> We can—and should —pay attention to dreams.

In the Bible, Jacob dreamed. Joseph dreamed. Daniel dreamed. Jesus's earthly father, Joseph, dreamed. We all dream. We can—and should—pay attention to dreams.

First the dream, then the awakening.

3

Conversion

Language, Dr. Pepper, and Ebenezer Scrooge

St. Paul. Constantine. Augustine. Martin Luther. John Newton. Olaudah Equiano. C. S. Lewis. Alice Cooper. Justin Bieber.

These are some of history's most famous Christian converts. Each of their conversions is unique and dramatic in its own way. For those who believe, all of these converts are reminders to hold onto hope for those who don't believe.

Although conversion is one of the defining ideas of the evangelical movement, conversion is not just an evangelical idea. It's not even a solely Christian idea or even necessarily religious.

Conversion as a kind of transformation can be found everywhere, in art and nature, in countless literary characters, and in the transformation of a caterpillar into a butterfly. As schoolchildren, we learn to convert fractions into whole numbers in math problems. When traveling abroad, we convert our own country's currency into another. Sometimes we convert an extra bedroom into a home office. All of these conversions suggest a real alteration or change, not only in being but in identity too.

When I was growing up, for example, a catchy Dr. Pepper television commercial centered on the concept of conversion. The commercial featured a spirited band of attractive young people singing and dancing to a catchy song about drinking Dr. Pepper. The benefits of doing so were so plentiful that its imbibers found their loneliness replaced by a sense of belonging and community inhabited by fellow "Peppers." "Wouldn't you like to be a Pepper, too?" the song asks in closing.

> Conversion as a kind of transformation can be found everywhere, in art and nature, in countless literary characters, and in the transformation of a caterpillar into a butterfly.

Now, there's nothing particularly religious about not wanting to be "alone in a crowd," as one phrase in the song puts it, or not wanting to be alone at all. But there is something very "evangelical" about this little ditty. Of course, the song is marketing a product. But in employing the language of evangelism and conversion to do the work of marketing, the song proves the lure of such language. On the other hand, evangelicalism has itself become a highly marketed product. What started out as a necessary call to replace nominal Christianity with a genuine conversion experience has devolved over time to marketing—not sharing the good news but selling it.

As the words to this tune show, genuine conversion—whether conversion to Pepperism or Christianity—entails a change of both belief and identity. The evangelical movement emerged during a time in church history when many identified as Christians but did not truly believe. Now, three centuries later, many who identify as evangelicals not only don't embrace evangelical beliefs, but they often don't even know what defines evangelicalism.[1] "Evangelical" as an idea has devolved into polling, political, and marketing categories. But there is a rich history of this evangelical emphasis on conversion—a history based on sound doctrine—that might be recovered. But first we need to uncover this history.

A Reorientation of the Soul

It is in the religious context that conversion carries the most weight and meaning.

In his seminal study, *Conversion: The Old and the New in Religion from Alexander the Great to Augustine of Hippo*, A. D. Nock defines "conversion" as "the reorientation of the soul of an individual, his deliberate turning from indifference or from an earlier form of piety to another, a turning which implies a consciousness that a great change is involved, that the old was wrong and the new right."[2] This description of conversion applies to religion in general. But while most religions include some form of conversion in their understandings, evangelical Christianity emphasizes conversion in a way that is distinct even within Christianity more broadly.

"Conversion" is an interesting word. It comes from a Latin word that means "a turning round, revolving; alteration, change," one that suggests the turn of one's entire being. The word has carried the current sense of a religious transformation since the Middle Ages.[3]

In Scripture, the idea of conversion is paramount, often expressed through various metaphors. Only a few places in the Greek New Testament use a word that is translated as the English word "convert."[4] These instances usually refer to someone from outside the Jewish tradition (a gentile) who turns to the faith. Most references in the New Testament to the kind of change that brings salvation come from different Greek words that are rendered into English with some form of the word "repent." "Repent" literally means a change of mind. An unbeliever can repent and receive Christ. But even the converted have much to repent of over the course of their daily lives. Both repentance and conversion refer to a decisive act of turning from sin to Christ. As Lakoff and Johnson demonstrate in *Metaphors We Live By,* much of the language we use has a physical basis that is lost once overtaken by its metaphorical meanings. "Turn" is such a word. Its original meaning refers to physical rotation or revolving. Now it has come to refer to movements beyond those made by physical bodies. Thus the metaphor of turning within the context of conversion brings multiple layers of meaning to the event: it is a change of direction, from death to life; it is a movement, a turn of the mind; and in the fullest sense it is also a turn of the body (bowing, praying, serving, obeying) and therefore an aesthetic experience. Another metaphor Scripture uses is seen in 2 Corinthians 5:17, which says that anyone who is in Christ has become a "new creation." Ephesians 4:24 describes the believer as having a "new self." But the biblical metaphor most often associated with evangelicals today is the one found in John 3:7: "born again."

> An unbeliever can repent and receive Christ. But even the converted have much to repent of over the course of their daily lives.

While the phrase "born again" is only one of the terms used in the Bible to describe conversion, this particular phrase became prominent in the popular imagination in the later twentieth century after Jimmy Carter became "the nation's first born-again president" and Richard Nixon's adviser Chuck Colson had his own conversion experience, which he wrote about in a 1976 book titled *Born Again.*[5] That year, 1976, a Gallup poll showed that 34 percent of Americans considered themselves to be evangelical or born again. *Newsweek* declared on its cover that this was "the year of the evangelical." The term "born again" peaked in popularity around 2010,[6] and it has declined ever since. (I think 2010 was about the time I started to notice Christians describing themselves as "Christ followers," a phrase that seems to have had a short shelf life. "Believer" seems to have maintained a steadier presence.) "Born again" continues to be the phrase most commonly used in surveys and polls in recent years to identify evangelicals, usually combining both terms in one question, such as, "Are you evangelical or born again?"[7]

The Language of Conversion

The way these descriptions of conversion go in and out of style demonstrates how, in some ways, conversion (like much of the Christian life) can be seen as "a process of acquiring a specific religious language."[8] In fact, the way in which religious language, including the language of conversion, is used in secular contexts to express significant life experiences has become its own object of study within the field of linguistics.[9] There can be no doubt for anyone who believes in the truth of Scripture that something happens—something supernatural and eternal—when one is converted (or born again, or made new in Christ). Yet, in our humanness, language can be an obstacle to the truth as well as an expression of that truth. "Born again" as a descriptor of being converted came into style and went out, just as other metaphors have and will. It is important to recognize that language not only reveals truth but can also at times limit or even distort our imaginations. In moving from one region of the country to another, for example, I encountered a use of the phrase "born again" that didn't align with how it is used in the Bible. I sometimes would hear people use it to describe a onetime experience (such as going forward at an altar call or praying the sinner's prayer) that was disconnected from whether the person still thought of themselves as a Christian. Within evangelicalism, we need only look at all the trite phrases and clichés that cycle in and out of our vernacular (and receive a justifiable amount of mockery from time to time—remember "smokin' hot wife"?[10]). No wonder Jonathan Swift, the eighteenth-century Anglican priest better known as a brilliant satirist, advised—earnestly, not satirically—in his 1719 *Letter to a Young Clergyman* against "the folly of using old threadbare phrases" in preaching.[11]

Biblical language (which, of course, for most of us is translated from its original language into our own) is never clichéd. But our use of it can be. We should take instruction from the fact that the Bible expresses its recurring ideas and concepts with a delicious menu of varied words and phrases. This truth is a subtle acknowledgment that human words are but an echo of the Word who not only is the source of all our words but is the "incarnational ordering" of those words.[12] Indeed, the root of the Greek word "logos" included in its meanings "to collect, gather," a meaning that was used in the context of ordering one's words in speaking.[13] No less than a "miracle," Charles Marsh writes in his memoir, *Evangelical Anxiety*, "is the way language can reconcile disparate parts of the self."[14] The Word incarnated is what reconciles us to God too. The Logos is a proper ordering, or reordering, as the case may be. This is the essence of conversion, a reordering of the fallen soul into proper relationship with God. Conversion is a literal event of individual, personal, eternal salvation. And yet its meaning manifests metaphorically too.

> We should take instruction from the fact that the Bible expresses its recurring ideas and concepts with a delicious menu of varied words and phrases.

Evangelicalism and Conversionism

Conversion has not been emphasized everywhere in the church or throughout church history in the way evangelicalism stresses it. Evangelicals today, especially those who grew up within the contemporary evangelical subculture, might find it difficult to imagine how conversion could *not* be central to the Christian faith.

I'm reminded of someone who had been reading Jane Austen's work and asked me whether there was a shortage of clergymen during Austen's time. This reader couldn't make sense of why clergymen like *Pride and Prejudice*'s Mr. Collins—who doesn't seem religious at all, let alone Christian—are so common in Austen's works and wondered whether the churches at that time were so desperate to fill the position that they'd hire just anyone. Actually, it was the opposite. Because the Church of England is a state church, its ministers are government employees. Clerical posts were in Austen's day political appointments more than divine callings.

The reclamation of the centrality of conversion emerged, then, from the nominally Christian culture that existed at the time of the evangelical movement's origins. Evangelicals tend today to emphasize making converts from among those of other religions or no religion, so it's a little ironic that evangelicalism arose within a context in which the vast majority of the culture claimed to be Christian regardless of whether they had actually been converted.

Sounds familiar, doesn't it?

The English Reformation began formally in 1534 when King Henry VIII broke from the Roman Catholic Church and established the Church of England as a national church. Christianity was the default religion, and the Church of England became the default church. As in other post-Reformation European countries with a state church, "the baptism of infants made children into citizens as well as church members."[15] It was easy in such a context to identify as a Christian (and be identified as one by others) without *believing* as a Christian.

It also meant that the church was filled with unbelievers by default. Every English citizen "was by mere fact of residence in a parish, a member of the parish church; and however ungodly his beliefs or behavior, the parish church was powerless to expel him."[16] With few exceptions, everyone who lived in a parish was a member of that church by virtue of being born there. Thus, one of the several "purifications" sought by the Puritans was to "purify" church membership by limiting membership to those who had actually been converted. Back then, it was kind of a novel idea!

Anti-Puritan sentiments were high, however, particularly around the years of the English Civil War (1642–1651), which centered on religious-political divides. Reformation fervor peaked in England with the execution of King Charles I by the Puritan-led Parliament in 1649. By 1657, English Puritans Thomas Goodwin and Philip Nye felt the need to remind the church, "It hast been one of the Glories of the *Protestant Religion*, that it revived the Doctrine of *Saving Conversion*."[17] Following the restoration of the monarchy through the return of Charles II to the throne in 1660, an even more anti-Puritan spirit overtook the nation. Until the implementation of the Toleration Act in 1689, dissent from the established church was essentially illegal, which is why nonconformist ministers like John Bunyan had been imprisoned for preaching outside the Church of England. Under the Toleration Act, however, freedom of worship (with certain restrictions) was granted to nonconformist Protestant Christians. (Some of these restrictions continued into the nineteenth century.)

> With few exceptions, everyone who lived in a parish was a member of that church by virtue of being born there.

One inevitable consequence of the establishment of a state church is that the pastoral office becomes a government post, thereby secularizing what is supposed to be a sacred calling (hence my friend's question about the clergymen in Austen's novels). David Bebbington describes the situation for ministers during the years surrounding and leading up to the Evangelical Revival in England in the early eighteenth century:

> Clergymen were expected to display the manners of the gentry, among whom they were educated at Oxford and Cambridge. Their pulpit ministry was partly designed to teach the lower orders their place in the order of things. Conscientious men there were in the Church of England, notably at episcopal level, but there was little effective check on clerical negligence. The church played a salient role in everyday life, but at the expense of imbibing a strong dose of secularity.[18]

This kind of nominal Christianity inevitably bred complacency.

Some of the best illustrations of the extent to which Christianity had become nominal can be seen in the stories of those ministers who underwent conversion experiences while already serving in the ministry. Such stories were increasingly recorded around the start of the evangelical movement. An early example during this period is Richard Kilby, who graduated from Oxford and Cambridge and was ordained as a minister long before being convicted that he had not been truly converted.[19] Another famous story is that of William Haslam, who was converted while preaching his own sermon on the Pharisees and suddenly recognized himself. Upon feeling "light and joy coming into his soul," he repented, and one witness exclaimed, "The parson is converted!"[20] A later example is Thomas Chalmers, a nineteenth-century evangelical leader in the Church of Scotland who, by his own testimony, had been a minister for nearly ten years before he was converted to Christ.[21]

Within such a context, apart from genuine conversion, one's claim to Christianity was merely perfunctory. A person might assume they were a Christian simply because they were born to Christian parents in a Christian nation, baptized in the church, and educated as a Christian. A context in which belief is *assumed* ends up working, paradoxically, like a vaccination *against* belief. Not surprisingly, then, in addition to the secularization of the office of the pastorate, a significant decline among the people in the practices associated with Christian devotion—from reading the Bible to attending church—took place in the eighteenth century, to the point that some churches were closing as a result of decreased participation.[22]

This parched religious landscape was ready for the sweet rain of revival. The evangelical movement's renewed emphasis on authentic, genuine conversion drew the replenishing waters down.

The same spirit was moving across the ocean in America too. Jonathan Edwards, one of the leaders of the American Evangelical Revival (the First Great Awakening, discussed in the previous chapter), underwent his conversion in 1721, while still a young man. Edwards had wrestled with many intellectual objections to the notion of God electing some to salvation and not others. But while reading 1 Timothy 1:17, he experienced in his heart "an inward, sweet delight in God and divine things that I have lived in since," he wrote some years later in his "Personal Narrative."[23] Edwards and other American revivalists would join with their British counterparts in a movement that would sweep across the transatlantic region and then the globe.

> A context in which belief is *assumed* ends up working, paradoxically, like a vaccination *against* belief.

Those counterparts in England were led by brothers John and Charles Wesley and their friend (though their foe in matters of doctrine and slaveholding) George Whitefield.[24] When Whitefield and then his Oxford classmates John and Charles Wesley experienced and proclaimed their own conversions, the Evangelical Revival began. While students at Oxford, the Wesleys founded the Holy Club, which came to include Whitefield among its members. The club aimed to spur members on to more pious lives. Critics of the club referred to members as "Methodists," mocking their efforts as an attempt to achieve holiness through methodical living. Eventually, the name stuck and was adopted by the denomination started by Wesley when he was ousted from the Church of England for his renegade approaches to evangelism.

Ironically, it was the failure of the works-based system of the Holy Club to offer the assurance of salvation that readied first Whitefield in 1735, then the Wesley brothers in 1738, to find assurance in the work of Christ alone. John Wesley's famous journal entry describing what happened to him on May 24, 1738, not only reflects a dramatic, singular experience of conversion; it also set an example of public testimony that would come to characterize evangelical experience:

> In the evening I went very unwillingly to a society in Aldersgate Street, where one was reading Luther's preface to the Epistle to the Romans. About a quarter before nine, while he was describing the change which God works in the heart through faith in Christ, I felt my heart strangely warmed. I felt I did trust in Christ, Christ alone, for salvation; and an assurance was given me that He had taken away my sins, even mine, and saved me from the law of sin and death.
>
> I began to pray with all my might for those who had in a more especial manner despitefully used me and persecuted me. I then testified openly to all there what I now first felt in my heart.[25]

The next year, Wesley began—as Whitefield had already done—to hold open-air services. The preaching of both men focused on conversion, what Wesley famously called the "new birth." In opposition to the established church leaders of the day, both Whitefield and Wesley emphasized conversion as "an individual, deeply felt experience."[26] In fact, experience is one of the four elements of the so-called Wesleyan Quadrilateral, a framework later developed to describe the principles undergirding Wesley's theological conclusions. Whitefield maintained his position as a clergyman with the Church of England (in contrast to Wesley, who was eventually banned from the Anglican communion) and revolutionized preaching and evangelism from within the institutional framework. The evangelical movement thus gained momentum both inside and outside the established church. (Significantly, the movement also included from its beginnings both anti-slavery and pro-slavery camps: Wesley was a staunch abolitionist while Whitefield owned slaves in America. The racial divisions we still see within evangelicalism have, sadly, existed from the start.)

The movement didn't just recover key doctrinal points such as conversionism, however. The movement also radically changed the style of faith and practice in the church. Many accounts attest, in particular, to Whitefield's presence, his rhetorical skills, and the emotional delivery of his sermons. To witness it was an experience. Whitefield's open-air preaching across England, Scotland, Ireland, Wales, and America revolutionized the church in ways beyond measure. By preaching outside the walls of the church building, limits on the size of the crowd were removed, also making it possible for these events to take place anywhere and at any time. People who normally attended church elsewhere could also go to hear Whitefield preach at another time or place without missing their own service. It also meant that he could draw believers from across denominations, especially in America, where a diversity of Protestant denominations flourished. The mingling of believers of various Christian denominations was a radical departure from the persecution (even to the point of brutal deaths) across the centuries until this era. Along with unbelievers, Christians of various stripes were drawn to evangelistic preachers like Whitefield and Wesley, and those preachers in turn crossed denominational boundaries in different ways for the sake of one unified purpose: evangelizing the unconverted.

This focus did not simply win more converts, however. It also shifted beliefs about conversion. As David Bebbington describes it, by the nineteenth century, "some of the more enthusiastic Evangelicals, eager to maximise conversions, began to teach that the crucial factor is a person's *will* to be saved." An emphasis on the individual will to be saved resulted in "carefully planned methods" that "could encourage the desire to believe."[27] In the Second Great Awakening of the nineteenth century, Charles Grandison Finney popularized what he called the "New Measures," strategies designed to encourage people to convert by their free-will decisions (a rejection of the Calvinist teaching of election).[28] Finney would cajole, berate, and scold his listeners to rise up from their seats and publicly come to faith in Christ at the "anxious seat," raising in his listeners their own emotional responses. Critics of these techniques, both then and now, surmise that many "conversions" that took place in these circumstances were not genuine.

This focus on conversions and ways to increase them brought other developments to church and Christian life, things that are familiar within evangelicalism today. These changes include more colloquial styles of preaching, the increased use of mass communication, less emphasis on instruction in doctrine, the wedding of populism to religious experience, and the birth of new sects and denominations.[29] These mass revivals also changed the conversion experience from something private to something public, a phenomenon relying on and building social trust, which had the further effect of strengthening families and a sense of community.[30] Yet, in Luke 12:52, Jesus warned his followers that such ties may be broken in order to truly follow him.

Conversion as Personal Experience

The emphasis on methods that result in (or seemingly result in) conversions is characteristic not only of evangelicalism but of the modern age that birthed the movement. Modernity is most simply understood as a turn from the authority of something external and objective (such as God or his infallible human regents) toward internal, subjective authority—in other words, the self. The "religion of the heart," as evangelicalism was often described in its early years,[31] was also referred to as an "experimental religion." In eighteenth-century usage, "experimental" meant something closer to what we would call today "experiential." But the association of "experimental" with scientific methods and experiences is not coincidental. Evangelicalism was birthed by the Enlightenment. It was the Enlightenment that brought a focus on not only the scientific method but also the individual—individual experience and individual subjectivity, emphases that were possible in large part because of the growth in literacy and print culture that allowed the masses to read the Bible for themselves. Evangelicalism "did not present itself to its adherents as a logical set of beliefs but rather as a series of vivid and compelling personal experiences."[32] The revivals across the transatlantic "introduced a new idea of conversion as a sudden, overwhelming experience of God's grace."[33]

> Evangelicalism was birthed by the Enlightenment.

The evangelical movement was right to reject the assumption that genuine Christianity could exist without the authentic conversion experience. However, the accompanying rejection of ecclesiastical authority also brought with it a new assumption of individual authority. Overreliance on the subjective authority of the individual can lead, not surprisingly, away from deep experiences of conversion to easy, shallow ones. From the stunning conversion of Saul on the road to Damascus—dramatic in both spiritual and physical ways, "a collusion between figurative and empirical ways of seeing and knowing; his three-day spell of blindness and his call to conversion are literal and allegorical at once"[34]—we devolve to filling out decision cards that we put in the offering plate, raising hands while everyone's eyes are supposed to be closed, or repeating the words of the sinner's prayer. It's not that God can't use these methods—he certainly does—it's rather that we choose to use them.

Paradoxically, in the midst of an age centered on reason, rationalism, and science—all of which are supposed to demonstrate the unity and universality of truth—a religious movement expressive of individual experience would become dominant. But it is perhaps not paradoxical after all: the bridge between these two seemingly contradictory impulses is "experiment."

But what experience gives, experience can take away.

Conversion as Cultural Phenomenon

Many cultural factors during the early years of evangelicalism made the field ripe for a harvest of conversions. The transatlantic region that was the center of the movement had experienced the tumult of the American Revolution, the French Revolution, and the industrial revolution. While the first two revolutions took place away from the homeland, the industrial revolution began in England, making it "the world's first modern technological society" and bringing the additional layers of anxiety and stress that attend any shift so dramatic and swift as that. Amid so very many changes, the appeal of the evangelical lifestyle of "self-discipline and seriousness" makes sense. These revolutions, too, brought smaller-scale revolutions and social reform movements, creating new class conflicts, popular movements, and social unrest that were new to a society that had been stable and relatively unchanging for so long.[35]

The conversion experience not only centered individual lives, but it was a unifying experience that bridged all social classes. From its beginnings, Christianity "demanded not merely acceptance of a rite, but the adhesion of the will to a theology, in a word faith, a new life in a new people."[36] The evangelical movement recovered an emphasis on the human will, which Christ demonstrated in his life when he invited people to follow him, marking a radical shift in the world's religions—and in the world. While social class and monetary means still divided people in the early modern era, the growing emphasis on individual agency revealed a common human condition: everyone has a will.

> While social class and monetary means still divided people in the early modern era, the growing emphasis on individual agency revealed a common human condition: everyone has a will.

John Wesley took his open-air preaching primarily to the working poor, whom no one had before thought of much beyond being a source of necessary labor. They had been neglected for so long—even by the church—that "few of them can have been obsessed by a sense of sin or filled with a desire for supernatural grace," A. D. Nock observes in his study of conversion. Yet, he notes, "those ideas were somewhere under the level of consciousness as a heritage from generation after generation of Bible-reading and sermon-hearing forefathers."[37] In other words, the social imaginary of even these neglected souls had been formed by the tenets of the English Reformation for two centuries.

While Wesley's Methodist movement had focused its efforts on the lower classes, the later Evangelical Revival sought to win over the upper and middle classes.[38] Hannah More is one example of a prolific and popular evangelical writer from the late eighteenth and early nineteenth century who wrote texts oriented to every class of reader, including the upper classes and royalty—and More successfully won over these readers. The notion that societal change is best achieved through the example set by those in higher society to those in lower society was particularly potent during the Victorian age. In a highly stratified society, such a flow of influence was much more likely than in a more democratized one. Nevertheless, this idea has persevered all these years, and it accounts, in part, for the infatuation among evangelicals today with seats at the table among celebrities and the powerful. The natural inclination to curry favor with such people is compounded by reasoning that, if those with great power and sway can be won over, their influence will then change the world accordingly.

Conversion as a Literary Theme

One of the earliest English novels, *Pamela; or Virtue Rewarded*, published in 1740 by Samuel Richardson, is an example of a conversion story that reflects the evangelical desire to win the powerful to Christ, not only for their own salvation but also for the good of all those under their influence. The conversion of the wealthy squire at the center of the novel comes through the virtuous example of the title character, Pamela, an impoverished servant girl who resists her master's many attempts on her "virtue" (even his attempt to rape her) and eventually sees him converted. The clear but unintended lessons of the novel are, first, virtue is not its own reward, but rather virtue might reward you with marriage to a wealthy man; and second, a virtuous woman has the power (and responsibility) to transform a wicked man. (The novel is also a very powerful early expression of the modern self, one who sees her soul as equal in human worth and dignity to anyone, regardless of social class or power—and this, too, is part of evangelicalism.)

Pamela was incredibly successful. One town rang the church bells when the part of the story depicting Pamela's marriage was published (see fig. 4).[39] One clergyman recommended the novel to his congregants from the pulpit.[40] An entire industry of Pamela-themed merchandise arose, including teacups, fans, unauthorized sequels and spinoffs, and stage adaptations.[41] Pamela was the nation's first bestseller.[42] And it was the product of an evangelical imagination, in turn shaping that imagination for years to come. Notably, critics of Pamela found in it too heavy an influence of antinomianism and "Methodism," the latter being a derogatory term at the time, applied first to the Wesleys and other members of their Holy Club at Oxford, then to evangelicalism as a whole (before it became the name of a denomination unto itself). The most troubling basis for these criticisms is the easy conversion Pamela's master undergoes in the narrative—a conversion that transforms him from Pamela's kidnapper and near-rapist to her beloved and respected husband. Critics at the time argued that such stories modeled the cheap grace (or license to sin) that some today accuse evangelicals of espousing. To read one of the first send-ups of the novel (Henry Fielding's parody, Shamela) is to encounter all of these critiques and more. In fact, some of what Fielding mocks about Methodism in Shamela reads like a scathing critique of today's evangelicalism.

In the chapter titled "Conversion" in William James's foundational work The Varieties of Religious Experience, first published in 1902, he writes,

> To be converted, to be regenerated, to receive grace, to experience religion, to gain an assurance, are so many phrases

which denote the process, gradual or sudden, by which a self hitherto divided, and consciously wrong, inferior and unhappy, becomes unified and consciously right, superior and happy, in consequence of its firmer hold upon religious realities.[43]

James's description of the "divided" self echoes the struggle Paul describes in Romans 7. Even after the change that comes through conversion, vestiges of our sin nature remain. While James (who is defining conversion in such a way that it can apply to all religious experience) says that conversion can be "gradual or sudden," evangelicals have traditionally emphasized it as the latter.

By the waning years of the nineteenth century, however, a growing cynicism about all things evangelical—including conversion—was settling in. Many adult children of evangelical Victorians rejected the faith of their parents, clearly foreshadowing today's phenomena of deconstruction and deconversion.

Thomas Hardy, the famous novelist and poet, was one of these who rejected the evangelicalism of his youth. Hardy shifted from boyhood plans of becoming a minister to atheism in his early adulthood, then finally to agnosticism. His shaken belief is evidenced everywhere in his literary works. In his 1891 novel *Tess of the D'Urbervilles*, Hardy is critical of—if sympathetic to—an evangelical family he portrays. He is less sympathetic to the novel's villain, Alec d'Urberville, who has an entire section of the novel—"The Convert"—named for him based on his adoption of evangelical Christianity. After being converted by an evangelical minister (the father in the family just mentioned), Alec—once a promiscuous libertine—becomes a revivalist preacher. His conversion turns out to be one of convenience, however, and it doesn't outlast the first lure of temptation, a plot point that contributes significantly to the novel's tragic end—and to expressing Hardy's real-life skepticism of evangelicalism.

A key part of how that tragedy plays out culminates in that section of the book named after Alec, titled "The Convert." After having run away following yet another devastation in her life, the heroine of the novel, Tess, encounters Alec—the original source of her ruin—once again. He is almost unrecognizable at first, in "half-clerical" dress, his "sable moustache" replaced by "neatly trimmed, old-fashioned whiskers."[44]

> It was less a reform than a transfiguration. The former curves of sensuousness were now modulated to lines of devotional passion. The lip-shapes that had meant seductiveness were now made to express supplication; the glow on the cheek that yesterday could be translated as riotousness was evangelized to-day into the splendour of pious rhetoric; animalism had become fanaticism; Paganism, Paulinism; the bold rolling eye that had flashed upon her form in the old time with such mastery now beamed with the rude energy of a theolatry that was almost ferocious.[45]

Alec's "transfiguration" is forced. It is not genuine but rather "*made to* express supplication."

Part of Hardy's purpose in writing this tale is to criticize evangelicalism. Thus, he allows his authorial knife another twist in the narrative's description of "the convert's" preaching:

> The sermon, as might be expected, was of the extremest antinomian type; on justification by faith, as expounded in the theology of St Paul. This fixed idea of the rhapsodist was delivered with animated enthusiasm, in a manner entirely declamatory, for he had plainly no skill as a dialectician.[46]

Translating Hardy's erudite verbiage into more common language: Alec couldn't make a logical argument, but he could make a claim and deliver it with emotion. Not only does Alec quickly abandon his newfound faith upon being reunited with the object of his passionate desire, but he also blames the woman for his fall—and takes her down with him. In this novel, as in nearly all of Hardy's work and in the work of many other late Victorians, his cynicism toward evangelicalism is on display, specifically the conversionism that Hardy thought came too easily and too superficially. For Hardy and other critics of the evangelical movement, too often the desire for purity encouraged hypocrisy, earnest ideals became mere performance, and the valuation of hard work turned into pursuit of material prosperity. The character of Alec d'Urberville is as cynical a depiction of an evangelical (at least in name) as I have seen in literature. Of course, Hardy's portrayal is that of an outsider. It is not how we evangelicals would wish to see ourselves. And yet, these corrupt kinds of conversions form part of our imaginary too.[47]

One of Hardy's close friends was Victorian poet and critic Edmund Gosse, the son of strict Calvinist parents who were part of the Plymouth Brethren. Gosse's parents raised him with the fervent belief from his childhood that he was among the elect. His mother hoped, he wrote in his 1907 memoir *Father and Son*, that "I should be the Charles Wesley of my age, 'or perhaps,' she had the candour to admit, 'merely the George Whitefield.'"[48]

The emphasis Gosse's parents placed on conversion is detailed throughout the memoir, from making new converts to emphasizing the drama of the conversion experience. Describing his father's evangelistic efforts among their neighbors, Gosse details what conversion meant for his father:

> There must be a new birth and being, a fresh creation in God. This crisis he was accustomed to regard as manifesting itself in a sudden and definite upheaval. There might have been

prolonged practical piety, deep and true contrition for sin, but these, although the natural and suitable prologue to conversion, were not conversion itself.

... On some day, at some hour and minute, if life was spared to them, the way of salvation would be revealed to these persons in such an aspect that they would be enabled instantaneously to accept it. They would take it consciously, as one takes a gift from the hand that offers it. This act of taking was the process of conversion, and the person who so accepted was a child of God now, although a single minute ago he had been a child of wrath. The very root of human nature had to be changed, and, in the majority of cases, this change was sudden, patent, and palpable.[49]

The fact that as a boy of nine, Edmund had not given evidence of a specific moment of conversion presented a quandary to his father, who believed Edmund was saved, desired his participation in communion, and yet, vexingly, could not point to an exact moment of his conversion. The problem was resolved by calling on two elders to examine the boy, which they did, happily reporting the next Sunday that young Gosse's "testimony to all the leading principles of salvation" had been "so distinct and exhaustive" that the elders recommended him for public baptism and admission to the communion.[50]

Early in adulthood, however, Gosse rejected his parents' faith, recoiling not only against what he viewed as severity in his father but even more against an evangelical experience that made no room for the literary and artistic imagination that his parents had worked hard to suppress in him during his youth.

It is ultimately impossible, of course, to determine with certainty whether those who seem to have walked away from the faith—whether in real life or in fictional accounts—were ever truly converted or simply never grew into maturity.

Yet, it's important to realize that converts can be converted to anything. Even the Bible warns against this in Matthew

23:15: "Woe to you, teachers of the law and Pharisees, you hypocrites! You travel over land and sea to win a single convert, and when you have succeeded, you make them twice as much a child of hell as you are." I don't know about you, but I don't recall ever hearing this verse mentioned before an altar call or a commissioning service.

Conversion as Revolution

The Bible's exhortation in Matthew 28:19 to "go and make disciples" does not command us to "go and make converts" (although conversion is implied, since disciples must first be converted). It tells us to make *disciples*—followers of Jesus who are baptized, instructed, and taught *how* to live lives in obedience to God's commands.

Three hundred years ago, the evangelical movement reminded the church that genuine conversion is necessary to being a Christian. One isn't simply born a Christian; one must be born *again*.

Now, centuries later, being born again has been so emphasized that nurturing that new life *after* birth—the process in the Christian life known as "sanctification"—is too often neglected. (Is it just coincidence that pro-life evangelicals are sometimes accused in the abortion debate of being pro-*birth* more than pro-*life*? While the charge is not entirely just, there *is* a tendency among evangelicals, who were reacting to a history that neglected conversion, to emphasize the new birth at the expense of what follows.) The good news of Jesus Christ doesn't end when one is born again. Overcorrection is a universal human tendency, but the course of virtue steers between the ditches on either side. Such virtue is as rare as it is radical.

Indeed in *The Wounded Healer*, Henri Nouwen characterizes true Christian conversion as "the individual equivalent of revolution." Nouwen earlier describes two opposing pulls in the universal search for transcendence: the inward pull toward mysticism and the outward one toward social revolution. In Christ, the two come together. "Mysticism and revolution are two aspects of the same attempt to bring about radical change," Nouwen explains.[51] Conversion brings radical change inside the believer that will by its very nature effect change in the world outside. We need look no further than to the first disciples, who turned the world upside down.

Evangelicalism's long emphasis on conversion—its stadium-filled services, its emotional altar calls, its formulaic prayers of salvation—leaves too little emphasis on formation, on sanctification. Personal salvation alone will not solve all problems, personal and social.[52] "Get people saved," one hears constantly in response to laments about social injustice and moral problems. If this were all that were necessary to eradicate injustice, there would be no (or at least far fewer) Christians who have bought and sold slaves, abused their wives, aborted their unborn children, watched porn, or gotten drunk on power.

Woe to us if we fail to see what exactly we are asking people to convert to.

4

Testimony

Grace Abounding *and* *"Evangelically Speaking"*

Everybody loves a good story.

Evangelicals love a good conversion story.

The more dramatic, the better. The starker the difference between "before" and "after," the more often the story will be retold. (Have you ever noticed how often the gritty details of the "before" part can be dragged out in these stories while the "after" is all but an afterthought?)

The power of all good stories—not just the ones centered on conversion—is in how they reflect the order of human existence: first comes the recognition that something is missing or out of order, then the desire to fill that need, and, finally, fulfillment and restoration. In the best stories, resolution comes in some surprising way or from some unexpected source. This is the universal story. As literary critic Northrop Frye puts it, the poet or storyteller's role "is not to tell you what happened, but what happens: not what did take place, but the kind of thing that always does take place."[1] In this way, every story is a metaphor. Every story invites us to compare—compare that story to this story, this story to our story—and to compare what is with what should be.

Metaphors help us make meaning of the world, and human beings are meaning-making creatures. The world revolves around facts, but our understanding of the world depends on the facts we consider and on the meaning we make of these facts. We cannot make meaning without imagination. And our imaginations are shaped as much (although not always in the same way) by things that are *not* factual as by things that are factual. The imagination begins with the concrete materials of the real world—what we see, hear, touch, taste, and smell—and makes meaning from there. Some of that meaning takes the form of thoughts. Some expresses itself in music, poetry, story, or love letters. As the famous saying (commonly attributed to Pablo Picasso) goes, "Art is a lie that tells the truth."

> Metaphors help us make meaning of the world, and human beings are meaning-making creatures.

C. S. Lewis describes something similar in a letter to a friend when he reveals a key moment in the long process of his conversion. In the midst of a late-night conversation about "metaphor and myth," Lewis came to the realization that while he was "mysteriously moved" by pagan myths, he rejected the power of the gospel story and its truth claims. He suddenly saw that "the story of Christ is simply a true myth: a myth working on us in the same way as the others, but with this tremendous difference: that it really happened."[2] Mythical stories prepared the field of Lewis's imagination to receive the truth of the gospel.

While the categories of fiction versus nonfiction, imaginary versus real, and truth versus lie are essential distinctions, a story as a form shapes our imaginations regardless of whether its basis is fact or fiction. Our visions are expanded not only by what *is* or *was* but by what *could be.*

Although the content of every story differs from others, the basic form of most stories remains the same. A story has a beginning, middle, and end. The middle is a point of conflict, the center on which the rising action and resolution revolve. *I thought I wasn't a dog person. Then one day Sam showed up at my door. My life hasn't been the same since.* In this three-sentence story, we have a before and after—and in between, a point of conflict that leads to a turning point or conversion. The before and after are defined by that turning point. "Before" isn't "before" until both the something it precedes and the consequences that follow take place. (By the way, is Sam a dog or a person? The answer to that question *is* the story.) The structure of every story, even this miniature one, reflects the grand narrative told in Scripture of creation, fall, redemption. In a more complicated way, this remains true even in stories told out of chronological order. Some kind of conversion or transformation is the hinge that confers meaning on what precedes and follows. This holds true whether the story is truth or fiction.

Now, nothing ruins a good conversion story like a lie. Some years ago, someone I considered a friend was exposed for falsifying details about his life in order to make his Christian testimony more dramatic—*extremely dramatic.* Not only this, but this highly embellished story conveniently played into a number of fears, stereotypes, and myths that were in vogue among American evangelicals at the time. Not surprisingly, this conversion testimony catapulted its teller into modest Christian fame, the sort of fame that leads to book deals, media appearances, and plum appointments in evangelical institutions. In the midst of increasing public accusations, I asked my friend directly whether the charges were true. He replied, unflappably, "Of course not." I chose to believe him.

I shouldn't have.

Some would say such naivete is baked into evangelicalism. That's probably true. It's definitely true of me.

The gullible are grist to the evangelical industrial mill.

For years, I wondered how those poor, illiterate medieval serfs could fall so easily for the tricks and schemes of those corrupt clergymen selling pardons and indulgences. The past few years have been, for me, a long and humbling realization that I am no better or smarter than those medieval peasants. Perhaps, even worse, it's not so much gullibility as it is that we've become so accustomed to these "evangelically speaking" stories that we have simply developed too great a tolerance for them.

> **The gullible are grist to the evangelical industrial mill.**

A Horse Is a Horse of Course of Course

There's fact. There's fiction. Then there's truth, which transcends both. To arrive at truth requires the work of the imagination. This is not to say that truth is imaginary. Rather, it is to recognize that imagination is what discerns meaning—and ultimately, hopefully, truth—from the facts.

The isolation of facts from the meaning or value of those facts is humorously illustrated in a famous scene from Charles Dickens's *Hard Times*. The scene takes place in a schoolroom presided over by a teacher named Mr. Gradgrind, whose name is quite fitting. His utilitarian philosophy of teaching is described in the opening lines of the story:

> Now, what I want is, Facts. Teach these boys and girls nothing but Facts. Facts alone are wanted in life. Plant nothing else, and root out everything else. You can only form the minds of reasoning animals upon Facts: nothing else will ever be of any service to them. This is the principle on which I bring up

my own children, and this is the principle on which I bring
up these children. Stick to Facts, sir![3]

During one class, Gradgrind asks a pupil, Sissy Jupe, to
define a horse. Sissy knows horses very well because her father
trains and rides horses in the circus. However, intimidated
by her teacher's badgering style, she stumbles to answer. The
next student provides Gradgrind with the exact answer the
schoolmaster seeks: "Quadruped. Graminivorous. Forty
teeth, namely twenty-four grinders, four eye-teeth, and twelve
incisive. Sheds coat in the spring; in marshy countries, sheds
hoofs, too. Hoofs hard, but requiring to be shod with iron.
Age known by marks in mouth."[4]

How little the mere facts of a horse convey the truth of its
marvelous beauty, power, majesty, and mystery!

Conversion stories—whether those of real life or those
found in imaginative literature—are powerful and good
because stories are the way in which human beings make
meaning and share that meaning, something Dickens's Gradgrind clearly fails to understand. But like all expressions of
human understanding, these stories—along with the language we use to create and tell them—are limited and fallen.
They cannot capture "the whole truth and nothing but the
truth."

Before and After

My own imagination was formed within a culture in which
having a conversion story to tell was almost as important as
the conversion itself. If you're like me, you grew up hearing,
"I know the year, the day, and the hour I was saved," and its
countless variations, in many churches, from many people,
and many, many preachers. I heard it so often that it was years
before I could admit publicly that I don't remember my own

day of salvation, the time when I asked Jesus into my heart and was born again. No, I don't remember my moment of conversion.

Although I can't remember the middle of the story, I do know the "before" and "after." I have one very early memory of sitting on a stoop after being chided for some now-forgotten act of childish disobedience, just wallowing in my sin. Another memory from a year or two later is in another town in another state in a new home. My family had just moved, and my mother was kneeling with me as I prayed and asked Jesus—whom I knew then to be my Savior—to help me. Somewhere in between those two memories—according to my mother's testimony—I prayed to receive Christ.

It is to my baptism, which took place while I was a young child—in a cold northern lake because our church was too small for a baptistry—that I look for the mark, seal, and assurance of my faith, my step of obedience and my public profession that Jesus is Lord and I belong to him.

Yet, not having a memory of that prayer of salvation—not having a conversion story—is something that held so much weight in my faith community that I dared not speak of it for a long time.

I'm in good company, though.

Despite the dramatic standard set by Saul when he became Paul after that sudden experience on the road to Damascus (see fig. 5), other famous Christians throughout church history had a slower go of it, including Martin Luther, Blaise Pascal, John Bunyan, and William Jay, just to name a few.

Richard Baxter, the renowned seventeenth-century Puritan divine, had a similar testimony. When he was about fifteen years old he read a devotional work by Rev. Edmund Bunny. Baxter felt a sense of awakening during this reading. Recalling this moment later, Baxter wrote,

It pleased God to awaken my Soul, and shew me the folly of Sinning, and the misery of the Wicked, and the unexpressible weight of things Eternal, and the necessity of resolving on a Holy Life, more than I was ever acquainted with before. The same things which I knew before came now in another manner, with Light, and Sense and Seriousness to my Heart.[5]

But Baxter was careful to point out that he could not say whether this was the moment of his conversion, for he did not know when that took place. "Yet whether sincere Conversion began *now*, or *before*, or *after*," he explains, "I was never able to this day to know."[6]

Jonathan Edwards stood firm on the needlessness of identifying a precise moment of conversion:

Conversion is a great and glorious work of God's power, at once changing the heart, and infusing life into the dead soul; though the grace then implanted more gradually displays itself in some than in others. But as to fixing on the *precise time* when they put forth the very first act of grace, there is a great deal of difference in different persons; in some it seems to be very discernible when the very time was; but others are more at a loss. In *this respect*, there are very many who do not know, even when they have it, that *it is* the grace of conversion, and sometimes do not think it to be so till a long time after.... The manner of God's work on the soul, sometimes especially, is very *mysterious*.[7]

It's a paradox. Evangelicals heavily promote child evangelism. On the other hand, evangelicals also encourage the sort of salvation testimony that requires not only a good memory of that decision but an understanding of it sophisticated enough to tell the story of that conversion well. Of course, somewhere in the fine print, if one digs deeply enough, is a disclaimer stating that these circumstances aren't necessary to one's testimony. Nevertheless, the emphasis on such stories carries an implicit veneration of them.

Not having a before-and-after kind of conversion experience is a worrisome thing for an evangelical. It sets your mind to racing backward in search of a lost memory and, failing to find one, leads you to say the sinner's prayer over and over, or to raise your hand at the end of the sermon one more time, or to go forward to the altar again (and again), just to be sure the deal is sealed.

> Not having a before-and-after kind of conversion experience is a worrisome thing for an evangelical.

Yet, as one of my colleagues wryly observed over a recent faculty lunch, "No parent prays for their child to have a dramatic testimony."

Testimony as Both Witness and Assurance

This "question of timing" of one's conversion has been a point of discussion since the Reformation.[8] Evangelicals tended not to be hard and fast about pinpointing the exact moment of conversion, but Revivalists and the Methodists "usually looked for a datable crisis" or "the change of a particular moment."[9] While some schools within the evangelical movement believe "once saved, always saved" and others do not believe in eternal security, both, in emphasizing conversion, stress deepening the conversion experience by remembering it. Not only the conversion testimony itself but the retelling of it, too, helps deepen assurance of salvation. Memories and the retelling of them are what give and increase the meaning of them in our lives. The same is true of our salvation stories.

For telling stories is a universal human activity, and retelling the stories of our identity and our origin (including new spiritual birth) is a way of reinscribing that identity and origin more deeply into our sense of self.[10] Through memory, the conversion experience moves from an objective, onetime event to a more subjective, layered experience. Conversely, the testimony transforms a conversion experience into a reified form by externalizing an internal experience, for both the writer/speaker and the reader/listener. Conversion narratives build identity, strengthen beliefs, create a sense of community with others who share that identity, and extend invitations to the unconverted to join.[11]

The use of the word "testimony" to mean "conversion story" is so prevalent within evangelicalism today that some of us who resist this conflation commonly resort to the running joke of responding "Which one?" when asked to share our "testimony." On the one hand, it's just semantics: we know that when evangelicals talk about one's "testimony" it's a shorthand phrase that is referring to our salvation story. On the other hand, though, words matter. The life of the faithful Christian ought to be chock-full of testimonies of the mysterious and ordinary workings of the Lord in our lives. Genuine conversion transforms how we see everything.

> It is nearly impossible within evangelicalism to separate the importance of conversion itself from the importance of telling the story of it.

Yet, there is a history behind this semantic quirk. The prominent place of the conversion narrative within the evangelical social imaginary has a story of its own. It is nearly impossible within evangelicalism to separate the importance of conversion itself from the importance of telling the story of it. Throughout the evangelical movement—and even in the years leading up to it—sharing one's testimony of conversion has been so connected to the conversion experience that conversion essentially has come to have "two parts, a heart-change and a narrative."[12] These narratives take different forms. Augustine's *Confessions*, for example, is an obvious early example. The genre of spiritual autobiography became extremely prominent among Puritans in the seventeenth century. Today, evangelicals love spiritual memoirs, which make up a good chunk of the ever-expanding publishing category known as "Christian living." As one academic study sums it up, "Conversion stories are the trademark of born-again Evangelical believers."[13]

The World's Most Influential Conversion Narrator

But the most influential conversion narrative ever published isn't a true account like those marvelous accounts by Augustine or the Puritans or Lauren Winner. The most influential conversion narrative in all of human literature, hands down, is John Bunyan's *The Pilgrim's Progress*.

Technically, using today's categories, *The Pilgrim's Progress* is a fictional conversion narrative. But Bunyan would not have seen it as such. For him, as he explains in the poem that precedes the story and serves as a kind of foreword, allegory is simply truth adorned by outer dress—in Lewis's terms, a true myth. The symbols that comprise the story (obscured or "dark" words) do not lie or feign (as his critics charged) but rather make truth clearer. He explains,

> Some men, by feigned words, as dark as mine,
> Make truth to spangle and its rays to shine.
> Solidity, indeed, becomes the pen
> Of him that writeth things divine to men;
> But must I needs want solidness, because
> By metaphors I speak? Were not God's laws,
> His gospel laws, in olden times held forth
> By types, shadows, and metaphors?[14]

Some lines later, Bunyan proclaims,

> My dark and cloudy words, they do but hold
> The truth, as cabinets enclose the gold.[15]

It is significant that before writing this work that would for centuries be the most published book in the world after the Bible, Bunyan wrote his real-life conversion narrative. His spiritual autobiography, *Grace Abounding to the Chief of Sinners*, was first printed in 1666, twelve years before the publication of *The Pilgrim's Progress*. (Both works were written while Bunyan, a Baptist Dissenter, was imprisoned for preaching without a license.) Undoubtedly, Bunyan's own conversion experience, followed by his careful retelling of it, was the fuel that lit the fire of *The Pilgrim's Progress*, a blaze that has been burning through Christendom for hundreds of years and is still bright.

Bunyan's pilgrimage to genuine Christian conversion began with reading two books that were among the sole possessions his wife brought into their marriage. Notably, the subject of one of these books, Arthur Dent's *The Plain Man's Pathway to Heaven*, was also conversion. Upon reading this testimony, along with the other book, Lewis Bayly's *The Practice of Piety*, Bunyan felt his first stirrings of religious desires. He began to attend church regularly but did not yet experience internal change. Amid ongoing temptations toward sin, he longed to find an example in Christian history worthy of emulation, observing that many ministers and theologians of his day wrote of the experiences of other people rather than their own experiences, in his words, of "only that which others felt . . . without going down themselves into the deep."[16]

But then Bunyan came upon Martin Luther's testimony in Luther's commentary on Galatians. There Luther wrestles in ways similar to Bunyan's own struggling, and Bunyan soon preferred, of all books, second only to the Bible, this one of

Luther's, one Bunyan describes as "most fit for a wounded conscience." After reading Luther's testimony, "I found, as I thought," Bunyan writes, "that I loved Christ dearly: Oh! Methought my soul cleaved unto Him, my affections cleaved unto Him; I felt love to Him as hot as fire."[17]

Unbeknownst to him, Bunyan's imagination was being refashioned until that time when it was ready to conform to the gospel. With prose that is sheer poetry (and worthwhile to slow down so as to read attentively), Bunyan describes that moment like this:

> As I was passing in the field, and that too with some dashes on my conscience, fearing lest yet all was not right, suddenly this sentence fell upon my soul, *Thy righteousness is in heaven*; and methought withal, I saw with the eyes of my soul, Jesus Christ at God's right hand: there, I say, was my righteousness; so that wherever I was, or whatever I was doing, God could not say of me, *He wants My righteousness*; for that was just before Him. I also saw moreover, that it was not my good frame of heart that made my righteousness better, nor yet my bad frame that made my righteousness worse; for my righteousness was Jesus Christ Himself, *The same yesterday, to-day, and for ever*. Heb. Xiii. 8.
>
> Now did my chains fall off my legs indeed; I was loosed from my afflictions and irons; my temptations also fled away; so that from that time those dreadful scriptures of God left off to trouble me: now went I also home rejoicing, for the grace and love of God; so when I came home, I looked to see if I could find that sentence; *Thy righteousness is in heaven*, but could not find such a saying; wherefore my heart began to sink again, only that was brought to my remembrance, 1 Cor. i. 30, *Christ Jesus, who of God is made unto us wisdom, and righteousness, and sanctification, and redemption*; by this word I saw the other sentence true.
>
> For by this scripture I saw that the Man Christ Jesus, as He is distinct from us, as touching His bodily presence, so He is our righteousness and sanctification before God.[18]

Here is conversion as it would be imagined for the next several centuries: in Christ alone and in an instant.

Yet, truth be told, that "instant" was a long time coming. *Grace Abounding* is filled with many near misses. Bunyan's conversion takes such a "diffuse, repetitive, and cumulative" character that it even has been described as a "double-conversion."[19]

> "I found, as I thought," Bunyan writes, "that I loved Christ dearly: Oh! Methought my soul cleaved unto Him, my affections cleaved unto Him; I felt love to Him as hot as fire."

Bunyan's slow, meandering journey to his spiritual rebirth contributes to the way in which *Grace Abounding* is not just spiritual autobiography and conversion narrative but also a work of apologetics in a vein similar to Augustine's *Confessions*. In narrating his many doubts, questions, and challenges to the Christian faith, Bunyan also offers resolutions. The reader has the chance to wrestle vicariously along with Bunyan, to ask the same questions and to arrive with him at his conclusions. In so doing, the reader goes through the same process far more quickly and efficiently than the years it took Bunyan to do so. *Grace Abounding* offers the reader a "morphology of conversion,"[20] a map for the spiritual journey. Bunyan's travail can thus be both universalized and truncated. He offers a path that, once cleared, becomes easier for others to follow.

Indeed, Bunyan's account has had a long and lasting influence, making appearances in later conversion narratives for years to come.[21] Together with *The Pilgrim's Progress*—which is in many ways an allegorical retelling of the real-life journey narrated in *Grace Abounding*—Bunyan's cumulative influence in shaping the evangelical imaginary is likely unmatched, particularly in the context of the testimony.

Notably, Bunyan was a man of active and vivid imagination, not only in his written texts but also in his dreams, memories, and understanding of himself and the world, a quality of his inner life vividly captured in *Grace Abounding*. He even expresses an essential understanding of the social imaginary when he writes of "unthought of imaginations" that drive a soul to distress.[22] Yet, looking back on his life, he attributes even the "fearful dreams" and "fearful visions" of devils and hellfire of his childhood to God's pursuit of him.[23] Later in his life, after encountering joyful Christians in Bedford and feeling the conviction of his conscience for his lack of saving faith, he recalls,

> Bedford was thus, *in a kind of a vision*, presented to me, I saw as if they were on the sunny side of some high mountain, there refreshing themselves with the pleasant beams of the sun, while I was shivering and shrinking in the cold, afflicted with frost, snow and dark clouds: methought also, betwixt me and them, I saw a wall that did compass about this mountain, now through this wall my soul did greatly desire to pass; concluding, that if I could, I would even go into the very midst of them, and there also comfort myself with the heat of their sun.[24]

In both *Grace Abounding* and *The Pilgrim's Progress*, Bunyan's approach to making a testimony of faith, done as a mode of apologetics, is described by Bunyan scholar David Parry as "a kind of imaginative preparationism." In other words, Bunyan appeals "to the imagination in order to entice the unregenerate mind to entertain and to become habituated to the thought world of faith." Such a reformation of the imagination helps create for readers social imaginaries more hospitable to religious belief.[25] Such an approach suggests that though "the message of salvation cannot be attained by unaided human reason or imagination, appeal to the imagination can persuade the reason to be open to the divine revelation that offers salvation."[26] What a contrasting tale is offered between Bunyan's embrace of the gifts and power of his imagination and Edmund Gosse's parents' denial of those same gifts to their son two centuries later. Bunyan's welcome of the imagination helped usher in the evangelical movement; Gosse's parents' rejection of it marked its decline.

The Conversion Narrative of Ebenezer Scrooge

Another conversion story that continues to be beloved, in its original form or in countless adaptations, isn't a religious conversion narrative at all, at least not on the surface. Nevertheless, Charles Dickens's *A Christmas Carol* ends the way all good testimonies do—with Ebenezer Scrooge having become, truly, a new creature.

Part of the brilliance of Dickens's tale is his depiction of the growing awareness that Scrooge undergoes during each journey with the spirits, each foray a separate pilgrimage bringing its own progress. When the miserly and miserable Ebenezer Scrooge awakens in his room on Christmas morning after his final sojourn during the night with various ghosts—those of his deceased business partner Jacob Marley, Christmas Past, Christmas Present, and Christmas Yet to Come—he converts, in every sense of the word:

> Yes! And the bedpost was his own. The bed was his own, the room was his own. Best and happiest of all, the Time before him was his own, to make amends in!
> "I will live in the Past, the Present, and the Future!" Scrooge repeated, as he scrambled out of bed. "The Spirits of all Three shall strive within me. Oh Jacob Marley! Heaven, and the Christmas Time be praised for this! I say it on my knees, old Jacob; on my knees!"
> He was so fluttered and so glowing with his good intentions, that his broken voice would scarcely answer to his call.

He had been sobbing violently in his conflict with the Spirit, and his face was wet with tears.[27]

This famous conversion scene reflects a great deal about the concept of conversion, from both an evangelical perspective and a broader one.

It's no coincidence that *A Christmas Carol* appeared in 1843, early in the Victorian period, which was shaped, perhaps more than anything else, by evangelicalism.[28] Dickens was not an evangelical, although he did seem to believe in Jesus as Lord and Savior, despite a lack of both orthodoxy and orthopraxy. He was writing within a culture and for an audience largely shaped by evangelical values and ideals. While he often criticized the hypocrisy and excesses of evangelicalism, he also reflected some of its core beliefs—not only conversionism but activism too. Like the evangelicals, Dickens believed in the possibility and necessity of social reform. He also understood, as *A Christmas Carol* shows, the power of the conversion story.

Most good stories (the longer ones, anyway) are pilgrimages. Some of these pilgrimages involve literal journeys—*The Divine Comedy, The Canterbury Tales, The Pilgrim's Progress,* and even *Jane Eyre*—that are also personal and spiritual journeys too. Nearly every pilgrimage ends—or begins—with a conversion (of some kind). Most importantly, these stories invite readers to participate in these pilgrimages. The modern distinction between fiction and nonfiction, between dream vision and waking reality, does not register on the soul embarked on such a journey.

Print Culture, Modernity, and Evangelicalism

The modern sense of the individual has been accompanied by the increased importance of identity. It makes sense, then, that the conversion narrative would be a way of not only articulating but also cementing the new identity of a convert. In his seminal study, *The Evangelical Conversion Narrative*, Bruce Hindmarsh documents the rise of this genre and its influence on the movement. Through "narrative identity," Hindmarsh explains, the reader, by reading the conversion narrative and then seeing in it "these stages in her life, correlating outward and inward experience," can "possess a well-ordered and integrated sense of herself—who she was, where she had come from, and where she was going."[29] This is a particularly modern and evangelical move in that such identity and the assurance it can bring cultivate a democratization of authority. Not just the cleric but even the layperson could be an "author" of their own story.

This democratization of authority arose alongside technological and political changes: publication of conversion narratives was possible because of greater religious liberty and more freedom of the press.[30]

It is not coincidental that a narrative understanding of one's life, identity, belief, and self would emerge at the same time as print culture. The spread of literacy and reading made possible by the printing press also cultivated introspection and heightened the experience of interiority, which are so bound up in creating one's sense of identity. Print media, as Neil Postman demonstrates in his classic work *Amusing Ourselves to Death*, tends toward, and thereby cultivates, a linear, sequential frame of mind.[31] Thus, alongside the rise of printed texts and literacy, Hindmarsh says, came an increasing theological emphasis on "the sequencing of salvation" in one's personal conversion experience.[32]

> Evangelicalism was in many ways the product of a reading culture.

Because of these developments, evangelicalism was in many ways the product of a reading culture. Testimonies beget testimonies. And, of course, this includes oral testimonies—whether those of ancient times or those shared on a park bench with a friend—but printed accounts not only circulate more but become objects in their own right. Thus, conversion narratives beget conversion narratives. As one scholar of the genre explains, "Conversion not only responds to but creates its own context. Converts sum themselves up in language. They follow models of conversion that have come before, they write themselves into existence, and they rely on their own words to do evangelistic work."[33] *The Pilgrim's Progress* was so influential because it appeared at a time when print technology and literacy were on the rise.

This symbiotic relationship between the evangelical movement and the culture of print has existed from the movement's beginning. Many prominent evangelicals from these centuries cite the influence of books in their journey toward conversion. They include John Newton, who read Thomas à Kempis's *Imitation of Christ*; Hannah More, who read John Newton's *Cardiphonia*; William Wilberforce, who read Philip Doddridge's *The Rise and Progress of Religion in the Soul*; and Legh Richmond, who read Wilberforce's *Practical View of Christianity*. It is a pattern that is hundreds of years old, and it laid the foundation for today's evangelical publishing industry, which has transformed not only evangelicalism but America itself.

Little Pilgrims

Indeed, one of the most beloved and enduring works of American literature is Louisa May Alcott's *Little Women*, which is the direct literary offspring of *The Pilgrim's Progress*. Images and motifs from the allegory recur throughout *Little Women*, and several chapter titles make direct reference to *The Pilgrim's Progress*. The very opening of the novel pays direct homage to Bunyan. The story begins (like *A Christmas Carol* does) at Christmastime, with the four young March sisters (notice the journey motif in the family's surname) grousing and grumbling to each other until their mother, Marmee, tempers the moment by recalling,

> Do you remember how you used to play *Pilgrim's Progress* when you were little things? Nothing delighted you more than to have me tie my piece bags on your backs for burdens, give you hats and sticks and rolls of paper, and let you travel through the house from the cellar, which was the City of Destruction, up, up, to the housetop, where you had all the lovely things you could collect to make a Celestial City.[34]

The girls respond with fond recollections—except for Amy, who says, "I don't remember much about it, except that I was afraid of the cellar and the dark entry, and always liked the cake and milk we had up at the top. If I wasn't too old for such things, I'd rather like to play it over again." Marmee corrects her, saying,

> We never are too old for this, my dear, because it is a play we are playing all the time in one way or another. Our burdens are here, our road is before us, and the longing for good-ness and happiness is the guide that leads us through many troubles and mistakes to the peace which is a true Celestial City. Now, my little pilgrims, suppose you begin again, not in play, but in earnest, and see how far on you can get before Father comes home.[35]

Amy, lacking hermeneutical sophistication, doesn't make the move from symbol to interpretation: "'Really, Mother? Where are our bundles?' asked Amy, who was a very literal young lady."[36]

Marmee explains that each of the complaints the girls had been rehearsing is the burden they need to shed. They are not to merely play *The Pilgrim's Progress* but apply the story and live out its pattern in their own lives. Meg understands exactly what the purpose of such a testimony is: "'Let us do it,' said Meg thoughtfully. 'It is only another name for trying to be good, and the story may help us, for though we do want to be good, it's hard work and we forget, and don't do our best.'"[37]

No one more than Bunyan would have been pleased with such a result, for as he wrote in his prologue to the allegory,

> This book will make a traveller of thee,
> If by its counsel thou wilt ruled be;
> It will direct thee to the Holy Land,
> If thou wilt its directions understand[38]

Bunyan's purpose in penning *The Pilgrim's Progress*, he makes clear, was to point others to the kingdom of God—which is, of course, the point of the entire testimony genre.

Good Genre Gone Wild

Religious conversion is, of course, a genuine human experience. So, too, is the desire to tell others about it.

But like all powerful things, such experiences can be manipulated. "Testimony envy" is a thing,[39] and the conversion narrative can easily become performative. The signs—coming to the "anxious bench," going forward to the altar, raising a hand, saying a rote prayer, or sharing a powerful story—can become mistaken for the substance. Documenting the role the conversion narrative had in many churches around the beginning of the evangelical revivals, Bruce Hindmarsh summarizes it this way: "No narrative, no admittance."[40] The pattern for conversion narratives has existed for so long and is so ingrained

> Religious conversion is, of course, a genuine human experience. So, too, is the desire to tell others about it.

in our imaginations that it has become formulaic, not only regarding spiritual conversion itself but often the journey that follows. Christians, along with Christian institutions, are not immune from the dynamics of peer pressure.

In *Pray Away*, for example, a documentary about the gay conversion movement (note that it is called a "conversion"), Julie Rodgers, a lesbian who once advocated celibacy for same-sex-attracted Christians but is now married to a woman, shares a story from her former involvement in an ex-gay ministry (often described as "conversion therapy"). Early on in that role, Julie says she was pushed into telling her story a certain way. After she shared with one of the ministry's leaders that she had been sexually assaulted in college, the leader told Julie he "wanted me to incorporate that into my testimony." Julie wasn't comfortable doing so. But, praising her for her speaking skills, the leader insisted that including this experience would make Julie's testimony more powerful. Finally, Julie says,

> I ended up telling the story. But I remember feeling, like, so angry that all of these really intimate experiences of my life were being orchestrated and put together in a way that pushed a narrative: "Men are bad, and I hate men. And because of abuse, I have turned to women."[41]

The pressure to spin a narrative along the path in which it is already spinning and has been spinning for decades or centuries is tremendous, as Rodgers's account confirms. But such pressure is counterproductive at best.

Another problem is that the dominant culture of evangelicalism has consisted primarily of stories that make too little room for the people oppressed by that dominant culture. The conversion of African slaves, Native Americans, and many others often occurred not because of, but despite, the testimonies of those who dominated them. As Robert Kellemen puts it in *Beyond the Suffering*, regarding such experiences among America's descendants of enslaved people,

> If spiritually famished African Americans were going to convert to Christianity, then they had to convert on the basis of Christ's life, death, and resurrection as revealed in the Bible, not on the basis of Christianity revealed in the lifestyles of the Christians they knew. Ironically, to find redemption in Christ, African Americans had to redeem Christianity as they saw it practiced.[42]

The connection between the conversion experience itself and its retelling is not rooted in doctrine or theology as much as it reflects defining characteristics of the age and the culture in which it is told. Different people and different times have different ways of telling stories.

Even in the modern, secular age that has been developing for hundreds of years, the expectations for the Christian testimony have also evolved. But the image embedded in our social imaginaries about what conversion should look or feel like can undermine the reality of the experience for some. I learned this truth by hard experience years ago. I was a full-time graduate student and working on a horse farm on the side. I had befriended the farm owner's wife, who had been asking me questions about my Christian faith. One day, she surprised me by saying she wanted to be saved. We talked more, and I led her in a prayer for salvation. When we were done praying, she lifted her head, opened her eyes, looked at me quietly for a few moments, and said, "I don't feel any different." I panicked. I didn't know what to say (nor do I remember what I did say). But I do remember that as soon as I got home, I called my pastor to ask what I should have said. And for the first time in my life, I heard—or at least heard in a way that made me really hear it—that conversion to Christ is not strictly or necessarily an emotional experience (although that might sometimes be part of it). This woman had learned enough about conversion to imagine it would have some sort of immediate emotional component—and I had not imagined enough about conversion to know it didn't have to include that.

He's the Real Thing

In *Sources of the Self*, Charles Taylor argues that an "inescapable feature of human life" is that in order to make sense of our lives and to have an identity, "we need an orientation to the good." Further, "this sense of the good has to be woven into my understanding of my life as a story." One "basic condition of making sense of ourselves," Taylor says, is "that we grasp our lives in a *narrative*."[43] We "determine what we are by what we have become, by the story of how we got there."[44] It makes sense that our identity as Christians would be rooted in the *story* of how we came to that identity—whether that story centers on one dramatic before-and-after moment or plays out more like a stop-motion film in which the movement is detectable only when all the frames are shown in sequence.

One study of evangelical conversion narratives done over the course of the last several decades documented a shift in the form these testimonies have taken, shifts that reflect the same changes in the modern sense of self that Taylor describes in his work. The study noted that over the years, conversion stories moved through three stages. The earliest type reflected "biblical scripts of dramatic conversion modeled after the conversion of St Paul and the prodigal son." But in the 1990s these types of testimonies gave way to what the researchers call "revitalization stories." These are narratives that chart a more gradual process of spiritual awakening, often within the context of a lifetime spent in Christian communities or churches.

More recently, a third kind of testimony has emerged. These narratives make more room for "failed transformation, even hinting at the possibility of deconversion." Such testimonies differ significantly enough from the form of conversion narratives that were prominent through the 1990s that the study refers to them not as conversion stories but as "life stories" in which the narrators "present themselves as pilgrims and life as a journey."[45]

We have come, if this research is right, back around to the testimony exemplified by Bunyan in both *Grace Abounding* and *The Pilgrim's Progress*. And yet this conversion-as-life-journey redux affirms Taylor's insights into the modern self, the ethics of authenticity, and the power of social imaginaries. This study of evangelical testimonies shows that today's conversion narratives have shifted the emphasis from the authenticity or credibility of the experience itself to the authenticity or credibility of the person who had the experience. In other words, it's a shift from asking "Do I believe this really happened?" to "Do I trust this person?" The shift parallels the modern turn to subjectivity over objectivity, and to expressive individualism.[46]

Thus the question in the current evangelical social imaginary isn't so much about whether Jesus is real as it is about whether the person telling the story is real. It's not a bad question. I don't know about you, but I have no doubts about how real Jesus is. Yet, I have increasing questions about the stories of some of those who claim to follow him.

5

Improvement

The Puritan Work Ethic, Paradise Lost, *and the Price of Progress*

You can't walk down the aisle of the grocery store without the words "new and improved!" jumping out at you from one product or twenty (see fig. 6).

There's hardly a sport or a team that doesn't honor the player who is most improved. The home improvement retail industry in the US brings in over $500 billion per year.[1] Across America, government entities, organizations, and committees devote themselves to neighborhood improvement projects. And the already gargantuan category of self-help books (a genre in previous centuries referred to as "improving literature") continues to grow steadily each year.[2]

Improvement is good! It's also such a ubiquitous idea that it can be difficult to distinguish real, good advances from clever marketing and feel-goodism.

Evangelicals are not immune to improvement fever. Not by a long shot. "Christian living," as it's called in the publishing industry, is big business. So, too, are the Christian conferences, Instagram accounts, TikToks, Bible studies, marriage manuals, television shows, workshops, classes, and webinars that promise to bring improvement to whatever area of life in which you need it—and plenty of areas where you don't.

Don't get me wrong. I'm in favor of Christian living! And improvement in general. Who isn't?

Christians especially believe in improvement. After all, the Christian life doesn't end with conversion. Being born again begins a new life, one that ought to be marked by ongoing growth and maturity, a diet of meat rather than milk, increasing Christlikeness and the ongoing display of the fruit of the Spirit. The Christian is to "improve," in a way, of course. But there's a reason this process in the Christian life is more accurately called by another name: sanctification. Sanctification—literally, the process of becoming holy—is a religious, not a consumerist, experience.

The steady beat to *improve, improve, improve* resounds loudly everywhere. It's nearly impossible to imagine a world in which improvement isn't valued for its own sake, as a constant, never-ending pursuit.

> The steady beat to *improve, improve, improve* resounds loudly everywhere.

Yet, improvement wasn't always assumed to be something we should constantly be pursuing like hamsters on the wheel. The fact is that the idea of improvement is, well, *new*. That is, it's new relative to all of human history. Improvement might even be considered one of the key characteristics that makes the modern age modern, a fact echoed in the familiar phrase "modern progress" (although, as we will see, improvement and progress aren't exactly the same). Like most things that characterize modernity, the idea of improvement is part of the evangelical social imaginary.

The Invention of Improvement

Like the evangelical movement itself, the notion of improvement began in England. According to Paul Slack in *The Invention of Improvement*, the word appeared there in the early sixteenth century, right around the time of the Reformation. It was first used in the context of making land more profitable through improvements, and it had no exact synonym in other European languages at the time. Unlike existing words such as "reformation" and "revolution," "improvement" suggested "gradual, piecemeal, but cumulative betterment" rather than a change that was sudden or dramatic.[3] Eventually, the word was applied metaphorically to betterment in other areas of life and society until its meaning gradually broadened into the many contexts in which it is used today.[4]

Because the concept of improvement developed in England, it became "one of the things which made the English different from everyone else."[5] The end of the seventeenth century is often considered the beginning of the "great age of improvement," and by the early eighteenth century,

> improvement was more than an everyday idiom of expression; it was a word essential to political discussion of national affairs and an integral part of English culture. It privileged certain kinds of public and private behaviour above others, encouraging innovative, industrious, and in every sense profitable activities, while discouraging their opposites. It sustained a story about England's progress and helped to bring it into being.[6]

Improvement became a distinctive component of the English social imaginary,[7] and, eventually, by extension, the early American social imaginary—and evangelicalism itself.

The idea of improvement included a number of accompanying activities and contexts that made articulation of the concept possible. These included "the use of calculation and measurement as instruments of understanding and control" within what was quickly becoming an "information-rich" culture. Measurement itself, and the increased reliance on it, produced the idea of progress (now that it could be measured) and the "conviction that moral and material progress" were both possible and desirable.[8] Indeed, like the sound of a tree falling in a forest, improvement wasn't really improvement if no one recognized it as such. Rather, improvement as a concept "depended on knowledge that it was happening."[9]

Perhaps no monument to such knowledge—knowledge that improvement was indeed happening—serves as a better symbol than the Crystal Palace, a gargantuan edifice of steel and glass of nearly one million square feet that held England's Great Exhibition in 1851. Essentially the first world's fair, the Great Exhibition showcased tens of thousands of objects, inventions, and technological improvements from thousands of contributors from around the world. When the event ended, the massive Crystal Palace—a miracle of technology and design, the crown jewel of the industrial revolution—was dismantled and reassembled in South London, where it was destroyed by fire less than a century later, proving Shakespeare's wisdom true: "Not marble nor the gilded monuments / Of princes shall outlive this powerful rhyme."[10]

The Price of Progress

Improvement requires a willingness to break from tradition and the past, which is part of the idea of progress.[11] This posture is not unrelated to evangelicalism's emphasis on conversion as a sudden turning or break from the past. Conversion is, after all, the ultimate improvement.

Progress, while connected to the idea of improvement, differs from it. The concept of progress gained traction after improvement did, arising in the eighteenth century and manifesting in a number of ways. As with improvement, "people have not always thought that progress was a fact."[12] Progress—the belief that history is "moving inexorably toward a more peaceful, intelligent, and commodious life" for humankind—is a product of the rationalism of the Enlightenment, one widely embraced by the start of the eighteenth century. Once such a notion gained widespread acceptance, it became "self-generating," cultivating "rising expectations" of ongoing improvements across societies.[13]

Yet not everyone was so hopeful about the human condition. Traditional thinkers and radicals alike contested the idea of true human progress.

Throughout his body of work, for example, famous English satirist Jonathan Swift roundly mocks the idea that human beings can "progress" in any meaningful way. For Swift, the notion that "moderns" are better or even could be better than the "ancients" is rooted in the deadly sin of pride. In many of his works, but most directly and devastatingly in *Gulliver's Travels*, Swift casts aspersions on excessive pride in human progress and its byproducts: projects, methods, experiments, inventions, and any science that dehumanizes. It's notable that Swift was an Anglican clergyman through and through—grounded in orthodox theology and church tradition. He predicted (and satirized) the sort of individualized religious experience that evangelicalism birthed as "enthusiasm"—defined by his contemporary Samuel Johnson in his *Dictionary of the English Language* as "a vain belief of private revelation."[14] (During the eighteenth and nineteenth centuries, critics would more and more associate "enthusiasm" with evangelicals.)

Another prominent critic of progress in the eighteenth century was painter William Hogarth, who satirized the notion of progress through several series of paintings using that term ironically, including *A Harlot's Progress* and *A Rake's Progress*, which depicted the decline (not improvement) of the two subjects (see fig. 7). Hogarth's paintings offered harsh social critiques of the conditions that would facilitate the fall of a young woman of poverty and a young man of means into moral decay.

Swift and Hogarth were not so much against progress as a *possibility* but rather against the *assumption* that the human condition could change, let alone improve. A more radical opposition to belief in progress came in the nineteenth century, most notably from Romantic poet-philosophers Samuel Taylor Coleridge and Percy Bysshe Shelley (and numerous others). The Romantics rightly understood that there could be no progress based on reason alone. They knew that our full humanity encompassed not just our rational nature but our emotional, imaginative, and spiritual nature too. Any moral calculus based on reason alone leads inevitably to inhumanity—whether that of the "new and improved" efficiency of the guillotine, the free labor of the slave trade, or the "final solution" of the concentration camp.

Somewhere between the two anti-rationalist camps—the traditional Anglicanism of Swift and radical Romanticism of Shelley—the first evangelicals landed.

Evangelicalism was (and is) inherently not conservative, not traditional, but rather innovative and therefore progressive (in a social and cultural sense, not necessarily politically or theologically). Recall the definition of evangelicalism given by John Stackhouse in chapter 1: evangelicals appropriate from tradition selectively and innovate as necessary in order to fulfill their mission.

Similarly, the founding of America was an exercise in newly emerging concepts of liberty, democracy, and self-rule—a "new and improved" version of government and nationhood.

The American Dream itself is a vision of successive, generational improvement; its essence is that no matter where you start, you can build a better life, one that will be even better for your children and their children.

One of the most famous advocates of self-improvement in nineteenth-century America was Horatio Alger, author of numerous juvenile novels (precursors to today's young adult genre). Alger's stories typically depicted impoverished boys who improved their material conditions through pluck and virtues of character that usually led to the notice and support of wealthy patrons, who gave the boys a leg up in the world. The most famous of these novels is *Ragged Dick*. Published in 1868 after being printed serially, *Ragged Dick* exemplifies the pattern of Alger's stories by portraying a young ruffian with enough good qualities to eventually achieve financial and social improvement. Alger was one of the key promoters of a dominant metaphor of America's Gilded Age (the last decades of the nineteenth century, so called for ushering in an explosion of wealth and prosperity). That metaphor, one that persists today, attributes material success to pulling yourself up by your bootstraps.[15] Martin Luther King Jr. famously pointed out later that "it's a cruel jest to say to a bootless man that he ought to lift himself by his own bootstraps."[16]

But there is another reason, besides King's pointed critique, to question Alger's vision for self-improvement. In 1866, Alger, who was an ordained Unitarian minister, was expelled from the ministry for sexual abuse of boys. These abuses were documented at the time but not widely known until a century later.[17]

There are times when a message should be rightly understood apart from the messenger. But sometimes the agenda in the message cannot be separated from that of the messenger. Horatio Alger's work is an example of the latter.

From Riches to Rags

To understand improvement as a concept, value, or underlying assumption that is specifically modern (and not universal) can lead to other important understandings. To be able to imagine a world in which improvement as a concept isn't part of the shared imagination helps us to see both the advantages and the limits of a world driven by an impulse toward constant betterment.

In his foundational book *Understanding Media*, twentieth-century communications theorist Marshall McLuhan observes that when a new technology is developed, we tend to consider only what we gain from that technology while overlooking what we lose. It's easy to see, for example, what we gained with the invention of the automobile but to forget about what we lose in a society in which we spend so much time zipping over the land sealed up in metal and glass rather than walking or riding on horseback at a slower pace. Considering what is lost is not to say that the new technology doesn't give more than it takes. But acknowledging that there are losses gives us a healthier, fuller account of reality as a whole and of the particularities of our own social imaginary, one in which certain ideas that encourage improvement are a given and other ideas are diminished. Improvement can be an improvement—but that doesn't mean it doesn't entail some loss.

> Improvement can be an improvement—but that doesn't mean it doesn't entail some loss.

"Improvements" not only alter *how* we relate to the world but also change the very meaning of the world and our lives in it. Martin Luther King Jr. offers a sober assessment of this aspect of modern life in our spiritual lives:

> Every man lives in two realms, the internal and the external. The internal is that realm of spiritual ends expressed in art,

literature, morals and religion. The external is that complex of devices, techniques, mechanisms and instrumentalities by means of which we live. Our problem today is that we have allowed the internal to become lost in the external. We have allowed the means by which we live to outdistance the ends for which we live. So much of modern life can be summarized in that suggestive phrase of Thoreau: "Improved means to an unimproved end."[18]

As the idea of improvement grew in the eighteenth century, so too did the "idea of national improvement,"[19] which brought with it the assumption that material progress will bring only benefits and incur no losses. "That's the price of progress," we often hear. We don't nearly as often ask what exactly that price is.

There's a poignant scene in *Everything Sad Is Untrue (A True Story)* by Daniel Nayeri in which he tells the story of moving to Oklahoma as a young boy from his native Iran. Daniel recalls taking a field trip with his class at school to see a museum—a house that was ninety-eight years old. "So every ninety-eight years, people move out of their houses and turn them into museums?" Daniel asks, incredulously. His own grandfather's home back in Iran is six hundred years old.[20]

One price that can be exacted is that some kinds of improvement require disposing of the old in favor of the new. What is disposed of includes material goods: whether old flooring or outdated fashion. It includes the intangibles too: leaving one job to take a better one or leaving a church for another down the road. Sometimes, of course, these are necessary and good decisions! But as the illustration from Nayeri's book shows, what is "old" and what is still perfectly fine is largely culturally determined. That cultural determination also includes the level of quality we expect—and are willing to pay for. The level of waste we routinely produce is telling. According to the EPA, the amount of waste generated in 1960 was 2.68 pounds per person per day. In 2018, it was 4.9 pounds.[21] Clothing generated from today's fast fashion is one major source of the world's garbage. Many of us (myself included) assuage our guilt about buying new, improved clothes by donating our old ones. But clothing donations—especially of poor-quality items—have increased so much that underdeveloped nations are begging richer countries to stop sending our throwaways to them. Not surprisingly, the US is the biggest source of used clothing, exporting an average of $662 million each year, constituting 40 percent of exports from within the top three exporters of worn clothing.[22] One quick search will bring countless news reports filled with images from nations across the world covered with mountains of discarded clothing that is unwearable, unburnable, and unusable. The problem has been described as "an environmental disaster."[23]

New and improved, indeed.

How the Reformation Brought About Improvement

While, as we've seen, the word "improvement" emerged within a particular context in England, the idea captured by the word is much older, broader, and deeper.

Improvement began as an effort connected to society as a whole, to the *civilization* that results from *civility*. The medieval codes of courtesy, which applied only to those in and around the court (hence the word), grew into an ideal that expanded into the broader population, Charles Taylor explains in *A Secular Age*.[24] In Taylor's account, this ideal of civility, which emphasizes individual will (to be civil, or to show manners, requires intention; it does not occur naturally), undergirds the entire shift from the premodern to the modern age. Taylor describes the shift as "a stance of reconstruction toward ourselves," a posture that stresses "modes of discipline," programs, "methods," and "procedures" directed toward "self-fashioning"[25] that lead to peaceful, rational collaboration for everyone's mutual benefit.[26]

In a chapter of *A Secular Age* titled "The Rise of the Disciplinary Society" (the chapter's title is helpfully descriptive), Taylor describes how the Renaissance ideal of civility combined with the Reformation's emphasis on piety to create a social and cultural transformation in which improvement, achieved through discipline, "came to be seen as a duty for itself."[27] First a duty, then an assumption. Once improvement (and, later, self-improvement) had become an assumed good, it became part of the social imaginary. One would hardly think to even question whether or not improvement is good. It now goes without saying within certain social imaginaries.

Before the concept of improvement as a universal and assumed good had taken hold, moralists had actually "condemned luxury and the pursuit of profit and material comfort."[28] But the value of the leisure and rest required for the contemplative monastic life was replaced by the value of work (and restlessness) reflected in the Puritan work ethic. For the Reformers, work was a form of works, and clearly not a means of salvation. However, the success of one's work (namely, the improvement and progress that result from it) could be seen as evidence of one's election.[29] The changes that both led to and followed from the Protestant Reformation were those applied first to systems, structures, and institutions, then to individuals in the form of self-improvement.

The way in which the theology of the Reformers led to the idea of improvement manifests in several ways. In *The Protestant Ethic and the "Spirit" of Capitalism*, Max Weber argues that first Protestant, then Puritan, theology led to a rational, utilitarian, and individualistic approach to life and work that replaced the older enchanted and communal view of life and work.[30]

Weber paints this contrast vividly by comparing the closing scenes of two central works of Christian literature. Dante's medieval Catholic masterpiece *The Divine Comedy* ends with the poet-sojourner absorbed by the ineffable mystery of the divine presence (see fig. 17). Centuries later, following the Reformation, the Puritan John Milton closes his epic poem *Paradise Lost* with the expulsion of Adam and Eve from the garden of Eden. The pair, having been instructed by the angel Michael to add to the knowledge they gained by ill means the honest gains of good deeds and virtues, join hands and head out into the wide world that lies before them. The contrast between these two works—the first quintessentially Catholic, the second purely Protestant—reveals seismic shifts, not only in theological doctrine but in competing images of human telos: to ponder (Dante) or to improve (Milton). This contrast reflects an age-old debate between the superiority of the contemplative life versus the active life. Remarking on the closing of *Paradise Lost*, Weber writes, "Anyone can sense immediately that this mightiest expression of earnest Protestant worldliness, that is, valuing life as a task to be accomplished, would have been impossible in the mouth of a medieval writer."[31]

Two centuries after Milton, John Henry Newman would echo the ending of *Paradise Lost* when he preached a sermon in which he began with the question, "Why were you sent into the world?" and answered it with, essentially, "*To work.*"[32]

Please Be Courteous

Bodies of imaginative literature over the centuries have expressed, embodied, and encouraged the idea of improvement on a societal and personal level, primarily through work.

Long before the Reformation, and the more general spirit of reform that accompanied it, a genre known as "courtesy literature" arose during the medieval period. These works taught readers, mainly of the aristocratic class, the manners expected of people in and around the court.

After the Reformation, when literacy, social mobility, and religious piety grew, courtesy literature was replaced by conduct literature. Conduct books, which were particularly popular in the seventeenth century, conveyed instruction not only in manners but also in behavior, morals, and religion. Reading itself became a primary means of improvement, one advocated by conduct books. One of the most famous and influential of these works, for example, Thomas Gisborne's 1787 *An Enquiry into the Duties of the Female Sex*, lists among the "duties" of "every woman, whether single or married, the habit of regularly allotting to improving books a portion of each day."[33]

Both courtesy books and conduct books are the direct forerunners to the etiquette books that became popular in the nineteenth and twentieth centuries, the sort that instruct readers on how to set a table or address wedding invitations and so on. All of these works presuppose the possibility of upward social mobility, because people who were born into families that already possessed these manners didn't need to read such instruction manuals. Such manners and traditions were handed down. (The Latin root word from which we get the word "tradition" means "hand." Thus, traditions are "handed down.") Conduct literature emerged from a newly emerging assumption that sufficient knowledge of proper conduct and manners would not be handed down from within the family of one's origin because one had attained (or was hoping to attain) a higher social status than that of one's birth. The attainment of such improvement had become possible to achieve, if not by birth then by one's own effort.

One such effort was reading.

The first novels were, in many respects, conduct books—instructions for better living—made more interesting by being in the guise of lively tales. What was novel about the novel was that it combined instruction and delight in a revolutionary (or, at least, improving) way. It is one of the great ironies of literary history that the Puritans, who were generally suspicious of fiction, played a significant part in developing the genre of the novel. While Puritans and evangelicals in the Puritan strain objected to earlier forms of fiction—drama, tales, romances, and stories of adventure—early novels demonstrated the possibilities for redeeming fiction. In both form and content, long prose narratives had the capacity to replicate the ongoing sanctification that occurs in a person's life journey. Drawing on the forms of Puritan spiritual autobiography as well as allegory such as *The Pilgrim's Progress*, the novel form combined personal introspection with the age-old symbol of the spiritual quest or journey into a long personal narrative, a unique but relatable story.

> The attainment of such improvement had become possible to achieve, if not by birth then by one's own effort.

And it was another Puritan writer by the name of Daniel Defoe who, half a century after *The Pilgrim's Progress*, helped turn serious conduct literature into a form that would become the novel. Defoe was a prolific journalist and writer, producing hundreds of publications, including pamphlets, political treatises, and fictional works that served as precursors to the novel. His most famous of these are *Robinson Crusoe* (1719) and *Moll Flanders* (1722). For almost two centuries, *Robinson Crusoe* was, along with *The Pilgrim's Progress*, one of the most popular and influential works ever printed (after the Bible).

The novel as a literary form developed around a more subjective point of view, one that in its subjectivity offered an inherent search for a meaning that was no longer merely a given—which is the essential quality that defines the modern age. Such a search gave shape to the narrative of the novel itself, unifying, particularizing, and relativizing it in a way that, paradoxically, lent it an indirect universality. In other words, to encounter a fictional character like Moll Flanders—a child born in prison who grew up to be a prostitute and thief before undergoing a dramatic conversion to Christian faith—a character so very likely to be unlike anyone reading the account, offers the opportunity to see what in Moll is similar to oneself. To witness Moll's "improvement" is a sideways lesson in how to improve oneself. If one so bad as she could undergo such radical transformation, why couldn't I?

It helped that Defoe had political and theological street cred with conservative readers, including evangelicals. When Queen Anne ascended the throne in 1702, religious Dissenters such as Defoe (who was a Calvinist Presbyterian) were targeted for persecution. Before writing his famous works of fiction, Defoe published a scathing satire on the oppression of religious freedom; he was arrested, tried, and convicted of seditious libel and sent to prison after spending three days in the pillory.

Although sometimes referred to as novels, Defoe's fictional works are, for a number of reasons, generally considered precursors to the novel. Combining genres such as journalism, narrative, and spiritual autobiography in these works, Defoe made significant contributions to developments in fiction that reflected specifically modern concerns. One of these is the Puritan (or Protestant) work ethic. Defoe's characters improve by their own diligent efforts, as is befitting good Puritans.

It was a couple of decades later, in 1740, that Samuel Richardson published the groundbreaking *Pamela; or Virtue Rewarded*, which we considered in a previous chapter. Drawing heavily from the popular genre of conduct books, *Pamela* is presented as a series of letters (followed by a journal) written by a poor, virtuous servant girl to her equally poor and virtuous parents about her troubles being pursued by her wealthy master. Pamela resists—through very hard work and strenuous effort—various temptations and attacks from her employer, and she wins him, not only to marriage (which occurs two-thirds of the way into the plot) but even more importantly to Christian repentance and sanctification.

What *Pamela* shares in common with *The Pilgrim's Progress* and Defoe's fiction—and with many novels of the eighteenth and nineteenth centuries—is the depiction of gradual improvement over sudden conversion. Such improvement in early novels and their precursors often features an individual in oppressive circumstances laboring through individual will and determination against various social systems and structures to achieve progress. As the genre of the novel developed, novels increasingly took into view not merely the rise of the individual but the improvement of society as a whole. This circle of improvement—the way in which individuals who improve help bring about social improvement and vice versa—is reflected through the history of the concept. It's reflective, too, of the dance that takes place throughout evangelicalism between the role of the individual and the community, the believer and the church, saving personal faith and the great cloud of witnesses. Conversion, sanctification, and perseverance are the true forms—and the modern, secular idea of improvement but a metaphor of those forms. And whether we are talking about improvement or sanctification, the notion that either can be achieved by individual will alone, apart from community, is a myth.

Methods of Improvement

Like improvement, the phenomenon of "methods" was newly emerging in the eighteenth century. When the Wesley brothers formed their Holy Club at Oxford, a systematic approach to spending time each day in continual prayer and devotion, they were mockingly jeered by their critics as "methodists" because of these methodical practices. This derisive nickname, as already mentioned, is the origin of the eventual name of what became the Methodist denomination. Weber observes that this pejorative term indicates just how new and odd such a devotional life—what would become the normal aspiration for evangelicals—was at the time. While pre-Reformation Christians tried to perform good works and "traditional duties conscientiously," Protestants and the later evangelicals viewed good works as evidence of sanctification. Thus, Weber explains, "the ethical practice of ordinary people was divested of its random and unsystematic nature and built up into a consistent method for the whole conduct of one's life."[34]

> Evangelical history, from its start to the present, is filled with examples of those who saw improvement (their own and others') as the outgrowth of their faith.

Evangelical history, from its start to the present, is filled with examples of those who saw improvement (their own and others') as the outgrowth of their faith.

For example, one of the most famous evangelicals of the eighteenth century, William Wilberforce, stepped into a context in which a vision of social and moral improvement was emerging. A few years after his conversion, he wrote these famous words in his journal in 1787: "God Almighty has set before me two great objects, the suppression of the slave trade and the reformation of manners."[35] Wilberforce, along with many of his evangelical peers, did indeed succeed toward both these ends. To think of the abolition of the slave trade as an effort at "improvement" may seem odd, but it works on two accounts. First, until improvement across all of society was imaginable, it would not be attempted, let alone accomplished. Once improvement of various dramatic kinds (including social, personal, and moral) became imaginable, it became possible. Second, as significant as abolition was, by no means did it end human trafficking, racism, or oppression. It was something, but not everything, as our continued struggles in these matters prove. It was an improvement.

Other efforts at social and self-improvement marked the years leading to and through the nineteenth century. Wilberforce's friend Hannah More embodied in one person many of the efforts of the age. She wrote conduct books for the poor and the wealthy. She wrote a bestselling novel aimed at the middle class, a story filled with lessons about education, marriage, and family. She published poetry, drama, antirevolutionary essays, and devotionals. In addition to voluminous writing, she opened Sunday schools throughout southwest England where the children of the laboring classes were catechized, taught to read, and instructed in skills that would help them find better work. The work of More, Wilberforce, and their like-minded friends was rooted in the evangelical ethos of activism, specifically oriented toward moral and social improvement. Courtesy literature, conduct books, and works like More's aimed at moral reform had in common a social concern. The improved manners and morals these works aimed to teach individuals would help improve society.

One can always count on Charles Dickens to offer the voice of conscientious objection to the whole ethos of his age. "Improvement" was no exception. In *Bleak House*, Dickens portrays Mrs. Pardiggle as a satirical picture of an evangelical do-gooder whose good deeds are done in a spirit of cruelty and condescension. Mrs. Pardiggle moralizes and reads the Bible to the poor people she visits, for example, but does nothing to alleviate their material distress. She forces her five children to devote themselves to her charitable causes, denying them joy or fun. All this is offered in the name of social improvement. Nevertheless, despite Dickens's satirical jab at such wrongheaded efforts, probably no other writer did more than him to effect real social improvements across society in the nineteenth century, particularly for children, criminals, and the poor.

The Rise of Self-Help

A new version of improvement literature that emerged in the nineteenth century centered on personal improvement: the self-help book. The first work of this kind was titled, appropriately, *Self Help*, published by Samuel Smiles in 1859.

"Heaven helps those who help themselves," declares the book's opening, a line that would become so famous that some would come to think it was the word of Scripture itself. Smiles continues, "The spirit of self-help is the root of all genuine growth in the individual."[36] And it is entirely toward the individual—largely apart from institutions and community—that the book is focused. In his preface to the later 1866 edition, Smiles explains that the object of the book "is to stimulate youths to apply themselves diligently to right pursuits,—sparing neither labour, pains, nor self-denial in prosecuting them,—and to rely upon their own efforts in life, rather than depend upon the help or patronage of others."[37] Smiles claims,

> Even the best institutions can give a man no active help. Perhaps the most they can do is, to leave him free to develop himself and improve his individual condition. But in all times men have been prone to believe that their happiness and well-being were to be secured by means of institutions rather than by their own conduct.[38]

Most of what follows consists of inspiring vignettes of almost entirely European men, whether greatly or lesser known, throughout history who demonstrated Smiles's vision of self-improvement. His vast array of exemplary people shows, he writes, that "great men" come from "no exclusive class nor rank in life." Rather, greatness is achievable by anyone who sets their mind to it. Even the greatest difficulties, in Smiles's rendering, become the "best helpers" by creating "powers of labour and endurance, stimulating into life faculties which might otherwise have lain dormant."[39] For Smiles, improvement and even greatness are merely matters of individual will—not birth, circumstance, opportunity, or social structures.

The same economic and other variables that made social mobility possible for the first time in human history made improvement in general—whether on a large or small scale—more appealing and attainable. Everyone wanted to emulate the lives of those in the superior ranks.

To have wealth was to be respectable,[40] but most people weren't born with it. In contrast, improvement was an egalitarian value. Anyone could improve from any starting point. Idleness, for example, was denounced among the rich and the poor. As Benjamin Franklin famously advised, "Time is money." Frugality could be practiced by both the haves and the have-nots. The "way to wealth, if you so desire it," Franklin urged, "is as plain as the way to market. It depends chiefly on two words, industry and frugality. Waste neither time nor money, but make the best use of both."[41] In a letter Franklin wrote to his grandson, who was away at school, Franklin remarked that there are "two sorts of people":

One who are well dress'd, live comfortably in Good Houses, whose Conversation is sensible and instructive, and who are Respected for their Virtue. The other Sort are poor, and dirty, and ragged and ignorant, and vicious, & live in miserable Cabbins or Garrets, on Coarse Provisions, which they must work hard to obtain, or which if they are idle, they must go without or Starve.[42]

Franklin went on to urge his grandson "to make good use of every moment" so as to become one of the better, rather than the "other sort." This ideal of the good house possessed by the supposedly better sort is captured in a 1789 painting by British painter George Morland, titled *Fruits of Early Industry and Economy* (see fig. 8).

Thus, the new virtue of duty, an obligation anyone could fulfill regardless of rank, replaced the old code of honor.[43] While gentility was a status granted only by birth, more and more the ability to be a "gentleman" or a "gentlewoman" evolved into a matter of character and manner rather than inherited class. John Henry Newman's *The Idea of a University* included a lengthy passage redefining the gentleman as some-one who gives ease and comfort to others.[44] While having material and economic means is one of the easiest ways to provide ease and comfort to others, good manners (which are free but must be acquired) can too. By emulating the wealthy, anyone could try to gain respectability in this way. On the other hand, the failure of anyone to succeed could then be attributed to poor character. This idea became common and is expressed by the fictional character John Thornton, a manu-facturer in Elizabeth Gaskell's novel *North and South* who blames the misery of the poor workers in his industrial town on themselves:

I believe that this suffering, which Miss Hale says is impressed on the countenances of the people of Milton, is but the nat-ural punishment of dishonestly-enjoyed pleasure, at some former period of their lives. I do not look on self-indulgent, sensual people as worthy of my hatred; I simply look upon them with contempt for their poorness of character.[45]

Not surprisingly, then, the signs of respectability—which overlapped greatly with the signs of success—became increasingly important. Wealth was one. But so, too, were the signs of wealth: conspicuous consumption and the display of that consumption. Keeping up appearances, so to speak. As we will see in a later chapter, Victorian architecture, decor, and clothing were characterized by excess, ornamentation, and abundance—improvement made manifest (see fig. 9). To the extent to which evangelicalism today is a commercial religion (and there is ample evidence that commercialism has been profoundly formative in the movement's identity, growth, and direction[46]), that commercial spirit took hold in the Victorian era, a period commonly called "the age of progress."

This appropriation of the signs of upper-class society by evangelicalism was paradoxical given that much about the lifestyle of the envied aristocratic class opposed evangelical practices and values. In fact, eighteenth- and nineteenth-century evangelicals aimed many of their reform efforts specifically toward the upper classes because reform of them would have the additional effect of setting an example for everyone else.

Evangelicals' emphasis on improvement (and that of the larger Enlightenment worldview) eventually held considerable sway. "It is not surprising," observes one historian, "that the early Victorian middle classes, seeking a code of behavior which would suit their professional needs and ambitions, eagerly espoused the model provided by the evangelicals."[47] By the middle of the Victorian age and beyond, self-improvement, especially economic self-improvement, had come to be regarded not merely as an aspiration but as a social duty: "To do the best for yourself was to do the best for society."[48] Art critic John Ruskin, who had deconverted from his earlier evangelical faith, advised, "See that no day passes in which you do not make yourself a somewhat better creature."[49] Today's hashtaggable idea of personal growth and improvement has a long history.

Evangelicalism's infatuation with secular notions of social progress and self-improvement is marked throughout the nineteenth and twentieth centuries. While evangelicals initially opposed nineteenth-century movements that emphasized the possibility that human effort could bring physical healing, mind cures, victory over sin—movements such as New Thought, the Keswick movement, and the Victorious Life—the influence of these popular teachings could not be entirely stemmed: therapeutic culture snaked its way into evangelicalism. Nineteenth-century revivalists such as D. L. Moody and Billy Sunday were among those whose teachings blended evangelicalism with notions of social progress and transformation through personal purity and piety.[50] In the twentieth century, spurred significantly by the popularity of Norman Vincent Peale's *The Power of Positive Thinking*, the self-help ethos became "a fully entrenched part of American life."[51]

> By the middle of the Victorian age and beyond, self-improvement, especially economic self-improvement, had come to be regarded not merely as an aspiration but as a social duty.

As religion became increasingly a private experience, and as the modern age became increasingly oriented toward individualism, "even evangelicals were integrating psychological concepts of self-worth into evangelicalism." Jesus became "the friend who helps us find happiness and self-improvement."[52] God became not merely omniscient, omnipotent, and omnipresent—but he became these things for the benefit of each individual—a kind of personal therapist, benefactor, and ever-present friend.[53] Therapeutic evangelicalism exists so you can "become a better you."[54] Eventually, it leads to a sense of saving yourself. Or being saved by improvement, a notion Flannery O'Connor skewers with a line delivered in earnest by the antihero of her novel *Wise Blood*: "Nobody with a good car needs to be justified."[55]

A recent glance at the bestsellers in Christian self-help books on Amazon showed Peale's book in first place, followed by books on topics such as boundaries, anxiety, hurry, self-discovery, washing your face, and becoming untamed. There's always room for improvement, I guess.

Evangelical culture is so steeped today in the self-improvement waters that it hardly needs to be stated. But it should also be

> "Nobody with a good car needs to be justified."

pointed out that this is the ethos of our age in general. Evangelicals and ex-vangelicals alike seem unable to resist the lure of selling Substack subscriptions, online courses, and personal coaching opportunities[56] as a way to improve by being more (or less) evangelical, more (or less) Christian, and less (or more) something else. In such a culture, even in the church, it can be difficult to distinguish conversion from self-help, spiritual growth from worldly success, sanctification from self-improvement.

But the converted person isn't merely "new and improved." She is a new creature.

6

Sentimentality

*Uncle Tom, Sweet Jesus,
and Public Urination*

What is it about so much contemporary "Christian" art that makes it so bad so often? Even the complaints have become cliché.

To be sure, there are many Christian writers and artists today who strive to defy this stereotype and succeed. Nevertheless, Christian art has a problem. It's easy to think this problem began with the cheesy evangelical movies and Christian rock of the 1980s and '90s. But the fact is that bad evangelical art has a long and interesting history. Of course, bad art can be bad for any number of reasons (such as lack of imagination, execution, or skill). But what tends to make evangelical Christian art bad is its sentimentalism.

What Is Sentimentality?

The word "sentimental" is most often used in a context in which an object is cherished not for its monetary worth but for the feelings it evokes, usually emotions associated with the memories or relationships the item represents. In fact, the word "sentiment" is nearly synonymous with *feelings* or *thoughts*. (Pedants take note: because to have sentiments about something means to have thoughts or feelings about it, there is no need to be critical or disapproving when people say, "I feel . . ." instead of "I think . . ." The meaning is essentially the same.)

Sentimentality itself isn't necessarily bad. But sentimental*ism* is an emotional response in excess of what the situation demands; it's an indulgence in emotion for its own sake. It is emotion that is unearned. As Victorian critic Leslie Stephen puts it, sentimentalism is "the name of the mood in which we make a luxury of grief, and regard sympathetic emotion as an end rather than a means."[1] To be wary of sentimentalism is by no means to reject feelings but rather is to recognize when emotion surpasses what is warranted. Like having candy for dinner every night, sentimentalism—meaning a way of life or worldview—can cause harm when it is not recognized as the indulgence that it is and then becomes a regular habit of life or a way of conceiving of the world.

Excessive emotion can develop from within ourselves, arising from our own individual propensities or personalities. But emotionalism can also be evoked by external manipulation. This is what sentimental art does: it attempts artificially to create feelings that exceed what the situation warrants.

> To be wary of sentimentalism is by no means to reject feelings but rather is to recognize when emotion surpasses what is warranted.

Television commercials using sweet puppies or cute babies to wring tears from our eyes in hopes of selling a certain brand of beer or phone service are obvious examples of the easily exploitative powers of sentimentality. So are romance novels, movies about Scottish warriors, and prints by Thomas Kinkade, the Painter of Light™.

Sentimentality sells, as Kinkade proves.

Kinkade was born again in 1980 while he was a college student. He showed tremendous talent as an artist from a young age. After some early artistic success, Kinkade shifted his style and his methods until eventually he was mass-producing the cozy, glowing cottage scenes that are said to hang in ten million homes.[2] His earliest paintings—the work of a serious artist—are nearly unrecognizable to anyone who knows the later works that made him rich and famous. Kinkade said in one interview that his moniker, Painter of Light, reflected his evangelical Christian beliefs, explaining, "Light is what we're attracted to. This world is very dark, but in heaven there is no darkness."[3]

A 2010 essay in *First Things* described him as "one of the most financially successful artists in the world," having sold more than ten million works, along with licensed products that include wallpaper, furniture, and stationery.[4] By the time he died in 2012 at the age of fifty-four, Kinkade's life and legacy had been marred by lawsuits over fraud, a DUI arrest, and an accusation that he had molested a female employee.[5] Additionally, and ironically, the man who had once denounced modernist art by calling it the "fecal school" of art and "bodily function" art[6] was said by witnesses to have developed a bizarre practice of urinating in public places.[7]

In 2013, the *Journal of British Aesthetics* published fascinating research examining the effects on viewers of repeated exposure to bad art. The bad works of art they used? Paintings by Thomas Kinkade.[8]

The Authority of Emotion

If the purpose of art is to recreate human experience, the purpose of sentimental art is to recreate emotional experience.

This can be harmless—such as when a souvenir from a vacation brings back warm memories of a cherished trip. But sentimentalism can do harm when emotions are evoked apart from or subordinate to other aspects of the human experience (such as intellectual, spiritual, or physical experience) and thus to the totality of what is real. Whether portraying things in terms overly sweet or overly sad, or whether interpreting people (who are complex) as one-dimensional heroes or villains, sentimentality smooths over the rough edges of reality and glosses over hard questions so as to tie things up neatly in a bow. Even glorified violence and prettified barbarity are forms of sentimentality because the emotions they evoke are distorted and thus detract from the ability of art to convey truth. There is a reason the ancients used the word "obscene" (which literally means "against the scene") for those things not fit to be portrayed on the stage.

It's not only art that can manipulate our emotions. Religion can too. And the connection between evangelicalism and sentimentalism is not just a coincidence of history.

A strength of the early evangelical movement was how it engaged with emerging ideas in philosophy, epistemology, and aesthetics. It might even be fair to say that evangelicalism, because it arose as a response to cultural forces more than doctrinal ones, has always reflected cultural currents, whatever they may be. This is both a strength and a weakness, of course. As a response to what had become the assumption of Christianity in the wider society, early evangelicalism rightly sought a more authentic Christianity, one rooted in an understanding of the whole person—affections, emotions, intellect, and will.

One school of thought that was growing more influential during the rise of the evangelical movement was sentimental philosophy. Sentimental philosophy grew out of a rivalry

> It's not only art that can manipulate our emotions. Religion can too.

between the two dominant Enlightenment-era epistemologies: rationalism and empiricism. Rationalists believed that abstract reasoning was the surest ground of knowledge, while empiricists, inspired by the new scientific method, thought that knowledge begins with the senses—what we can see, hear, touch, taste, and smell. Much discussion and debate was taking place concerning the relative powers of rational judgment versus affective responses resulting from sensory experience. This debate is the reason the term "sentiment" came to the fore, as it refers not only to conscious ideas and thoughts, as mentioned above, but also to "non-cognitive attitudes and states of all kinds—emotions, feelings, affects, desires, plans, and dispositions to have them."[9] The word comes from the same root as "sense," which encompasses not only the perceptual senses but also "sense" in terms of the impressions we form, impressions that begin in sensory experience—as in our *sense* of things.

This emphasis on sense emerged from the ideas of English philosopher John Locke. In his 1690 work *An Essay Concerning Human Understanding*, Locke argues, "Ideas in the Understanding, are coeval with Sensation; which is such an Impression or Motion, made in some part of the body, as makes it be taken notice of in the Understanding."[10] In other words, Locke believed that our ideas began with our physical, bodily experience and were then processed through the mind.

Later, the Scottish school of philosophy called "common sense realism" developed this vein of thinking in emphasizing the role of inductive reasoning (based on facts derived from observation and experimentation) rather than deductive reasoning (drawn from theoretical concepts and abstract principles). Scottish realism, based in common sense, argued that truth was accessible to all. The influence of common sense (or Scottish) realism on Protestantism (and subsequently the evangelical movement) was so significant that this school of philosophy has been called "the key to Puritan sensibilities."[11] Its influence is present today in strains of evangelicalism that are hostile to any whiff of elitism or intellectualism. Whatever is true, such thinking goes, is accessible to the common person through basic reason and sense—expertise and credentials be damned.

The Bible, too, came to be understood within this new conceptual frame as a sort of "storehouse of facts,"[12] a way of seeing the Bible that would have been inconceivable to the early church fathers (and had dramatic consequences when later scientific theories questioned the facts presented in the Bible). This school of thought also led to a view of the Bible that made less room for metaphors, literary complexity, or layers of meaning, which was a clear departure from earlier hermeneutical approaches, including those of Martin Luther and John Calvin.[13]

> Whatever is true, such thinking goes, is accessible to the common person through basic reason and sense, expertise and credentials be damned.

The Pietist tendencies of the Puritan ancestors of evangelicals were based on a rationalist approach to sanctification. This approach to virtue formation emphasized practices and habits (or methods, in the case of the Wesleys and their Holy Club) that could develop good character and build strong personal faith. But, influenced by the sentimentalism increasingly in the air, some evangelicals began to stress the role of emotion within individual faith experience. This development partly explains why evangelicalism came to be called a religion of the heart.[14] Eventually, evangelicals came to see "the repetitive engagement of the emotions" as a means of forming habits that would develop virtuous character.[15]

Again, emotions themselves do not comprise sentimentality. Rather, sentimentality entails a *repetition* of previous emotional experience. So while evangelicalism tends to think it eschews the ritual, liturgy, and "vain repetitions" (Matt. 6:7 KJV) of earlier church practices, it has its own habits or repetitions—its stock phrases, images, actions, and tropes—too often performed with little or no awareness or reflection.[16] When these repetitions aim solely to replicate certain emotional experiences, they fall squarely within the realm of the sentimental.

The Cult of Sensibility

Much has been made in recent years of expressive individualism, a modern understanding that assumes happiness or the good life depends on the fulfillment of one's own individual beliefs, desires, and goals as well as the ability to express these.[17] This increased experience of the inner world of the self as well as the sense of the interplay between the self and the world is called subjectivity.

In many ways, evangelicalism grew as a reflection of the new understanding of the self and of individual experience offered by sentimental philosophy. This shift in religious understanding took place within a much larger cultural context that placed a similar emphasis on the inner life. Subjectivity contributes, for example, to the evangelical movement's emphasis on the felt conversion experience as the basis for Christian faith rather than mere inheritance. In some ways, then, the story of evangelicalism is the story of the attempt—sometimes successful, sometimes not—to rejoin what no man should put asunder: the rational and emotional, the objective and subjective, the interior and external aspects that comprise the totality of what it means to be human.

Sensibility—a prevalent concept in the eighteenth century—is one expression of this emphasis on interiority that developed alongside the rise of the evangelical movement. Sensibility denoted a person's perceptiveness or responsiveness, a meaning more closely connected to sensory experience (the five senses) than what we mean today when we refer to something as "sensible" (reflecting common sense). The concept of sensibility was linked to "emotion," which means, most literally, *a movement out of*—in other words, an agitation or responsiveness that begins inside the body and moves outward. For example, Jane Austen's novel *Sense and Sensibility* centers on this meaning of "sensibility"; the two terms used in its title roughly correspond to what "reason" and "emotion" mean today. Austen, who published this work in 1811, was satirizing (among other things) sensibility because (as we will see below) it had grown so popular in previous decades that it had become a movement called the "cult of sensibility."

The cult of sensibility, which peaked in the mid-eighteenth century, elevated one's ability to be "sensible" toward (or emotionally responsive to) affecting situations, especially suffering. (Today, we would use the word "sensitive" rather than "sensible.") According to the cult of sensibility, our moral judgments, our abilities to discern good and evil, arise from properly attuned emotional responses evoked by the powers of sensory perception, a harmonizing of experiences of the inner life and the outer world. "Proper moral action" was understood to be "predicated on proper moral feeling."[18] To be capable of feeling strong emotions (sensibility), particularly pity at any form of suffering, whether human or animal, was considered to be moral and virtuous.[19] Because perceptions are capable of being directed and refined, education and experience played an important part in developing moral feeling. Thus, art that offered practice in bringing out such emotions served to instruct and thereby to advance moral improvement, a power seized on by Christians:

> Although the cult of sensibility was short-lived, its influence on the broader culture, including evangelicalism, was long-lasting.

By connecting sentiment to sensation, Christian culture raised a series of questions about the relations between mind and body, senses and spectatorship, and whether the wellsprings of faith lay in mystery or invigilation. By valuing sensory impressions, intense feeling, and active agency, Christian artworks offered a discomforting model for a public exhibition culture concerned with the comportment of spectators.[20]

Although the cult of sensibility was short-lived, its influence on the broader culture, including evangelicalism, was long-lasting, becoming a defining characteristic of the Victorian age (and beyond).[21] As one historian explains,

> In both Britain and the United States, the Victorian extension of this idea of sensibility as a moral quantity amounted to the definition of a kind of intrinsic character element of the socially refined and cultivated person. Sensibility in the nineteenth century was something that one had or one lacked in varying degrees, in the same way that Victorians saw culture as something possessed in quantities. To have sensibility was to have a capacity for sensitivity to moral and aesthetic experience. To lack sensibility was to be a moral and/or social idiot, unable to discriminate right from wrong, good art from bad, things to be valued from those to be deplored. In some ways, this notion of sensibility is similar to what today would be described in positive moral terms as a "sensitive" character—a person who feels deeply, is inclined to have "hurt" feelings, but who is compassionate and caring, capable of higher moral feeling.[22]

This link between aesthetic sensibility (feeling the right emotional response arise from sensory perception) and moral sense (making the right judgment)[23] led naturally to valuing the outward signs of emotional sensitivity—tears, ecstasies, and swoons. It wasn't a big leap to come to consider the signs themselves the marks of virtue.

Entire bodies of art and literature developed around sensibility. These works offered emotion-laden scenes that encouraged audiences to tremble in fear, weep in sadness, or rejoice in happiness as appropriate. For example, Richardson's novel *Pamela*, discussed earlier, elicited all of these responses, and the novel is considered a landmark in the genre of sentimental literature. *Pamela*'s sensational scenes depicting an innocent girl under physical and emotional attack, retaining her "virtue" through it all (and being rewarded in the end), advanced the cult of sensibility's idea that emotional responsiveness cultivates virtue and morality. Sentimentalists held that readers who can feel with Pamela her trials and temptations, as well as the relief that comes from her triumphs, are training their sensibilities toward the way of virtue. Two and a half centuries later, when an American presidential candidate replied to a question related to the economy with the equivalent of "I feel your pain,"[24] he was channeling a long history of sentimental philosophy.

Not everyone was on board the sensibility train, however. In 1782, a few decades after *Pamela* was published, poet and playwright Hannah More—who would soon become an evangelical—published her acclaimed poem "Sensibility." While praising sensibility, which was so very much in fashion (and More was quite fashionable herself during these years), the poem presents a gentle critique too. For one thing, the poem observes, sensibility is too vague and "still eludes the chains / Of definition." The poem also warns against confusing the signs of feeling for genuine acts of compassion, calling out anyone "who thinks feign'd sorrows all her tears deserve, / And weeps o'er WERTER,[25] while her children starve."[26] In other words, the poem suggests, true morality is in how we actually live, not how much emotion we feel from the imagined suffering portrayed in art and literature. Although Aristotle, Sir Philip Sidney, and others have argued (rightly) that good art can train the emotions in such a way that leads to virtuous action, the lesson offered by literature must be received and applied in order for virtue to develop. This is the point of More's complaint. Virtue is an action, not just a feeling.

Reform School

The Christian obligation to help a suffering stranger is an idea as old as the parable of the good Samaritan (which itself is an expansion of many teachings throughout the Old Testament). But the idea of proactively bettering the condition of entire social classes—the masses—was an emerging one within the early evangelical movement. It would come to define the movement, what David Bebbington termed "activism," one of the four characteristics that define evangelicalism as described in chapter 1. In fact, it was in large part owing to the early evangelicals that the larger society began to see human suffering in a different way—as a result of systemic injustices that could and should be eased. Tremendous scientific and social improvements were becoming possible because of the scientific revolution. But it was in great part the result of the evangelical emphasis on the individual—first individual salvation, then individual morality, then individual improvement overall—that it became more possible to think about the alleviation of unnecessary suffering. (Of course, this focus on the individual meant that suffering also tended to be understood as centering on individuals. This helps explain why the evangelical movement has tended to be blind to injustices that have been baked over time into systems and institutions in ways

> The Christian obligation to help a suffering stranger is an idea as old as the parable of the good Samaritan (which itself is an expansion of many teachings throughout the Old Testament).

that are often hidden from individual, conscious awareness.) Whereas the prevailing view for time immemorial had been that poverty, sickness, and calamity were God's will for those who suffered those fates, the evangelical reformers of the eighteenth century imagined that such improvements were not only possible but attainable and desirable. They therefore set out to abolish the slave trade, educate the poor, improve conditions for laborers, and stem cruelty to animals.[27] The reforms sought and achieved by evangelicals in the later eighteenth century and early nineteenth century set the stage for the "age of progress" that would define the Victorian period.

Eighteenth-century evangelicals based their vision for widespread social reform on the virtue of benevolence (which means, literally, "good will"). What underlies benevolence is "a forgetfulness of self in the recognition of our common humanity."[28] It is a fine virtue. Sentimentality, however, in centering one's own emotional responsiveness, is a "deterioration" of benevolence.[29] Because it focuses on the self and one's own emotional response, sentimentality does away with the most important thing needed for benevolence: the forgetfulness of the self. Thus, the rise of sentimentality has been linked to the decline of robust Christian faith.[30] Where evangelicalism slides into sentimentalism, it can be counted as participating in this decline.

Sentimental philosophy, along with the art it inspired, bears both gifts and curses. One great good it brought has been in making us more sensible (or sensitive) to the experiences of others around us—in other words, to empathize, although it wasn't called that then. In fact, the English word "empathy" was coined only about a century ago, well after the rise of sentimentality, when it was translated from a German word that means "feeling-in." (Notably, one other translation that was considered was "aesthetic sympathy," a phrase that points to how empathy refers to feelings as both conscious thoughts and bodily or aesthetic sensations.)[31]

Perhaps no Victorian wielded the power of sentimentalism more effectively than Charles Dickens. Although his novels transcend the narrower (and generally inferior) subgenre of sentimental novels, Dickens's use of techniques of sentimental art is part of what made his masterpieces so wildly successful. Dickens painted sympathetic pictures of suffering, usually those of people least deserving it (often orphans, widows, the poor). Such misery in real life was, of course, all around—in the lives of countless neglected or abused orphans, workers, inmates, and women. But such unnecessary affliction was so common and so unquestioned for so long that it had become practically invisible. By making this suffering manifest in affecting scenes within gripping narratives, Dickens helped people first to imagine suffering, then to finally see the real suffering that had been right in front of them all the time.

Dickens was not the first to highlight needless suffering in his art, of course. Poets in particular had been exploring issues of social justice, suffering, and moral sentiments for some decades. The Romantic poets William Blake and William Wordsworth are noteworthy for paying attention in their art to the pains of the commoner, a subject deemed unworthy for traditional aesthetics. But even before these luminaries of poetic imagination, lesser-known evangelical poets Hannah More and William Cowper helped transform poetry and other literary forms away from the cool, neoclassical aesthetic toward more humane, emotional, earthy warmth.

But it was the novel form, still a newly developing genre, that reached a critical mass in readership and truly transformed the modern social imaginaries, including the evangelical imagination.

On the opposite side of the Atlantic, Harriet Beecher Stowe published *Uncle Tom's Cabin* in 1852. A truly sentimental novel, *Uncle Tom's Cabin* was written by a white person in order to move the sympathies of white readers toward abolition of slavery. The novel did exactly that. One oft-repeated (though possibly apocryphal) legend is that upon being introduced to Stowe, President Abraham Lincoln greeted her by calling her "the little woman who wrote the book that started this great war."[32]

But the same sentimental quality that so moved *Uncle Tom's Cabin*'s readers is also what renders the novel objectionable. While it humanized slaves enough to draw the ire of slave owners, the palatability of its message to those who did receive it sympathetically depended a great deal on racist tropes and stereotypes that did harm along the way—as any form of sentimentalism, ultimately, will do.

It was the novel form, still a newly developing genre, that reached a critical mass in readership and truly transformed the modern social imaginaries, including the evangelical imagination.

Popular novelists like Dickens (who was a Christian, although not entirely orthodox and not at all fond of evangelicals) and Stowe (whose Christian faith tended toward evangelical) proved the theories of moral philosophers from previous centuries who recognized that sensibility can cultivate morality. But, as *Uncle Tom's Cabin* demonstrates, what sentimentality gives, sentimentality can take away. While sentimentality can move one to sympathize with others in their suffering, it can also, ironically, cultivate self-centeredness as "one enjoys feeling a burst of kindness for those less fortunate than himself."[33] This helps explain why sentimentality and sentimental art can be found on both sides of the liberal/conservative political divide: everyone likes to feel good about themselves. Moreover, as Lauren Berlant argues in her examination of the role of sentimentality in American culture, the personal feelings aroused by sentimental art and literature (such as *Uncle*

Tom's Cabin) may ultimately, and paradoxically, impede the social, political, and structural changes needed to address the cause of suffering. Because in sentimentalism the focus is too much on the personal and private rather than the public, even politically motivated sentimental rhetoric replaces "the ethical imperative toward social transformation" with a more "passive and vaguely civic-minded ideal of compassion."[34] Sentimentalism inches toward change; it does not revolutionize.

Sentimentalism reflected and enabled subtle shifts in Christian belief. For example, the emotional deathbed scenes that were so common in Victorian novels—particularly in the novels of Dickens and Stowe—were, one critic says, "clearly connected with the religious crisis" of the age. Such emotional scenes were "intended to help the reader sustain his faith by dissolving religious doubt in a solution of warm sentiment. When the heart is so strongly moved, the skeptical intellect is silenced," and the believer is reassured.[35] Reassurance of one's saving faith is good, of course. But not if that blessed assurance is founded in feelings alone.

Sentimental Jesus

While the sentimentality of eighteenth- and nineteenth-century evangelicals was oriented toward societal reform, in the twentieth century, as individualism and consumerism came more and more to reign, sentimentality came to reflect that growing individualism.

It would be difficult to find a more exemplary cultural artifact of this marriage of sentimentality and individualism than Warner Sallman's *Head of Christ*.

The most famous image of Jesus in the modern world, this painting powerfully demonstrates the double power of popular art: first, to reflect existing ideas, then to deepen their hold within a social imaginary.

For much of the twentieth century, *Head of Christ* was omnipresent. The original, painted by Sallman in 1940, was reproduced not only in prints of every size and quality but also in Bibles and church bulletins, on prayer cards and plaques, and even on clocks and lamps. Countless millions of people have had their own image of Jesus—ethereal, luminous, serene, and sexy—formed by this picture, often without even being aware of the source, never even imagining that Jesus could look any other way.

Head of Christ did not emerge ex nihilo. The story of how the work was created and how it ended up being reproduced more than 500 million times[36] offers a story within the story of how a social imaginary is formed and manifested.

Sallman had been commissioned to create the cover art for the monthly magazine of his denomination, the Evangelical Covenant Church. As he later retold the story, the image that became *Head of Christ* came to him as a vision following agonizing days and hours of futile effort, just before his deadline, in what he described as a "glorious appearing."[37] Sallman had more than a miracle to help him, however. Having studied at the Chicago Institute of Art, he was familiar with earlier paintings of Jesus, on which he modeled *Head of Christ*. In addition, having worked in the advertising industry, Sallman had marketing savvy that would help him create cover art that would appeal to the magazine's audience. By drawing on previous paintings of Christ and on contemporary trends in portraiture, Sallman created an image both fresh and familiar.[38] *Head of Christ* mimics the pose that was then popular for graduation photos[39] and celebrity close-ups amid a rising "cult of personality"[40] whose "legacy of personal promotion and facial display"[41] continues even today.

In this way, Sallman managed to create a Jesus who was at once celebrity and Everyman.

Except not quite *every* man. Portraying a white, or at best a racially ambiguous, Jesus, *Head of Christ* was not so much historically accurate as it was familiar, palatable, and desirable to Sallman's target audience. This audience consisted first of readers of the magazine, then later a far wider audience: consumers of the various reproductions of the painting. As is typical with popular art, the painting depicted "what an audience is pre-disposed to see."[42] Jesus's warm, radiant countenance is "earnest and accessible,"[43] offering "a compelling visualization of the values and devotional and religious ideas" of mainstream evangelicalism.[44] In portraying Christ the way the painting's admirers believed he would look, the work reflected their "mores, theology, social agenda, and ecclesiology,"[45] serving as a kind of Protestant version of Christ's "real presence."[46]

Of course, there is a chicken-and-egg scenario here: Which came first? Sallman's image of Christ or the glamorous celebrity Jesus that had already been conceived within the womb of the American evangelical social imaginary? Whichever the answer, the result is the same. For, as James K. A. Smith explains, "Over time, rituals and practices—often in tandem with aesthetic phenomena like pictures and stories—mold and shape our precognitive disposition to the world by training our desires."[47]

In recent years, the inaccurate race of Sallman's Jesus has been a frequent object of criticism,[48] but even before that, the image was embroiled in a different controversy: not around whether Sallman's Christ was too white, but whether he was too feminine.

While studying at Moody Bible Institute, Sallman had been exhorted by one of his professors to paint "a virile, manly Christ."[49] But as soon as *Head of Christ* gained popularity, opinions were divided on this question. Some saw in the painting a gentle and warm Jesus ("a vision of domestic Christian nurture"[50]), while others found the embodiment of masculine strength.[51] One person complained, "In Sallman's *Head of Christ*, we have a pretty picture of a woman with a curling beard who has just come from the beauty parlor with a Halo shampoo, but we do not have the Lord who died and rose again!"[52] Artist Marion Junkin derided the work as "a prettified portrait for the sentimental,"[53] while one evangelical minister, in recommending it to young people in particular, said that "just to look at that noble countenance, which expresses character, sympathy, consecration, composure, devotion, strengthens my spirit and purifies my soul."[54]

Some aspects of both masculinity and femininity are connected to biological sex, of course, while other aspects are rooted in historical and cultural context. (When one advocates for masculinity, is it the masculinity of King James I in his velvet cloak and crinkled ruff, or is it that of Chad, the cartoon figure of the alpha male popular in manosphere memes? Does the hardy peasant woman sowing the fields to help feed her large family in nineteenth-century Russia meet the criteria of femininity set by today's evangelical social media influencers?) It's helpful to consider how some aspects of cultural expectations around masculinity and femininity originate in feelings that have grown up around our contextually based perceptions of what constitutes "masculinity" and "femininity." Often, exaggerated expressions of masculinity and femininity (like those found in cosplaying militia groups or plastic-surgery-enhanced housewives of certain counties) are at base just a form of sentimentalism: indulgence in the feelings aroused by our own personal and cultural associations more than reality.

The debate surrounding *Head of Christ* is perfectly illustrative of this phenomenon, given that there is no biblical or historical record of Christ's physical appearance, particularly in terms of his masculinity (except, as stated in Isa. 53:2, that he *lacked* physical beauty and majesty). A veritable Rorschach test, Sallman's paintings of Jesus (he created many) allowed viewers to see in them (or to find missing) what they had already been taught to imagine Christ to be—and to have that image cemented in their understanding.[55]

More was at play, too, than merely images of Christ's physical appearance. Form and content ultimately cannot be separated, and the forms Sallman created taught something about his Christian faith and the faith of those who gazed upon them. For example, hanging Sallman's *Head of Christ* in the home communicated that Jesus was the "head of the household."[56] Similarly, Sallman's 1942 *Christ at Heart's Door* (an image that had predecessors in earlier art but was popularized by Sallman's version) borrowed from and, in turn, further emphasized evangelicalism's belief in the personal, private, and domestic aspect of the salvation experience.

> Form and content ultimately cannot be separated, and the forms Sallman created taught something about his Christian faith and the faith of those who gazed upon them.

As sensationally popular as *Head of Christ* was, only a couple of decades later the image was already considered outdated and became "suddenly Victorian." Just as Sallman had drawn from earlier images of Christ, his work, in turn, yielded its own crops of imitators, updated to reflect ever newer sensibilities.[57]

Such a series of modified imitations embodies the repetition that characterizes sentimentality. Repetition familiarizes and, in the case of sentimentality, overfamiliarizes. This is why sentimental art (and sentimental thinking of any kind) traffics in familiar tropes and stock characters. Sentimentality reinforces rather than refines beliefs. It softens edges rather than clarifies. It serves to comfort rather than correct. There is, of course, a time and a place for reinforcement, softness, and comfort. But these must be balanced by

challenges—including emotional and aesthetic challenges—
that strengthen rather than pacify, that enlarge perception
rather than narrow it.

▩ "How Nice to Be Moved"

In the classical tradition, truth, goodness, and beauty are
understood to be three transcendental qualities or universal
realities that originate in and lead to the eternal and divine.
The Christian tradition emphasizes the trinitarian relationship of these transcendent realities, each of which finds its
source in and reflects God (as reflected by Augustine's address
to beauty quoted in chap. 2). Beauty is the quality that makes
truth and goodness manifest.

It is easy to confuse the beautiful with the sentimental
because in some ways both are aesthetic experiences. The
root meaning of "emotion" is *stirring, agitation,* or *movement,*
which later came to mean "feelings." At the most fundamental
level, an aesthetic experience is an affective experience, one
that moves us. To be moved by something is to experience a
bodily response, such as a quickened heartbeat, widened eyes,
gathering tears, a gasp, a nod, or a smile. Sentimental art can
move us or evoke emotion, just as true beauty does. But not
all movements are equal.

Consider this famous passage from Milan Kundera's novel,
The Unbearable Lightness of Being, which points to the difference. Kundera is defining "kitsch," which is cheap, deriva-
tive, sentimental art. Kitsch comes in many forms, including
amusement park souvenirs, garden gnomes, knickknacks,
Hobby Lobby wall decor, Lifetime movies, and so on (see
fig. 10). Kundera explains kitsch this way:

> Kitsch causes two tears to flow in quick succession. The first
> tear says: How nice to see children running on the grass!

The second tear says: How nice to be moved, together with all mankind, by children running on the grass![58]

Kitsch, like sentimentalism, indulges emotion for the sake of the emotion itself. And as Kundera points out, that second emotion is self-aware and self-satisfied. Again, emotions are not bad. They are good. They are essential to our humanity. But divorced from their proper purpose of rightly driving our thoughts and actions, sentimentality is akin to pornography, as Flannery O'Connor memorably puts it. For both sentimentality and pornography sever the *experience* (emotional in the first case, sexual in the latter) from its *meaning* and *purpose*.[59]

In reality, you can't have beauty apart from truth. Beauty apart from truth and goodness is mere sentimentality.

Yet, just as it is easy to satisfy our physical hunger with fast food rather than good food, so, too, is it easy for our appetites to be whetted and then filled by cheap forms of art and beauty, and for our emotions to be seduced by false versions of truly aesthetic experiences. Indeed, living in the age of late capitalism, defined by the marriage of consumerism and mass production, causes us to be surrounded, overwhelmed even, by opportunities for easy sentiment and cheap luxury.

> **In reality, you can't have beauty apart from truth. Beauty apart from truth and goodness is mere sentimentality.**

Easy sentiment isn't limited to the world of art and entertainment, however. The habit of quick and easy emotional experiences naturally transfers from objects to people and relationships. Indeed, evangelicals today "live in an aesthetic world where emotion is the currency to interact not only with other human beings but also with God."[60]

In *Good Taste, Bad Taste, and Christian Taste: Aesthetics in Religious Life*, Frank Burch Brown examines the theological implications of taste. Taste, Brown writes, plays a significant part in forming religious perceptions and identities, in creating and reinforcing religious differences, and in making possible a wide variety of religious and moral discernments and experiences. Matters of religion and morality cannot be reduced to aesthetics; neither can aesthetics be reduced to religion and morality. But these spheres overlap and interact in ways that we have barely begun to appreciate.[61]

Most of us in modern-day America have effortless access to art, music, and literature—we have abundant works of great truth, goodness, and beauty, and we have an even more abundant supply of false imitations. This means it is easy to forget how much sacrifice is required to truly experience what real beauty invites us to. Even the enjoyment of natural beauty usually exacts a sacrifice: for most of us, a walk in the woods requires time, attention, and energy that we are constantly tempted to spend on other things. Whatever is easily consumed—without effort or thought or cost—is rarely the genuine thing. What soothes, mollifies, and rouses not a second thought is often cheap and sentimental—and our desire for it is an indictment of the deformity of our souls.

> What soothes, mollifies, and rouses not a second thought is often cheap and sentimental—and our desire for it is an indictment of the deformity of our souls.

We also have effortless access to religion (at least in the free world).

In this effortlessness—the ease, the lack of sacrifice, the mere assumption—lies the danger of the sentimental. Whenever and wherever evangelicalism substitutes the sentimental for the sacrificial, we are in danger of getting the gospel wrong.[62]

In *Homespun Gospel*, Todd Brenneman offers insightful connections between the sentimentality that characterizes much of modern-day evangelicalism and the great crises emerging within too many evangelical churches and communities. Evangelical sentimentality is not limited to warm, fuzzy feelings about God, Brenneman says.

> It is also a means to perpetuate the evangelical community and instantiate religious authority. . . . It perpetuates a specific worldview, not through intellectual assent to beliefs but through the internalization of emotional habits of seeing that world through sentimental eyes. Contemporary evangelical sentimentality is a conservative force to perpetuate authority.[63]

The authority of sentimentality is not unique to evangelicalism. This kind of authority is inherent in the modern condition, where authority is increasingly subjective and personal rather than objective and transcendent. Yet, some of the built-in features of evangelicalism cultivate sentimental forms of authority. The evangelical mantra that Christianity is "a relationship, not a religion," for example, while seeking to correct the error of an impersonal, ritualized religion, can also become an error in the other direction—toward an entirely subjective, emotional experience. Namely, sentimental religion. "Friendship evangelism," which seeks to use personal relationships for the purpose of evangelization, takes this direction even further.

Evangelical leaders, especially celebrity ones, tend to relate to the public on a more relational, personal basis than do their more traditional high church peers. Pastors and choir members are more likely to don street clothes or casual wear than vestments and robes, making them look more like friends than church officials. This is not bad or wrong in itself. In fact, I think it is to be preferred. However, such an approach can make it easy to gloss over the fact that leaders have authority, power, and influence over others even if they wear khakis and polo shirts and prefer to go by their first names. The informality of such power can make us blind to it. The failure to recognize power that doesn't look like power creates conditions ripe for abuse of that power. The tricky thing about sentimentality within evangelicalism is not just that it exists—but that we hardly know it exists (if we know it at all). And yet, it is deeply forming and directing us.

Of course, this is true of most elements of a social imaginary—the water we swim in, to return to the metaphor invoked in chapter 1. But there are different kinds of water: seawater and freshwater, for example. Because the late-modern age in which we live is

> The failure to recognize power that doesn't look like power creates conditions ripe for abuse of that power.

largely shaped by expressive individualism—which is inherently sentimental—sentimentalism is naturally something we easily assume rather than become aware of. Returning to the metaphor of the parts of a house, sentimentalism might be the furnace, which is felt but not seen. The unexamined sentimentalism that characterizes evangelicalism today encourages us "to encounter life through emotionally charged engagement."[64] But, Brenneman says, "there is generally minimal *cultural self-consciousness* about the presence and use of sentimentality in evangelicalism."[65]

A lack of introspection can make people vulnerable to veiled forms of authority that don't present themselves as authority. Sentimentality, as we have seen, is one form of authority that is largely unexamined. There are many others.

Sensible Sentimentality

Sentimentality and sensibility were never only about emotion. Both concepts are related not only to our capacity for sensory experience (which animals share with humans) but also to the intellectual faculties that, through the senses, receive perceptions and form impressions. Even having an impression depends on more than mere sensory ability. An impression requires attentiveness to the sensory event and reception of it in the mind (whether consciously or subconsciously). Think of the way we find ourselves subconsciously humming a song we heard earlier in the day, perhaps without even having noticed the song playing at the time. In this way, sensibility, which is a kind of aesthetic experience, is as connected to the rational mind as it is to emotional response. Most significantly, sentimental philosophy, recognizing that the body and mind are connected, understands that sensory experience constitutes "the basis of intellectual and imaginative constructs."[66]

While we are right to be suspicious of sentimentalism wherever it might be found (even, or perhaps especially, in our own tradition), in seeing how it originated as a response to an opposite impulse, we might not only correct its error but also avoid erring in the opposite direction through overcorrection (by placing too little value on our emotional register). Virtue, as the classical tradition teaches, is the moderation between two extremes. It is a kind of harmony.

7

Materiality

Jesus in the Window, the Virgin Mary on Grilled Cheese, Gingerbread Houses, and the Sacramentality of Church Space

One day, when I was a girl of about six, I was playing on the swing set in the backyard of my little friends who lived next door to me. I was seated on the swing facing the rear of the house. As I pumped higher and higher, I looked up at the second-floor bedroom window in front of me, which was covered with a screen. Each time I swung toward the house, the light shifted in the screen, and each time I rose up, the shape of a face appeared there. It was a man's face. It had a beard and was haloed by shoulder-length hair. It was Jesus.

"I see Jesus! I see Jesus!" I shouted in utter ecstasy to my girlfriends, who quickly hopped onto the empty swings and pumped as fast as they could in hopes that they, too, would see Jesus in the window.

I don't think they did.

But I remember that face in the screen like it was yesterday. Even more, I remember my elation. I was sure the Lord was there in the window, gazing down at me, kindly and serenely. I realize now that he looked just like Warner Sallman's *Head of Christ*.

I don't remember whether at that age I was aware of the mystical sightings around the world that made the news or history from time to time: the imprint of Jesus in the Shroud of Turin or a pancake, the Virgin Mary on a grilled cheese sandwich, or Julian of Norwich's vision of a bleeding Christ adorned by a crown of thorns.

My family was Baptist, but my next-door neighbors were Catholic. Inside their house hung numerous pictures, beads, and icons of a sort I'd never before seen. Outside, in their yard, among the flowers and shrubs, stood a statue of Mary ensconced by a gleaming porcelain bathtub, a jarring juxta-position—even then I saw that—of the sacred and the profane.

Was it any wonder then that I saw Jesus on their window screen?

A Material Girl, Living in a Material World

Human cultures consist of many things. Some of these things are intangible and of the mind: manners, institutions, orga-nizations, values, preferences, and religions. Some of these things are concrete and material: tools, buildings, furniture, clothing, works of art, crafts, and decorations.

Religion is traditionally counted within the category of the intangible—the spiritual, transcendent, and immaterial realm. Much of the debate around what evangelicalism is and who counts as evangelical (or counts themselves as evangelical) is centered on questions that fall within this category of the intangible, including beliefs, values, and traditions. And let's not forget politics and voting. Especially politics and voting.

Evangelicalism is, to be sure, a movement defined foremost by intangible characteristics that include beliefs, behaviors, and ideas. Awakening, conversion, testimony, and sentimentality are examples. This focus on the world of ideas, beliefs, and thoughts—often held in opposition to the realm of the physical, material, and bodily—has been around a long time. We see it in the idealism of Plato. We see a more modern strain of such dualism in Descartes: *Cogito, ergo sum* (I think, therefore I am). But while much of what we attempt to understand about evangelicalism focuses on the abstract rather than the concrete (including the focus of this book—ideas, images, and metaphors), the sensible world also matters.

Evangelical culture,[1] like all cultures, manifests itself materially too.

You might be thinking that last sentence could qualify as the understatement of the year. After all, you've gone into Christian bookstores that carry all the Jesus junk, seen the hobby and craft supply chains, been cut off by cars with Jesus bumper stickers, and maybe even worn a T-shirt emblazoned with "Lord's Gym" or "This Blood's For You."

Material culture is alive and well within evangelicalism.

To be fair, this culture of objects, their production, and consumption—the knickknacks, the kitsch, the plaques, the WWJD bracelets, the floppy hats and tall boots, the skinny jeans, and designer coffee drinks ubiquitous among evangelicals—merely reflects the larger late capitalist, conspicuously consumeristic culture. Evangelicals are, in this regard, apparently no different.

Material culture simply refers to the physical objects and structures of a society as well as all the behaviors that engage with these material artifacts: the way they are created and used, along with their meanings in people's lives or in a society. Evangelicalism has a material culture. To study it is to learn more about the movement and its people. As Lauren Winner explains in *A Cheerful and Comfortable Faith: Anglican Religious Practice in the Elite Households of Eighteenth-Century Virginia*, material objects "invite the study of religious practice because objects imply practices and practitioners." Winner argues that material objects can reveal as much about a culture and a belief system as written records or literary texts can, a provocative observation about a word-centered religion such as Protestant Christianity.[2]

Material culture (both itself and as a field of study) exists because humans have material existence—we have bodies, and the things in the world have physical properties—and because humans have culture. The ways we use our bodies are practices learned in community. As material-culture scholar David Morgan puts it, "People count, cut their meat, bathe, put on their clothing, sit, squat, gesticulate, wave, and laugh in ways peculiar to the social bodies to which they belong—their tribe, city, nation, race, or religion."[3] Our bodies adopt postures, make gestures, take on expressions, and engage in movements that are both actions and signs. They "are signs embedded in a medium experienced as continuous with the physical world" but often "operate below the level of consciousness."[4]

Material culture, it's important to clarify, is not the same thing as materialism. Materialism—whether the philosophy that locates all explanations and meaning in the material world apart from the spiritual one, or the other meaning that refers to the excessive pursuit of material goods—is a values system or worldview. Material culture is much broader—not to mention more morally and ethically neutral—than these. To be human is to live in and with material goods and to participate in the creation and consumption of the same.

> Material culture (both itself and as a field of study) exists because humans have material existence—we have bodies, and the things in the world have physical properties—and because humans have culture.

To discuss evangelical material culture is to consider something applicable to all human beings but in the ways that are distinct to and particularly meaningful within evangelicalism. It is to consider "the social operation of feeling propelled by images, objects, spaces, sounds, and movement"[5] within evangelicalism. Obviously, that covers a lot of ground. Sounds alone—from the hymns of Charles Wesley to Larry Norman[6] to CCM to Christian rap—could take entire books to cover. And they do. But let's consider, even if cursorily, some images, objects, and spaces as examples of the way in which materiality is inseparable from spirituality.

Evangelical Material Culture and Protestant Iconoclasm

When considering that the evangelical movement emerged directly out of the Protestant Reformation, it might seem counterintuitive that images like *Head of Christ* (not to mention countless other Christian paintings, T-shirts, statuettes, plaques, prints, wall hangings, decals, and decorations) should find such a powerful place in the evangelical social imaginary. After all, the Reformers centered the word over the image. Indeed, some of the Reformers were iconoclasts, going so far as to destroy priceless graven images such as the ancient Ruthwell Cross. "Protestant reformers privileged the ear over the eye, hearing over seeing, the word over the image, and the book over the statue."[7]

Yet, early Protestantism's rejection of images is not as wholesale or complete as is often believed. As ample specimens of illustrated Bibles, religious books, and Christian-themed crafts from the seventeenth century and beyond prove, many Protestants have treasured pictures. The fact is that despite the word-centered culture of Protestantism and evangelicalism, visual culture has always been present, albeit in ways less obvious than is usually recognized within Roman Catholicism, for example. Indeed, "the commerce and mass production of devotional images" has always been "a characteristic and constructive element of Protestant piety."[8] The Reformation "did not eliminate images but rather substituted acceptable images in acceptable places for unacceptable images in unacceptable places."[9]

This early Protestant visual culture was nonetheless usually connected to texts. The old statues of saints in the Roman church were replaced by prints of biblical scenes. Both are forms of visual and material culture, but the latter is more textually based. Even the purely visual art that was not directly tied to a text that could be found in Protestant spaces—such as altar art, woodcuts, and paintings—tended to be narratival. So, while early Protestantism boasted a rich, varied visual culture, these images usually either told a story or supported the telling of a story.[10] Protestantism's word-centered theology created images that worked less as an image than as an aid to the words. Thus, even images were to be understood "literally"—to be *interpreted* rather than simply absorbed or felt aesthetically.

> Early Protestantism's rejection of images is not as wholesale or complete as is often believed.

As a matter of doctrine, the Reformers replaced the office of priest with the priesthood of all believers. But in practice, this diffusion of authority was made possible by material means. These means included the mass printing of Bibles and other documents (especially pamphlets but also books) as well as the physical press that produced them. As a result of this technology and the artifacts it generated, literacy expanded and with that the ability of the masses to engage in the doctrinal debates circulating in print. The Reformation emphasized the centrality of the Word and spread throughout the world because of the ability to print the Reformers' words.

Seeing Is Believing

Visual culture is one subset of material culture. Visual culture most obviously includes the visual arts, but it encompasses much more than that. In *The Embodied Eye: Religious Visual Culture and the Social Life of Feeling*, David Morgan explains it as "the *cultural* function of visuality." The word "function" is important. Think of how the appearance of where people meet, live, and work—homes, parks, town halls, and churches—influences what happens in those spaces. The visual culture of a place creates a "sensory world" that primes those gathered within it "to think, feel, and see *communicatively*."[11] We see not only as individuals, Morgan explains, but as part of a social body. We see with eyes not wholly our own because what we see is oriented and practiced by the community and the culture of which we are a part.[12] Visual culture habituates us to certain ways of seeing. This point offers an important connection between the sentimental basis for the moral life (examined in the previous chapter) and material culture. If sympathy is the fruit (manifested by attention to and identification with the experience of others), then imagination—the ability to "see," both literally and metaphorically—is the root.

A sacrament is often described as an outward sign of an inward state—in other words, a *visible* sign.

Evangelicals aren't big on sacraments. At least, not officially. But we do believe, at some level, that the external reflects the internal, which is the heart of sacramental theology: "As he thinks within himself, so he is" (Prov. 23:7 NASB). "If you confess with your mouth that Jesus is Lord and believe in your heart that God raised him from the dead, you will be saved" (Rom. 10:9 ESV).

It's commonplace now to critique the state of contemporary worship spaces. In place of vaulted ceilings and flying buttresses, we have sound-deadening ceiling tiles. Instead of choir lofts and pipe organs, we have canned music and computer slides. Instead of stained glass windows depicting the miracles from Holy Scriptures, we have drywall and EXIT signs. There is much to justly lament in anemic church architecture. But there is also much that we might miss by focusing on what is lacking. If we compare ancient European cathedrals with the plain style of old New England churches, for example, we might think the latter comes up short. But in his extended examination of plain American churches, Morgan offers insightful observations.

The bare aesthetic of traditional Protestant worship spaces is not, Morgan argues, a rejection of beauty but rather a different aesthetic experience that reflects different beliefs and values. Rather than being simply against images, Protestants express materiality in a different way. White walls unadorned by art, for example, are "a compelling metaphor for the notion of starting over" after the Reformation.[13] Traditionally, Protestants (and perhaps contemporary evangelicals more generally) emphasize through their visual culture the "reliability and authority of texts or voices." Morgan points out that "a plain style of architecture and furnishing endorses a corresponding body practice that enhances listening as the principal medium of the sacred."[14] Even a matter as simple as the pews being arranged in rows facing the pulpit creates a visual space and embodied means of reinforcing the priority of the Word both spoken and heard.[15] Thus, the worship spaces of Protestant churches historically "underscore the iconicity of words, which Protestants elevate above materiality as they do souls above bodies."[16]

Visual Art in the Age of Print Culture

The print culture that arose as a result of the Reformation (among other cultural shifts) transformed art too. As previously discussed, print culture gave birth to the novel form. While poetry was written (primarily) to be heard, and drama (primarily) to be performed, the novel was written to be read. It is a narrative art.

Paintings created around the time of the rise and establishment of print culture took on a more narrative form too. In the eighteenth century, William Hogarth's various series of paintings satirizing the idea of "progress" narrate dramatic and morally instructive stories, scene by scene. By the Victorian era of the next century, a style called narrative painting arose, a genre reflecting the didactic, prosaic mood of the age as well as the rising popularity of the novel.

Indeed, such paintings were "read" like novels, sometimes even over successive viewings. This interactive nature is what made the genre so popular. Narrative painting "empowers" the viewer, "encouraging him or her to work at the image, to take a part in unravelling its meanings, and even to determine that it is to be 'read' in the first place."[17] Henry James, on a visit to the Royal Academy in 1877, observed (disapprovingly) that some viewers of the paintings "projected themselves into the story" of the paintings. They seemed to read the paintings rather than view them, thus betraying form for function. For James, these paintings "embodied the worst excesses of Victorian sentiment."[18]

Narrative paintings often presented scenes from ordinary life and strove for a realism attempting to portray what the painters considered to be a "truthful view of the world."[19] The tendency of narrative paintings (recall *The Awakening Conscience* from chap. 2, for example) to include many intricate details, whether realistic, symbolic, or both, added to the interpretive layers of the painting's "story." Ironically, however, as one critic observes, "heavy-handed realism" ceases to be realistic when "it announces itself as such."[20] Moreover, these paintings more often *created* a vision of life (whether romantic or moral) rather than accurately *reflecting* it[21] (something many see today's Instagram accounts doing in a similar fashion). In these ways, narrative paintings departed from more traditional standards of visual art. In the classical, traditional understanding, a painting captured a moment rather than telling a story.[22] This change represented more than just a shift in aesthetic tastes. It "was bound up in the ideas of national identity that defined the Victorian narrative painting. The genre, in its construction as 'British,' had consolidated the growth of empire,"[23] a point whose significance will be made clearer in the chapter on empire that follows.

Material culture as seen in narrative paintings reflects social and moral values as well as the religious (evangelical) belief that gave rise to these values. It is a fairly straight line from this genre of visual art to other, more contemporary forms of evangelical art that serve to tell a certain kind of story and portray a certain kind of truth about the world.

One essay on William Holman Hunt's painting *The Awakening Conscience* shows that Hunt's approach to art as a means of relaying moral stories was not uncommon. Throughout the nineteenth century, Christian artists in various disciplines—literature, painting, design, architecture—increasingly saw art as a vehicle for evangelism. Christian art increasingly used "sensory forms and depictions of Christian subjects in heightened states of emotion to promote an affective connection with the viewer" in hopes that a "sensory encounter with a religious work of art would be a transformative, spiritual process."[24] The mastery of technique and attention to realistic and minute detail within these kinds of paintings reflected the view that the power of sensory experience could create a specific kind of spiritual, religious experience.

Painting a Picture of Material Culture

Sallman's *Head of Christ* offers an illuminating example of evangelical material culture. The previous chapter considered the painting as a sentimental object, an image that both reflected and promoted certain ideas, values, and assumptions—all part of symbolic culture.

But that's only half the story of this painting's role within evangelicalism. The other half of the story is in how this work gained so much influence, which occurred within the larger material culture of its time.

The popularity of *Head of Christ* owes not only to the image itself but also to "the material and historical circumstances of its marketing and the appeal of its visual properties within a particular cultural context."[25] In the case of this painting, its many imitators, and other works by Sallman, that cultural context includes what has been described as a Protestant "iconography of the face."[26]

If it sounds strange to think of iconography and Protestantism together, then consider the ways in which iconographies of the face exist all around us, not only in religious contexts but in secular ones too: the selfie, the duck face, the various filters that overlay cat ears or puppy noses and whatnot on Instagram photos and TikTok videos. As explained in the previous chapter, graduation photos and celebrity close-ups had become ubiquitous in the mid-twentieth century. These current trends are simply updated versions of this form of iconography.

The circulation, and therefore the influence, of Sallman's art was as much a phenomenon of the material culture of mass production and commercialization as of religious fervor. Sallman's fame, as well as his sales, grew first through his regular travels to local churches to give "chalk talks," a kind of popular event at churches featuring a guest artist who would create a chalk drawing from start to finish on stage before the congregation while delivering an inspirational message.

But Sallman's popularity was magnified greatly by the forces of technology, consumerism, and even a global war. A very particular technology that existed at that time is also part of the story. That technology was a lithograph process that recreated the signature glow of the original *Head of Christ*, making reprints even more desired by consumers. By 1944, 14 million prints had been made.[27] These prints were used "extensively" in youth programs and Sunday schools.[28] But the widest circulation came through mass distribution of the image on prayer cards given to enlisted men during World War II.[29] Eventually, the portrait became so popular that it was stamped on appliances, home decor, and various trinkets, as were other works by Sallman. (Even today you can venture onto eBay where a search for Warner Sallman merchandise will turn up hundreds of specimens.) In sum, it was not merely the original image of Christ that captured so many imaginations but its wide circulation, made possible by technology and the opportunity a global crisis created to offer a tangible and portable means of comfort to young men facing the trauma of war.

> The circulation, and therefore the influence, of Sallman's art was as much a phenomenon of the material culture of mass production and commercialization as of religious fervor.

While the roots of consumerism and material expression within Protestantism go back to at least the seventeenth century,[30] the conspicuous consumerism enveloping the phenomenon of the *Head of Christ* arose, not coincidentally, alongside the emergence of therapeutic religion.[31]

Along with other possible functions of religious materials, one function is to make those who possess them feel good. Yet, this is just as true of nonreligious goods and people too. The work of Norman Rockwell, perhaps the most popular and beloved American painter, has been described as constituting a "modern, secular icon: the collective mental space of a social imaginary."[32]

The material culture of the nineteenth century and following —made possible by the industrial revolution and its means of mass production—helped bring about a greater emphasis within the evangelical movement on seeing rather than hearing, a reversion in some ways to pre-Reformation religious experience. So while material culture is part of every human society, materialism (as defined above) became part of evangelical material culture through the combination of a variety of factors, including the technology that made mass production and goods more widely available and affordable, as well as the conspicuous consumerism that served as a visible sign of one's success in fulfilling the Puritan work ethic.

Just as the earlier evangelical emphasis on individual improvement that arrived through broader efforts at social reform took root during the Victorian age, so, too, did the materialism that signified such improvement. Homes built in the Victorian era were ornate and ostentatious in both architecture and decoration. Exteriors boasted gables, turrets, finials, porches, lattices, arches, dormers. Some of these homes are referred to as gingerbread houses—and for good reason. Interiors were swollen with pooling drapery, lush carpets, heavy furniture, damask wall coverings, and decorations galore. Even those ubiquitous oversized nineteenth-century leather-bound, gilt-edged Bibles "functioned more like religious furniture than biblical texts."[33] (My own volume of *The Domestic Bible*, published in 1864, weighs nearly seven pounds and is not much smaller than a desktop printer; see fig. 11.) Likewise, Victorian dress, for both men and women, was layered, ruffled, buttoned, snapped, furred, gloved, booted, and hatted. Hair— whether on the face or on the head—was equally ostentatious, a covering that paradoxically called attention to itself (see fig. 9). The popularity of Christian-themed arts, crafts, and decor showed that "merely believing was not enough; Christians had to visually demonstrate their piety."[34]

By the early twentieth century, commercialized religious art became less popular not because of changes in belief but because of changes in aesthetic values and, consequently, in fashion.[35] As modernism (with its minimalist style) overtook aesthetics in the early part of the twentieth century and as knickknacks and such declined in popularity, secular businesses reduced their offerings of religious products. The space left by secular businesses when they abandoned production of religious decor left an opening for Christian businesses to fill. And fill it they did—abundantly—thus continuing the tradition of "Victorian sentimental faith" through the twentieth century.[36]

This mass production and rampant consumerism became a subject unto itself, one taken up by some mid-century artists, most notably pop artist Andy Warhol, whose famous *Campbell's Soup Cans* (1962) both embodied and critiqued the commercialization that increasingly characterized modern material culture, including art. Sallman, like Warhol, had also worked in commercial art before becoming a well-known artist. Perhaps the greatest difference between Sallman and Warhol is the latter's obvious self-awareness in bringing together mass production, commercialism, and art in his work as a form of ironic critique. Warhol's work, unlike Sallman's, was anything but sentimental.

Thomas Kinkade, whose work was discussed in the previous chapter, was also a phenomenon of modern material

> Just as the earlier evangelical emphasis on individual improvement that arrived through broader efforts at social reform took root during the Victorian age, so, too, did the materialism that signified such improvement.

culture and conspicuous consumerism. Millions of Kinkade's works have been produced and sold—not by his own hands but by an industrialized process employing hundreds of artists, apprentices, and workers in a warehouse from which hundreds of pieces were produced and shipped daily to consumers, galleries, or licensed stores selling Kinkade merchandise exclusively. It became "a business empire that made Kinkade at least $53 million in personal income between 1997 and 2005."[37] In 2000 alone, Kinkade's company brought in $120 million in sales, a figure that didn't even account for the profits generated from public trading on the New York Stock Exchange.[38]

All of this materiality, particularly its technological aspects, pales in comparison to what we see happening—in all of culture, not just evangelicalism, but certainly within that—with the globalized influence of Facebook, Twitter, and TikTok. These forms are newer and, because of digital technology, even more ubiquitous, but the human nature behind them hasn't changed. Nor have the particularities of evangelicals.

The Sacred and the Profane

Because religious experience emphasizes the spiritual, it's easy to minimize the role the material realm plays in these experiences. This tendency is even truer in the context of a long-standing Western tradition that pits the spiritual and material against one another.

However, in *Material Christianity*, Colleen McDannell shows how "the material dimensions of Christianity" cultivate and shape the immaterial aspects of a faith community such as language, thoughts, and habits. The reality is that physical, bodily, and material expressions of religious belief are crucial to conveying its norms and ideals.[39] Thus the material and spiritual aspects of our faith cannot be separated any more than the human soul can exist apart from the human body.

Our inherited dichotomy of the sacred versus the profane distorts our understanding of religious experience. The focus on the spiritual over the material has separated religious experience from many other aspects of life, "from home life, sexuality, economic exchange, and fashion."[40] The sacred/profane dichotomy also privileges more cerebral, abstract realms of religious experience, often the sort of experience that belongs to the elite, one that looks down on the more concrete, earthy expressions of religious life that tend to characterize the masses, the laypeople, the less educated and enfranchised[41]—say, for example (and generally speaking), folks like evangelicals. On the other hand, this assumed division between the sacred and the profane can lead to false impressions and accusations by salt-of-the-earth folks of creeping secularization and religious decline within the intellectual or artistic classes.[42]

> The material and spiritual aspects of our faith cannot be separated any more than the human soul can exist apart from the human body.

In *The Sacred and the Profane*, Romanian philosopher Mircea Eliade offers a powerful insight about the relationship between the world of the real or material and the world of the sacred or spiritual. "The sacred," Eliade writes, "is pre-eminently the *real*, at once the source of life and fecundity."[43] Thus the religiously oriented person ought not dismiss or denigrate the world of concrete, tangible matter, Eliade argues. Rather, the

> religious man's desire to live *in the sacred* is in fact equivalent to his desire to take up his abode in objective reality, not to let himself be paralyzed by the never-ceasing relativity of purely subjective experiences, to live in a real and effective world, and not in an illusion.[44]

FIGURE 1. *Whitefield Preaching at Moor Fields* (1865) by Eyre Crowe, in *The Church of England: A History for the People* by H. D. M. Spence-Jones (1910) | Stapleton Collection / Bridgeman Images

FIGURE 2. John Bunyan's dream vision, *The Pilgrim's Progress* | John Bunyan after, 1679. Robert White © National Portrait Gallery, London

FIGURE 3. *The Awakening Conscience* (1853) by William Holman Hunt | Photo: Tate

FIGURE 4. *Pamela Is Married*, from painting series *Four Scenes from Samuel Richardson's "Pamela"* (1743–44) by Joseph Highmore | Photo: Tate

FIGURE 5. *Conversion of Paul* (1767) by Nicolas Bernard Lépicié | Public Domain / Wikimedia Commons

FIGURE 6. "New and Improved," Van Camp ad (1941) | Ashlee Glen

FIGURE 7. *The Tavern Scene*, from painting series *A Rake's Progress* (1732–35) by William Hogarth | Public Domain / Wikimedia Commons, Collection: Sir John Soane's Museum

FIGURE 8. *Fruits of Early Industry and Economy* (1789) by George Moreland | John Howard McFadden Collection, 1928 / Phildelphia Museum of Art

FIGURE 9. Portrait of a Victorian woman
| Ashlee Glen

FIGURE 10. Kitschy plate
depicting *The Last Supper* by
Leonardo da Vinci | Ashlee Glen

FIGURE 11. Victorian Bible (with *Self Help* by Samuel Smiles sitting atop)
| Ashlee Glen

FIGURE 12. Nativity scene from a fifteenth-century illuminated manuscript, Besançon Book of Hours, Fitzwilliam Museum, manuscript 69, folio 48r | Public Domain / Wikimedia Commons

FIGURE 13. "Family Devotion," Currier & Ives, 1871 | Library of Congress

FIGURE 14. Illustration by Frederick William Quartley, in *Avventure di Robinson Crusoe* by Daniel Defoe (Naples: Gaetano Nobile, 1842), 42 | Public Domain / Wikimedia Commons

FIGURE 15. Stained glass window cross by Carol M. Highsmith at Sixteenth Street Baptist Church, Birmingham, Alabama | Library of Congress

FIGURE 16. *Being Caught Up in Slow Motion* (2019) by Anthony Falbo | Accessed on Fine Art America

Canto 31 : The Saintly Throng in the Form of a Rose

FIGURE 17. Illustration by Gustave Doré of heaven from Dante's *Paradiso*, canto 31

| In *The Divine Comedy by Dante, Illustrated, Complete*, trans. and ed. Henry Francis Cary (London: Cassell, 1892)

Material culture plays a part in all religions and belief systems to one extent or another, of course. But material culture is, or should be, particularly meaningful within Christianity. After all, the incarnation of Christ upends the long-standing dualism between spirit and matter, the sacred and the profane, categories that are more the work of theorists than they are of those who are living and practicing the Christian faith.[45]

The language of the Bible reflects how the spiritual and physical are inseverable. The Bible is filled with material, physical manifestations that serve as metaphors or anagogical images for spiritual truth. One of the most obvious of these is marriage—a union of two complementary physical bodies in a covenant that symbolizes the spiritual (and incarnational) relationship of Christ and his church. But the Bible contains so many more of such types (prophetic symbols) and figures. Both Noah's ark and the ark of the covenant, for example, are types of the church. The burning bush foreshadows the Holy Spirit. Adam, Joseph, Moses, and David are types of Christ. The floodwaters that covered the earth prefigure the waters of baptism. In fact, another way to think about types is to think of them as images or pictures. Each baptism depicts in miniature the story of what Christ did for us in his death, burial, and resurrection.

One of my favorite types—woven throughout the Bible, church history, and Christian art—is skin. Before Sinai, in the garden of Eden, the skins with which God covered Adam and Eve after they sinned were a type, or foreshadowing, of the skin that would cover God himself in the incarnation and that would then "cover" the sin of all believers. As David Lyle Jeffrey explores in depth in *People of the Book: Christian Identity and Literary Culture*, even the animal skins (vellum) on which early Scriptures were later written also remind us of this skin covering. This motif continued through church history, according to Jeffrey. Medieval paintings frequently depict Mary, other biblical figures, and church fathers anachronistically holding the Bible.[46]

One scene in manuscript 69 in the Fitzwilliam Museum (see fig. 12), a mid-fifteenth-century illuminated manuscript created by an unknown artist (one viewed by art historians as not particularly skilled), offers another of many variations of Mary being depicted as a reader, most commonly in the context of the annunciation, reading the Word at the moment when the Word became incarnate.

Such images, even though anachronistic (bound books did not exist when Mary bore Christ, of course), symbolize the centrality of reading to Christian faithfulness and point out the concrete, tangible nature of the Word. In many of these paintings, the subject is depicted with a finger inserted into the book's pages, suggesting active reading and reflecting, too, how Thomas needed to put his fingers into Christ's body in order to know and believe. God's Word, both written and incarnate, beckons us to come close and engage in a tactile relationship.

As we read in John 1:14, "The Word became flesh and made his dwelling among us. We have seen his glory, the glory of the one and only Son, who came from the Father, full of grace and truth." Some of us human beings even got to touch him. One of us held him in her womb—as the old, orthodox hymn sings to Mary: "He whom the entire universe could not contain was contained within your womb."[47]

As McDannell explains, "Since religion is emotive as well as cognitive, people use their sight, touch, smell and voice to stimulate pious feelings. Human beings seemingly cannot appropriate religious truths . . . without involving their bodies. . . . The human body is not only an avenue for expressing and appropriating religious feelings, it also drives people to ask fundamental religious questions."[48] Similarly, David Morgan points out, religious belief "is not simply assent to dogmatic principles or creedal propositions, but also the embodied or material practices that enact belonging to the group."[49]

Evangelical T-shirts, coffee mugs, and bumper stickers may be poor substitutes for the physical, material types shown in Scripture and all around us in the natural world that reveal eternal events and truths. But even so, they are expressions of an innate recognition that the God of our faith is not just transcendent but is here with us—and, like us, not just spiritual but material too.

8

Domesticity

Angels and Castles and Prostitutes, Oh My!

A man's home is his castle."
This proverb has a long history and a wide application. Unlike many old sayings, this one's origins are traceable. Those traces are tightly connected to the social changes that brought the rise and influence of evangelicalism.

Once upon a time, a castle—the literal kind—was the home of a king or lord, someone who ruled others and was served and worshiped by them. It was also a sovereign's refuge from enemies and outsiders who wished to usurp or destroy him. Then one day, the idea developed that every home was the castle of the man who owned it, even the lowliest of men.

This concept seems to have emerged in the seventeenth century as the feudal age was fading more and more into the past and more men gained the ability to own land and a home. English laws concerning property and privacy rights evolved accordingly, including the right to refuse forcible entry whether by a stranger or a sovereign.

Yet, much more is embedded in this idea than merely laws about illegal entry. Beyond the matters of ownership and legal rights, there is a sense in these words about what a home *means*, what it symbolizes, and how it functions in the larger world.

First, the canard assumes that a home belongs to a *man*. This was a safe assumption given that married women in England and America were generally not allowed to own landed property until the nineteenth century.[1]

Second, it expresses an emerging domestic ideal, one that finds ultimate meaning and security in hearth, family, and home. This ideal is so ingrained in our culture today that it's hard to imagine a world in which it would be otherwise. Within evangelicalism especially, domesticity and its concomitant ideas are so deeply embedded, it's easy to assume these ideas have always existed. Of course, family is a natural and God-ordained institution, one that goes all the way back to Genesis 1:28, and home is a logical extension of the family. But one needn't look far to find cultures and societies that fail to uphold this ideal or to uphold it universally, particularly in the modern manifestation that emphasizes the nuclear family above other family structures.

Domestic Bliss

Domesticity as a primary value emerged in both early modern England and America from a variety of concurrent and related phenomena: increased industry and trade at home, expanded exploration away from home, the ongoing threat of wars abroad, the rise of Great Britain as a world power. All of these made the comforts of home more dear.

Evangelicalism's developing views of women, family, and their respective roles also played a key role in developing the domestic ideal. This domestic ideal centered on the family unit but had direct implications for all of society. Evangelical leaders in the eighteenth century—foremost among them John Newton, William Wilberforce, and Hannah More— sought moral and social reform across all of society, from the upper to the lower classes. These reforms included rectifying injustices from slavery to child labor to animal cruelty. The reforms also included advancing a view of marriage more rooted in Christian theology. For much of European history, marriage between people, especially those of some means, was based on political and economic interests. This was so much the case that many writers in the eighteenth century were addressing the problem of parents forcing their children into marriage to partners of the parents' choosing. Evangelicals argued that marriage should be based on a vocational view rather than an economic one. They understood marriage to be a way for each spouse to support the other in loving God and neighbor in service to the kingdom, a model known as companionate marriage. This evangelical understanding cast the family and home in a new light and helped transform society's view of both marriage and home life. When Queen Victoria ascended the throne in the nineteenth century, she dramatically embodied this image of family through her long, affectionate marriage to Prince Albert and the nine children they had together.

This view of marriage has lasted long enough that it is the one most of us hold to today. The companionate marriage reflects the biblical ideal much more than a model that prioritizes joining landholdings in order to enlarge a family estate. Yet, it can also be argued that the ideal of the companionate marriage contributed to a newer understanding of marriage as

> **Evangelicals argued that marriage should be based on a vocational view rather than an economic one.**

a union of any partners who choose companionship (sexual or otherwise) for as long or as short a time as they so desire, an understanding that has led to concepts of marriage largely unintended by earlier evangelicals.

The domestic vision encouraged by evangelicalism was also assisted by the industrial revolution, which, like the evangelical movement, also began in England. By producing new sources of wealth apart from land, industrialization allowed the middle class to expand more than ever before. But industrialization also required masses of people to move out of rural areas and into the cities where the work was located. This resulted in a hugely dramatic shift: while in 1801, only 20 percent of the British population lived in a city, a century later 80 percent did.[2] Urbanization dramatically changed the cultural landscape as well as individual lifestyles. Home took on new meaning within this changed context, and domestic life became increasingly self-contained.

Before the industrial revolution, much work, by both men and women, was done at home. Women worked side by side with their husbands by keeping accounts, running the shop, or writing correspondence. Work life was not as separated from leisure time as it would come to be. Relaxation tended to be social, taking place in public places. Gentlemen, poets, and statesmen met in clubs and coffeehouses, while laboring men gathered in gin shops or on the streets.[3] But when men went to work in factories, women no longer had a role in helping their husbands with their work. (To be sure, many women also worked in factories, but even then the different skills required also divided male workers from female ones.[4]) Men went to the workplace, women stayed home, and home became a place of refuge from the dirty, noisy, stressful urban setting of business and commerce, a haven from the dehumanizing forces of the work world. Working men were exhorted to exchange the taverns and the gaming tables for the pleasures and comforts of home and to pursue "a quieter and more serious style of life than that traditionally" practiced by gentlemen and emulated by men of the middle classes.[5] By 1869, John Stuart Mill could observe in *The Subjection of Women*, "The association of men with women in daily life is much closer and more complete than it ever was before. Men's life is more domestic."[6] Home was thus redefined as a refuge for men, kept for them by women.

Because of the evangelical movement's presence across the transatlantic, this development was a particularly English and American phenomenon. Indeed, contemporary accounts show that while English and American families became more and more ensconced in homelife, their continental European counterparts were often found spending time together outside the home, whether in cafés, restaurants, or on city streets.[7] In the more evangelical-influenced England and America, in contrast, domesticity took a new place in the social imagination, one rooted in "the conception of the home as a source of virtues and emotions which were nowhere else to be found, least of all in business and society."[8]

There was yet another reason for this increased emphasis on domestic life. Thanks to advances in health and medicine, families were growing larger than those of previous centuries[9] (although this number would peak after the middle of the nineteenth century[10]). The eighteenth century witnessed what has been called the "invention" of childhood. Improved health conditions increased the likelihood of more children surviving past infancy. More mothers nursed their children rather than farming that job out to wet nurses. (One of the central conflicts in the plot of Richardson's sequel to *Pamela* is Pamela's desire to breastfeed her child, which her husband opposes because he fears it will ruin her figure. In promoting Pamela's view, Richardson was way ahead of his time.) With more children living longer, recognition of the formative role of education and nurture in a person's life grew, and Romantic philosophers such as Jean-Jacques Rousseau gave unprecedented emphasis to childhood as a crucial stage of development. Children were no longer seen simply as miniature adults. Children of the poor were no longer laboring like their parents six days a week. The offspring of the wealthy were no longer being raised merely as replacements for their parents, destined either to manage the family wealth as future heirs or (in the case of girls) to be future producers of subsequent heirs. It is no coincidence that children's literature emerged as a dominant literary genre during the Victorian era.

The Art of Architecture

By the nineteenth century, the home was said by leading voices ranging from ministers to novelists to architects to be "a vehicle for the promotion of values."[11] Thus, the home itself often attested to the domestic ideal. Not the metaphorical home—the literal one.

Homeownership was then, as now, highly desired. Not only was owning a home linked to religious virtue and moral character,[12] but so too was the design of the home. Commentary and criticism on architecture became increasingly influential during this time, and publications with home designs, accompanied by explanations for the moral and social import of certain floor plans, grew popular. The values of the domestic ideal were reinforced as architects and designers promoted privacy and gendered uses of rooms within homes, while lawns and porches served as buffers between the public and private spheres.[13] The way separations were designed between dwellings, too, promoted the "isolation of families" compared to designs used in continental Europe, England's Registrar General reported following the census of 1851.[14] For example, as one German visitor to England observed, urban dwellings in British homes were divided into separate homes side by side, while those in Germany were divided by floors within the same building.[15] Similarly, a French writer commented that the Englishman was notable for "plan[ning] his house as a small castle, independent and enclosed."[16]

Charles Dickens comically portrays this idea of the home as a castle through the memorable character of John Wemmick in *Great Expectations*. When Wemmick invites Pip, the main character of the story, to visit him at home, Pip finds there a "little wooden cottage," the smallest house he ever saw, surrounded by a moat (which was really just a ditch with a plank across it), complete with a gun-mounted battery. Showing his guest around, Wemmick tells Pip proudly, "At the back, there's a pig, and there are fowls and rabbits; then, I knock together my own little frame, you see, and grow cucumbers; and you'll judge at supper what sort of a salad I can raise. So, sir . . . if you can suppose the little place besieged, it would hold out a devil of a time in point of provisions."[17] Wemmick was no sovereign or lord—except as one in his home, which was literally his castle. Indeed, serving as clerk to a lawyer whose dealings tend toward distasteful, Wemmick has so shut off his public (work) life from his private (home) life that he has two different personalities and sets of rules that reflect and govern each sphere. As he tells Pip, "The office is one thing, and private life is another. When I go into the office, I leave the Castle behind me, and when I come into the Castle, I leave the office behind me."[18]

Interestingly, however, Dickens's sweet (and sharply incisive) portrayal of Wemmick's domesticity is not centered on the typical nuclear family. Wemmick is (for most of the story) an old bachelor, living only with his "aged parent," demonstrating that the domestic ideal can be wider than is usually imagined today.

Another example from Dickens of this wider vision of the domestic ideal, one more expansive than the nuclear family, occurs in *A Christmas Carol*, where the domestic scene plays a crucial part in the conversion of Scrooge. Despite the utter poverty of Ebenezer Scrooge's beleaguered worker, Bob Cratchit (so beleaguered thanks to Scrooge's miserly ways), Cratchit's domicile is filled with joy, laughter, and love. The scenes involving this family, in particular the youngest child Tiny Tim, are among Dickens's most memorable and sentimental. Here and in so many other examples, the family is the seat of faith and the locus of redemption. Indeed, Scrooge's transformation at the end of the story comes not at the foot of the cross but at the family table, for blessed is the one who eats "at the feast in the kingdom of God" (Luke 14:15).

A Man's Home Is His Chapel

Thus, a man's home might be more than just his castle. It could be a place of worship too.

This understanding goes back, as Charles Taylor explains it in *A Secular Age*, to the Protestant Reformation's rejection of the old divide between secular and sacred and its rejection of monasticism and celibacy. From a sociological perspective alone, the "new emphasis on the home and on domestic virtues" is "perhaps the most far-reaching consequence of the Reformation in England."[19]

Before the Protestant Reformation and the broader effort at reform around it, which Charles Taylor describes in *A Secular Age*,[20] the people of medieval European societies were divided into what was commonly called the three estates: clergy, nobility, and peasants. These estates are sometimes described according to their corresponding roles: those who pray, those who fight, and those who work. Notably, women aren't accounted for in this scheme. When the Reformation declared all work, all space, and all of life sacred, it made room for the sanctuary of the home and private life. And it made room for women. Rather than serving the feudal lord through their labors in someone else's field, both men and women could serve the Lord their God through their labors both in the home and without.

In erasing the division between secular work and space and sacred work and space, the Reformation intensified the categories of public and private. The domestic realm became the sphere for private life, one that developed alongside the rise of the individual and the growing interior life of the individual—theoretically, the interior life of all individuals, not just the monastic who had devoted his life to contemplation in separation from the world. In rightly seeing all the world as sacred for the believer, the Reformers infused ordinary life—everyday callings, everyday spaces, and everyday relationships—with holiness. No longer was serving in the church the only holy calling. Rather, all the business of everyday life—making, marketing, and mending—could be holy too. Likewise, it was not just the space within the walls of the church that was sacred, but it was farm, field, workplace, and home too.[21]

> In erasing the division between secular work and space and sacred work and space, the Reformation intensified the categories of public and private.

This doctrinal teaching had a political corollary as well. In their opposition to government authority based on inheritance, seventeenth-century English Puritans emphasized a vision of the family as a "self-enclosed social unit" whose authority could not be thwarted by the state. "Against genealogy"—power handed down by inheritance—the Puritans "posited domesticity."[22]

To promote these theo-political views, the Puritans published a number of tracts and treatises delineating in binary categories the specific roles of husbands and wives, further deepening the domestic ideal.[23] The husband was to be not only the provider for the family in his work outside the home—in the public sphere—but the leader in the home too—in the private sphere (see fig. 13). As homes came to be seen as sacred, one duty of the head of the household became, increasingly, to ensure family worship and family prayers (which included servants too).

This image of the home as a sacred temple could be part of a secularized form of religion too, as seen in the writing of Victorian architect and art critic John Ruskin, who had claimed evangelical Christianity earlier in life but eventually rejected it. For Ruskin, home became a sanctuary instead:

> This is the true nature of home—it is the place of Peace; the shelter, not only from all injury, but from all terror, doubt, and division. In so far as it is not this, it is not home; so far as the anxieties of the outer life penetrate into it, and the inconsistently-minded, unknown, unloved, or hostile society of the outer world is allowed by either husband or wife to cross the threshold, it ceases to be home; it is then only a part of that outer world which you have roofed over, and lighted fire in. But so far as it is a sacred place, a vestal temple, a temple of the hearth watched over by Household Gods, before whose faces none may come but those whom they can receive with love,—so far as it is this, and roof and fire are types only of a nobler shade and light,—shade as of the rock in a weary land, and light as of the Pharos in the stormy sea;—so far it vindicates the name, and fulfils the praise, of Home.[24]

Ruskin offers a beautiful (if, perhaps, overly sentimental) picture of the home. But the home cannot replace the church. Indeed, G. K. Chesterton lamented of the Victorians: "Theirs was the first generation that asked its children to worship the hearth without the altar."[25]

Father God, Mother Dearest

Just as the home at times came to replace the altar, so too the family (or at least the father) could become confused with God. Charles Kingsley, a Victorian-era priest in the Church of England, taught that the purpose of human relations, particularly familial ones, was "to teach us their divine antitypes." Thus, the role of father, son, wife, and other family members are, he said, "symbols of relations to God."[26]

Such symbolic interpretations work in two directions, however. The roles within a family become understood not only as a symbol of humanity's relationship with God but also as "a microcosm of the ideal society."[27] As roles within the family were emphasized for their correspondence to the family of God, so too God was understood in more personal terms as a father figure, and human beings were cast more and more as children dependent on him, as orphans until adopted by him.[28] Notably, many of the main characters in Victorian novels were orphans, a testimony to the power of a particular social imaginary at work. To be sure, the sense of being orphaned was not merely a religious metaphor but an existential one as well, as religious faith became during the modern age not an assumption but a choice, which is the essential definition of secularity as Charles Taylor renders it in *A Secular Age*.[29]

> Just as the home at times came to replace the altar, so too the family (or at least the father) could become confused with God.

While God is our Father, this particular metaphor does not confine him, nor should it limit our understanding of our relationship to him. He is not only our Father but our Creator, Lord, Judge, and so many more roles identified in Scripture. Moreover, an earthly father is not a stand-in for God with equal authority and power, as some sects teach.

Like all metaphors, God as Father is misunderstood when it is seen as complete and closed off from all other comparisons.

Likewise, the teaching of Ephesians 5:23 that "the husband is the head of the wife as Christ is the head of the church" was broadened into vague and overgeneralized applications. For example, Mary Anne Hearn, a nineteenth-century Baptist writer and educator who published under the pen name Marianne Farningham, declared, "The most important person in the household is the head of the family—the father. There can be no doubt of this really, and none will hesitate to admit it." Even if the father spends less time at home than the rest of the family, the entire household depends on him, she continues. Despite this assertion's straying far from the text of the Scriptures, she confidently concludes, "All this is so thoroughly understood that it may seem quite unnecessary to mention it here."[30] Notably, Mary Anne Hearn never married or had children.

Sarah Stickney Ellis, a Victorian-era Congregationalist writer of conduct books aimed at the women of the rising middle classes, exhorted women in *The Wives of England* to embrace "the superiority of your husband, simply as a man." Ellis continued, "It is quite possible you may have more talent, with higher attainments, and you may also have been generally more admired; but this has nothing whatever to do with your position as a woman, which is, and must be, inferior to his as a man."[31]

> **Clearly, the domestic ideal can slip into idolatry.**

On the other hand, Lydia Huntley Sigourney, nineteenth-century American poet and writer of conduct books, advised that the home was a "sanctuary" and that the wife should "become a priestess at its altar."[32] Clearly, the domestic ideal can slip into idolatry.

It's an ideal that was certainly not embraced by the apostle Paul. Not to mention Hannah More, Nannie Helen Burroughs,

Amy Carmichael, Henrietta Mears, John Stott, and countless other figures, both known and unknown in church history, who have lived faithful, fruitful lives that did not conform to the domestic vision advanced by evangelicalism.

The Rise of the Domestic Goddess

Paradoxically, while husbands were held to be superior, wives were often placed on pedestals of their own. Such a vision of women is most famously portrayed by the English poet Coventry Patmore in his long, narrative poem, *The Angel in the House* (1854), a fictional, romanticized account of Patmore's real-life courtship and marriage. His poem is now iconic (or infamous) for its idealized representation of the Victorian woman. Just four lines from the poem capture the essence of the ideal and its effect:

> She is so lovely, true, and pure,
> > Her virtue virtue so endears,
> That often, when I think of her,
> > Life's meanness fills mine eyes with tears—

Not only is it the wife's role to please her husband, the poem asserts, but doing so is her chief joy:

> Man must be pleased; but him to please
> Is woman's pleasure; down the gulf
> Of his condoled necessities
> She casts her best, she flings herself.

She hangs on every kind word from her husband and blames herself for his harsh ones:

> How often flings for nought, and yokes
> Her heart to an icicle or whim,

Whose each impatient word provokes
    Another, not from her, but him;
While she, too gentle even to force
    His penitence by kind replies,
Waits by, expecting his remorse,
    With pardon in her pitying eyes;
And if he once, by shame oppress'd,
    A comfortable word confers,
She leans and weeps against his breast,
    And seems to think the sin was hers . . .

And, in yet another paradox, while the domestic woman was expected to be protected by a man, it was she, in her angelic nature, whose role it was to draw her husband closer to God:

I loved her in the name of God,
    And for the ray she was of Him;
I ought to admire much more, not less.
    Her beauty was a godly grace;
The mystery of loveliness,
    Which made an altar of her face,
Was not of the flesh, though that was fair,
    But a most pure and living light
Without a name, by which the rare
    And virtuous spirit flamed to sight.[33]

Of course, not everyone agreed with the notion that it was women's nature to improve men's morality. Making the case for legal and moral equality of men and women, John Stuart Mill refuted the image of women as naturally morally superior to men by wryly observing that "there is no other situation in life in which it is the established order, and considered quite natural and suitable, that the better should obey the worse." Indeed, he continued, "If this piece of idle talk is good for anything, it is only as an admission by men, of the corrupting influence of power; for that is certainly the only truth which the fact, if it be a fact, either proves or illustrates."[34]

On the other hand, Ruskin, the erstwhile evangelical and esteemed critic quoted above, may have rejected the traditional faith, but he held fast to traditional views of men and women, writing,

> The man's power is active, progressive, defensive. He is eminently the doer, the creator, the discoverer, the defender. His intellect is for speculation and invention; his energy for adventure, for war, and for conquest, wherever war is just, wherever conquest necessary. But the woman's power is for rule, not for battle,—and her intellect is not for invention or creation, but for sweet ordering, arrangement, and decision.[35]

Rigid ideas about masculinity and femininity were never limited to evangelicals—they were in the air. Evangelicals simply breathed the same air that everyone else did. We still do. So much so that what evangelicals uncritically assume is "biblical" turns out to be simply Victorian.

The Angel in the House is not highly praised for its poetic qualities. In fact, it received little notice in England upon being published—but after becoming popular in America, it gained lasting attention at home and beyond. The poem gained so much influence through the nineteenth and early twentieth centuries that in 1931, Virginia Woolf declared that "killing the Angel in the House was part of the occupation of a woman writer."[36]

The ideal captured in *The Angel in the House* came to be described as "True Womanhood." This "cult of true womanhood," as it came to be called, promoted for women "four cardinal virtues—piety, purity, submissiveness, and domesticity."[37] This image of the domestic woman "established its hold over British culture through her dominance over all those objects and practices we associate with private life."[38]

Yet, ideals seldom hold up to reality, and the reality is that many women had to work beyond keeping their house or making an altar of their face. Before the industrial revolution, women who weren't of the upper class worked in agriculture, as wet nurses, or as servants. After the industrial revolution and its urbanization, many women from the lower and middle classes worked in factories or sold goods at shops or on the streets. In the second half of the nineteenth century 25 percent of women had paying jobs outside the home.[39] A tragic number of them entered prostitution: there were 50,000 known prostitutes in London in 1850,[40] a time when the population was about 2.5 million.[41] There had to be men keeping those prostitutes busy, and they weren't likely doing so at home. At first blush, it might seem surprising that an era characterized by duty, domesticity, family values, prudishness, and restraint would have one prostitute for every fifty people. On the other hand, perhaps it makes perfect sense.

The age-old dichotomy that casts women as either angel or whore does not seem to have lessened under evangelical influence.

Not All Women

Yet, it's important to note that domesticity has contributed much to human flourishing. Inasmuch as the home is a refuge from the workaday world (for both men and women), it nourishes the inner life, not entirely unlike the monastery once did. I say this as an evangelical woman who lives a rich, robust public and professional life, a woman who, in being childless, does not fit the domestic ideal, and yet treasures more than anything my home life.

Some would not agree that I have evangelicalism to thank for this. I think I do. As one historian points out, "There was a sense in which the Evangelicals liberated women by giving them a positive role to play in their families and in society." This may be why the model of womanhood portrayed in so many evangelical writings became popular in the nineteenth century, advancing a vision for women that expanded well beyond evangelicalism.[42] Indeed, some of the most historically significant, world-changing Victorians were women, many of them devout Christians. Foremost among these influential Christian women is, of course, Queen Victoria. Others include novelists and poets Charlotte, Emily, and Anne Brontë; poet Christina Rossetti; nurse and reformer Florence Nightingale; social reformer Elizabeth Fry; novelist Elizabeth Gaskell; and suffragist, reformer, and women's advocate Josephine Butler (who was an evangelical). Leading American Christian women of the same century include abolitionists Harriet Tubman, Sojourner Truth, and Harriet Beecher Stowe. Some of these women were wives. Some were mothers. Some were neither. None (save, perhaps, the queen) fit the domestic ideal of their age—or ours.

> Some of the most historically significant, world-changing Victorians were women, many of them devout Christians.

At the same time, a treacherous double standard has been applied within the evangelical vision of the domestic ideal. The commonly held view, one expressed by Jerry Falwell Sr. in his 1980 book *Listen, America!*, that "historically, the greatness of America can be measured in the greatness of families,"[43] was not applied historically to enslaved families who were bred and broken, routinely and repeatedly, by their white masters, often in the guise of Christianity. The evangelical domestic ideal was only for some, and it was (and sometimes still is) carried on the very real flesh-and-blood backs of others.

The Art of Domestic Life

In addition to corresponding theological and cultural shifts, popular literature and art reinforced the growing ideal of "domestic piety."[44]

As we have seen throughout this book, desires often begin and grow at the precognitive level of hypocognition. Images and ideas from our surroundings enter our minds, sometimes rising to the surface, sometimes remaining below it. A social imaginary is formed from the prevailing images and ideas within a culture or subculture. Some of these ideas develop in very intentional, practiced ways—as with theological doctrines or applications (such as evangelicalism's important emphasis on conversion)—while simultaneously simmering in the background too. Other elements of a social imaginary are less formal or defined, and so they have an even greater influence by being amorphous.

Domesticity and the desire for it grow in both ways.

While many arguments, treatises, sermons, essays, poems, works of art, and other cultural expressions put forth ideas and images related to domesticity (whether for or against), their effect—as with many ingredients of a social imaginary—is more than the sum of their parts. We understand today, for example, how social media images of body types, lifestyles, and home settings cultivate desires in those who consume them. The cultivation of such desires existed long before social media.

> A social imaginary is formed from the prevailing images and ideas within a culture or subculture.

As a result of broader discourse in the eighteenth and nineteenth centuries on the links between morality and aesthetics, Victorian Christians began to make connections between their religious faith and their domestic setting.[45]

Protestantism had long been influenced by a "Calvinist distrust of religious art," but eventually the ideals of Romanticism,[46] along with "the Victorian predilection for conspicuous consumption," won out, and many evangelical homes began to give material expression to their religious beliefs, particularly through decor.[47] As one historian describes it, "A mother's domestic sentiments, artistic accomplishments, and spiritual devotion (and through hers, her family's) came to be measured by her ability to decorate her home" whether through ready-made items or her own crafts.[48] Through the elevation of the "acquisition and display of domestic goods,"[49] what started as adornment of the home to reflect religious beliefs eventually reversed, making the home the "storehouse of moral and spiritual values."[50] Thus, increasingly, from about the 1840s on, the "marketplace played an active role in shaping and reinforcing Protestant domestic piety."[51] Consumerism gained the status of religious practice,[52] and many of these consumable goods were meant to be put on display.

For example, the narrative paintings discussed in an earlier chapter often reflected "the values of domesticity" both in their subject matter and in their form, and they were produced in smaller sizes that made them suitable for hanging in homes.[53] These paintings did more than simply decorate, however. The portrayals of love and romance typical of these paintings cultivated unreliable, even false, ideas about love, marriage, and domestic life. Indeed, one art critic observes, "It is no wonder that many women were bitterly disappointed in their experiences of love and marriage, for they did not so much 'weave' their own romances as have them woven for them in the public discourses of which the narrative painting formed a part."[54] We could say the same today of many other forms of narrative art, from chick flicks to Amish fiction to Instagram reels.

▩ A Woman's Home Is Her Castle

Modernity's shift to subjectivity—the turn away from a sense of oneself based on an external, objective authority "out there" toward a sense of self based on an internal, subjective existence within but separate from the world—was expressed more intensely in the changing consciousness and status of women.

In fact, it could be argued that "the modern individual was first and foremost a woman."[55] The social, political, and personal consequences of the tenets, first of the Reformation, then of evangelicalism, affected everyone, of course, but they wrought changes that were more magnified in the lives of women (and eventually children and oppressed people).

Furthermore, Protestantism's doctrinal emphases on individual salvation, the equality of souls, self-improvement, and social reform wrought immeasurable changes—not only outwardly in home and society but inwardly, too, in the imagination and in desires. The very possibility of change—change in one's religion, one's social status, one's life—brought with it the desire for such change. Woman's status as a more contested figure—one whose role, place, limits, and possibilities were the site of scrutiny and debate—made her more subject to commercial, consumer, and creative goods, all of which serve to reflect and cultivate desire for improvement, progress, and change.

This desire was given form in countless ways, but with the rise of print culture, many of these images expressed themselves in literary form. One literary critic explains that "modern culture depends on a form of power that works through language—and particularly the printed word—to constitute subjectivity."[56] For much of the three-hundred-year history of the evangelical movement, expectations, and thus desires, were produced by words within the context of a print culture.

Instead of TikTok and Twitter, evangelicals of the eighteenth, nineteenth, and twentieth centuries had tracts, treatises, sermons, and novels to fill their imaginations.

Novelists in particular "began to represent an individual's value" in terms of "essential qualities of mind" rather than title, social status, or economic class.[57] This was a dramatic shift that led to the social and personal values we take for granted today. The individuals who novelists depicted in portraying this shift were more often than not female—characters such as Moll Flanders and Pamela, and later, *Pride and Prejudice*'s Elizabeth Bennet, *Vanity Fair*'s Becky Sharp, the titular Jane Eyre, *Wuthering Heights*'s Catherine Earnshaw, and *North and South*'s Margaret Hale. There were plenty of male protagonists too. But the novel was first, and for a long time, seen as particularly suited for female readers, not only because of its subject matter but because of its language—the prose of everyday speech rather than the Greek, Latin, or versified English of lettered and powerful men. Thus, "a modern, gendered form of subjectivity developed . . . and determined how people understood themselves and what they desired in others."[58] Men in fiction were represented less as "political creatures" and more as "products of desire and producers of domestic life." Social, economic, and political differences were subordinate to gender differences. In transforming the idea of what made women desirable, the novel granted women (and thus the individual in general) a new kind of authority, lessening the traditional power once given to family lines.[59] (Note the echo of what Charles Taylor argued above about the way the

> Protestantism's doctrinal emphases on individual salvation, the equality of souls, self-improvement, and social reform wrought immeasurable changes—not only outwardly in home and society but inwardly, too, in the imagination and in desires.

Reformers replaced genealogical authority with familial authority.) Fiction, in this way, became both "the document" and "the agency" of cultural change.[60]

The desires and expectations of women were further cultivated by other literary forms too. Domestic fiction, a subgenre of the novel developed during the nineteenth century, consisted of stories infused with lessons of virtue and piety drawn from ordinary daily life for white, middle-class women. Magazines for women also proliferated during the nineteenth century. Their pages were filled with stories, essays, and advice oriented around the ideal of True Womanhood. Then, as now, these forms of media cultivated desires by putting forward such images and ideals. These publications had a similar influence on people of that time that magazines, movies, and social media have on consumers today.

In the seventeenth century, even before novels and magazines, because of the emerging sense of agency and choice made possible by modernity, conduct literature geared toward women taught them and their families how women could make themselves desirable to men of means by cultivating personal qualities beyond a woman's inherited rank and wealth. In other words, a woman might not have a fortune, but she could have other means to make herself desirable. But first she had to learn how to do so.

Whereas women had once been found desirable based on the circumstances of their birth—wealthy women would marry wealthy men, while poor women would marry poor men, in both cases nearly always within geographic proximity—the modern qualities deemed desirable were related to character and no longer limited to political or social identity.[61]

This new idea that women could through their character, virtue, education, and manners make themselves more attractive as potential marriage partners to men of rank and wealth served also to deepen the gendered differences between men and women. A man of fortune, rather than simply looking to marry a woman of fortune, might now prioritize personal and character attainments in a woman.[62] Women had become domesticated.

The rise—and triumph—of the domestic woman in the eighteenth and nineteenth centuries expressed "a specifically modern form of desire" that transformed "the criteria for determining what was most important in a female."[63] By the end of the twentieth century, we could say that it equally, or nearly equally, worked this way for both sexes. Marrying someone for their inner character qualities rather than their landholdings or dowry is one of the most significant developments of modern life.

> Domesticity is about creating a home that houses a body that houses a soul that houses the Lord.

Domesticity is not about who works at home, who cooks the meals, or who takes out the garbage. It's not about the luxuriance of the drapes, the finish of the appliances, or the tackiness of the wall art. It's not about the merits of a townhouse over a tiny house over a McMansion.

Domesticity is about creating a home that houses a body that houses a soul that houses the Lord.

And that's why a woman's home is her castle, too.

9

Empire

"The White Man's Burden," His Man Friday, the Jesus Nobody Knows, and What Johnny Cash Really Knew

S ome words are like woven tapestries. The top side displays the design and beauty intended by the maker to be seen. The underside is the chaotic negative of the visible side, holding the whole picture together, not meant to be seen.

Words are formed to weave certain ideas together so as to present a glossy picture, underneath which we are not supposed to look. (Movements, communities, cultures, and social structures can be like that too. It is from these that words and their meanings emerge.)

For example, when I was a child, the word "colony" conjured images of a quaint, old-fashioned village where ladies in bonnets churned butter by hand, men plowed and planted the fields with horses, and cherubic children played games rolling big wooden hoops atop cobblestone streets.

The word "reservation" once held similarly rosy associations for me. As a youngster, my family often visited friends who lived on land that went by this name. I thought of that place as special, set aside as an honor as one does in order to dine at a fine establishment.

The same is true of the word "empire." Once upon a time, it was a word linked to fairy tales and magic carpets. Later, I came to associate the word with strength and power used for the good of all. "Empire" could be used, for example, to describe a successful business enterprise. For a time, I lived in "the Empire State," home of one of the largest cities in the world and what was once the tallest tower in the world, the Empire State Building. Some empires had more sinister associations—like the Star Wars franchise's *The Empire Strikes Back*. Always the word possessed mythic proportions.

The power and influence of empire is not merely the stuff of fairy tales and myths, however. It is very real and is often exerted in the most ordinary ways. At a conference table. During a meeting. In a hallway exchange. In an email.

Empire building is almost as old as humanity itself. In its oldest and most literal sense, "empire" refers to political dominions made when one nation or state takes over another. We tend to associate these kinds of empires with ancient history, from the various Chinese dynasties to the Roman Empire, to the Mongol and Ottoman Empires, and so on. One cannot read these names without being reminded that, no matter how mighty they might be or how long they might last, empires fall. Such empire building isn't just a relic of the past, however. Russia recently invaded the neighboring nation of Ukraine in a modern-day act of barbaric empire building. Every day there are new reports of horrific atrocities being committed against ordinary, innocent people by a violent aggressor.

Most empires are built this way: through violence, blood, and terror.

But sometimes empires are built more subtly: through coercion, trickery, or deceit. Sometimes empires are built in the name of progress, tradition, or religion. Sometimes all it takes is a network of good ol' boys (whether literal or metaphorical). Sometimes empires are built simply through clever marketing. Sometimes they are built through all of these methods. Whichever way they are made, empires expand by dominating—rather than loving—their neighbors.

The first empires were land empires. As postcolonial literary critic Edward Said notes in *Culture and Imperialism*, "Everything about human history is rooted in the earth."[1] Various terms express the different manifestations of empires: "empire," "imperialism," and "colonialism," for example. According to Said, empire refers to a *relationship* of domination; imperialism refers to the *practices* and *attitudes* of domination; and colonialism refers to the implantation of *settlements* on another's land.[2] Even if the *relationship* changes (e.g., a nation is freed from occupying forces), imperialistic *postures* and *perspectives* can linger long afterward. As Said says, the struggles of empire are not only about land but also "about ideas, about forms, about images and imaginings."[3]

> Whichever way they are made, empires expand by dominating—rather than loving—their neighbors.

Empires aren't established only on land, however. They are also established in our hearts. This is actually where they begin.

The Sun Never Sets on the British Empire— Until It Does

Throughout most of history, empire building was led by rulers and governments. During the first wave of British expansion in the sixteenth and seventeenth centuries, as the age of exploration was booming, European countries, especially those with ready access to the sea, were discovering the wealth to be gained from bringing goods such as spices, dyes, sugar, and cotton from faraway lands back home. Colonization of these lands, usually by private companies, followed. In fact, the United States is described as "the first new nation" to come "through a colonial, not a social revolution."[4] Later, in the age of New Imperialism that began in the latter half of the nineteenth century as European nations participated in the Scramble for Africa, expansion was led mainly by merchants, not monarchs. Modern empire building became not only the work but even the dream of ordinary men. It still is.

The American colonies began, of course, as British ones. Following the loss of those colonies, England's growth into the world's biggest empire in the following century represented a stunning comeback. The British Empire would become the largest political empire in human history. At its peak, near the end of the nineteenth and into the twentieth century, Great Britain ruled one-quarter of the territory around the globe and one-quarter of the earth's population. Across the planet, one in four people was the subject of Queen Victoria. The old saying that "the sun never sets on the British Empire" was literally true: at every point in a twenty-four-hour day, it was daylight in at least one of the British territories.[5]

> It was almost inevitable that British imperialism would be thoroughly entangled with evangelicalism.

This was—not coincidentally—the age of evangelical expansion as well. It was almost inevitable that British imperialism would be thoroughly entangled with evangelicalism. Indeed, it was. And because it was, it still is. European expansion into other lands was often justified, even promoted, by claims that it would bring Christianity to "pagan" lands. The explosion of missionary societies in the nineteenth century took place within the larger context of exploration and colonization. In America, early colonists declared the conversion of the native people to Christianity as a reason, even a justification, for settling in the new land.[6]

What, You Too?

Often overlooked in this rationale for colonization was that the roots of Christianity go back at least to the earliest centuries in some of these "pagan" lands. Christianity came to North Africa, for instance, in the first or second century, and it was established in Ethiopia by the fourth century. The Eastern Christian tradition goes back at least as far. One friend of mine can trace his own family's Christian roots in India back to the first centuries of the church. He says that "the Indian Christian tradition was so well established by AD 325 that the First Ecumenical Council in Nicaea had at least one delegate from the Indian Church." His ancestors' faith, he wants to make clear, is not "a colonized one."[7]

Such oversights of evangelicals (both then and now) are the working out of a social imaginary built on an imperialist worldview that provides "a structure of attitude and reference"[8] that leaves out as much as it leaves in, one that reflects what Said describes as an "imagination of empire."[9]

An example of such a deficient imagination is powerfully illustrated by a story Willie James Jennings tells in *The Christian Imagination*. The story centers on a simple, everyday event: neighbors chatting with neighbors in their yard on a lovely day. Yet, this otherwise uneventful scene reveals the workings of a social imaginary centuries and generations in the making.

The incident takes place when Jennings, who was twelve at the time, and his mother are outside their home working in the garden. The Jenningses are Black. Two white men enter the yard and introduce themselves as members of a nearby

church. They tell Mrs. Jennings about their church and share
the gospel with her. What is striking to Jennings, even as a
young boy, is that the white men have no idea who the Jenningses are, no idea that his father is the pastor of their own
church in the same neighborhood as the white men's church,
or that his mother is "one of the pillars" of their church, and
most inexplicable of all, that the men seem to assume that
Mrs. Jennings is not a Christian. The men leave shortly after
Mrs. Jennings patiently explains these facts. Looking back
on the event as an adult, Willie Jennings does not attribute
the visitors' error to malice. Rather, he
writes, it merely "signaled a wider and
deeper order of not knowing, of not sens-
ing, of not *imagining.*" Even so, this inability to know, sense, and imagine, Jennings
explains, reflects "a sinful division" within
the Christian faith.[10] It is evidence for what
Jennings calls a "diseased" imagination.
The division Jennings points out developed through an imagination colonized
by the notion of empire.

> The idea of
> empire is so
> embedded in the
> modern Western
> imagination that
> it has shaped our
> understanding
> of nearly every
> facet of life.

In fact, the spread of the gospel during the missionary age
is so intertwined with the West's expansion through imperialism that it is almost impossible to imagine an evangelical
movement that is not an empire-building enterprise, not a
movement rooted in political and cultural domination, and
not propagated by the power of money, business, and capitalism rather than the power of the Holy Spirit. (It is almost,
but not quite, impossible to imagine such a movement; it is
possible because such a movement is there in Scripture in
the early church.)

The idea of empire is so embedded in the modern Western
imagination that it has shaped our understanding of nearly
every facet of life, from how we conceive of and measure

success, to how we develop national policy, to how we teach history, to how we orient and order our personal lives, to how we think the gospel is to be advanced. Because evangelicalism was so connected to the British Empire, imperialistic practices and attitudes are seldom far from the evangelical imagination. Names of events, organizations, and movements such as the Salvation Army, Pioneers, the Billy Graham crusades, Campus Crusade for Christ (now called Cru), the original crusades (of course), theonomy, Christian nationalism, and all forms of dominionism reflect the spirit of empire building within evangelicalism.

This triumphalist spirit of empire was cultivated on an individual level too. "Do great things for God!" was for a generation (or two) of evangelicals not just an encouragement but an expectation that became a mandate. One younger friend who grew up evangelical told me she had the sense that if she didn't grow up to do something great or radical, then she would have failed as a Christian. (Thankfully, she knows better now.) These mantras, perhaps unintentionally but certainly negligently, ignore the truth that ordinary kindness, commonplace service, everyday work, and faithful love also usher in the kingdom of God.

The elements that define the evangelical movement—particularly its emphasis on conversion and activism—fit naturally into the expansionist spirit that defined modernity from its beginning. Expansion of knowledge, landholding, power—this is what made the modern age modern.

The Literature of Empire

The novel developed alongside the rise of the British Empire as a literary form perfect for the expression of the newly emerging sense of the individual. This new, modern, autonomous self became a kind of colonizer of the world, at least of this particular corner of the world, achieving control over life in ways that before had been scarcely, if at all, possible: moving up in social and economic class, choosing a marriage partner, even adopting a religious practice or denomination.

Such agency is exerted over life in more subtle ways too, and these also are reflected in the form of the novel, not merely its subject matter. Through its use of narrative perspective and by centering on individual character growth, the novel embodies what might be called the "authority of the observer."[11] The colonist—whether the literal one in the empire or the metaphorical self of the modern novel or modern world—becomes a kind of authority. The "power to narrate," Said says, is "one of the main connections between" culture and imperialism, yet the ways in which the injustices and cruelties of imperialist practices are enabled by the stories, art, and philosophies of the colonizing culture are not always recognized.[12] The "enterprise of empire," Said says, "depends upon the *idea* of *having an empire*."[13] Or, as William Blake once scribbled in the margin of a book, "Empire follows Art, and not vice versa as Englishmen suppose."[14]

Perhaps no novel illustrates this "idea of having an empire" more than Daniel Defoe's *Robinson Crusoe*, which paints a picture of individual conquest that is both physical and spiritual (see fig. 14). Published in 1719, before the novel was widely recognized or accepted as a literary genre, *Robinson Crusoe* purported to be the true account of one Crusoe, written by himself, of the life he spent stranded on an island for twenty-eight years, where he built a one-man empire, fashioning two homes, cultivating crops, and raising livestock, not only surviving but thriving. Crusoe is a type of the self-reliant, self-made man. Significantly, Crusoe's conquest of the land parallels his self-conquest, illuminating how tightly tied are the notions of political empire and spiritual empire.

Indeed, the vision of empire consumes Crusoe's imagination while on the island. Despite living alone for most of his twenty-eight years on the island, he thinks of himself as ruler and emperor, at one point surveying the land "with a secret kind of pleasure (tho' mixt with my other afflicting thoughts) to think that this was all my own, that I was king and lord of this country indefeasibly, and had a right of possession."[15] Later, upon rescuing and taking in a few near-victims of the native cannibals, Crusoe says, "My island was now peopled, and I thought myself very rich in subjects; and it was a merry reflection which I frequently made, how like a king I look'd."[16]

Along with such notions of empire, Defoe's Puritan theology, which also shaped the evangelical movement, is evident throughout the narrative in ways both subtle and dramatic. One of the dramatic moments occurs nine months after Crusoe arrives on the island (a time span laden with obvious meaning), when he becomes extremely sick. After a torturous night marked by a "terrible vision" in which a man with a spear descends from a "great black cloud, in a bright flame of fire" and threatens to kill him, Crusoe turns to a Bible he had salvaged from the shipwreck and begins to read. His spiritual eyes open for the first time, and he is born again.

Yet, despite this spiritual awakening and genuine conversion, Crusoe never comes to question the underlying assumptions of his slaveholding religion and imperialist worldview. He rescues one native from cannibals roaming the island and names him Friday. Despite referring to Friday as his "man" or "servant," Friday is actually Crusoe's slave. Yet, Crusoe believes only that Providence brought Friday to him in order that Friday might receive the gospel and be saved. Friday's eventual conversion to Christianity and overall "improvement" reinforce the myth that enslavement was an "initiation" or "an apprenticeship in superior white ways and white culture," even if an involuntary one. Such defenses reflect the fact that slavery "was about theology and money simultaneously."[17]

Notably, the shipwreck that stranded Crusoe occurred during a slave expedition. But this is not the sin Crusoe recognizes and repents of following the night of his terrible dream. Indeed, the wealth Crusoe accumulates by the end of the story is the fruit, not of his own, but of slave labor. The power of a culture, of a social imaginary, is so great that it can indeed dull the conscience's role in the conviction of sin. Crusoe's (and Defoe's) inability to see past this moral blind spot is but one example of this truth, one example within an infinite supply.

In addition to a defense of imperialism and slavery, *Robinson Crusoe* provided a template for personal testimony and evangelical missions for centuries to come. Its influence is immeasurable in this regard. The work became "a flag for empire and travelled in the luggage of merchants, missionaries and generals," its influence long outlasting the British Empire itself.[18] Two centuries later, James Joyce called *Robinson Crusoe* the "true symbol of the British conquest."[19]

But *Robinson Crusoe* was also a symbol for the larger sense of modern empire, including the American empire. Crusoe's ability to develop and cultivate a home in this island frontier foreshadows how "America itself would evolve and develop—by trial and error, perseverance, and attention to detail."[20] It is no surprise that Defoe was beloved by one of America's most industrious, innovative, and self-reliant men, Benjamin Franklin.[21]

Most novels do not treat the theme of colonization as literally as *Robinson Crusoe* does. Yet, one cannot read Jane Austen, Charles Dickens, or Charlotte Brontë—just to name a few—without breathing from their pages the air of British imperialism, even if unacknowledged. The ghost of British imperialism lingers into the twentieth century even in such a seemingly innocent place as C. S. Lewis's Chronicles of Narnia. The father of Digory Kirke, the boy who starts it all in *The Magician's Nephew*, is at the series' beginning working in India, which was still under British rule during the time the story is set.[22]

By the end of the nineteenth century, empire as a theme was often front and center for many British thinkers and writers.[23] Perhaps the most influential literary expression of the modern imperialist spirit is Rudyard Kipling's 1899 poem, "The White Man's Burden."

Kipling is best known for *The Man Who Would Be King* (1888), *The Jungle Book* (1894), *Kim* (1901), *Just So Stories* (1902), and the poem "If—" which remains a favorite for school graduations and recitations. Kipling, born in India to British parents, is considered the "poet of British imperialism" because of his insightful treatment of both British colonizers and natives of colonized India. Kipling was heavily influenced by evangelicalism. The grandson of Methodist clergymen on both sides of parents, and schooled early in life by strict Calvinist guardians in England, Kipling exhibits these influences through his works' heavy didacticism as well as a musical rhythm reflective of church hymnody.[24]

Kipling first began writing "The White Man's Burden" in 1897 but didn't finish the poem until 1899, when the start of the Philippine–American War inspired him to publish it as an encouragement to the United States to assume colonial power of the Philippines (which it did).[25]

"The White Man's Burden" is a potent expression of the spirit of modern imperialism, presented as more complicated than simply a raw grab for power and land. Indeed, it famously portrays as a "burden" the duty of the "white man" to "civilize" non-white nations and peoples. Here is the poem in its entirety:

> Take up the White Man's burden—
> Send forth the best ye breed—

Go bind your sons to exile
To serve your captives' need;
To wait in heavy harness,
On fluttered folk and wild—
Your new-caught sullen peoples,
Half devil and half child.

Take up the White Man's burden—
In patience to abide,
To veil the threat of terror
And check the show of pride;
By open speech and simple,
An hundred times made plain
To seek another's profit,
And work another's gain.

Take up the White Man's burden—
The savage wars of peace—
Fill full the mouth of famine
And bid the sickness cease;
And when your goal is nearest
The end for others sought,
Watch Sloth and heathen Folly
Bring all your hopes to nought.

Take up the White Man's burden—
No tawdry rule of kings,
But toil of serf and sweeper—
The tale of common things.
The ports ye shall not enter,
The roads ye shall not tread,
Go mark them with your living,
And mark them with your dead!

Take up the White Man's burden—
And reap his old reward,
The blame of those ye better,
The hate of those ye guard—

The cry of hosts ye humour
(Ah, slowly!) toward the light:—
"Why brought ye us from bondage,
Our loved Egyptian night?"

Take up the White Man's burden—
Ye dare not stoop to less—
Nor call too loud on Freedom
To cloak your weariness;
By all ye cry or whisper,
By all ye leave or do,
The silent sullen peoples
Shall weigh your Gods and you.

Take up the White Man's burden—
Have done with childish days—
The lightly proffered laurel,
The easy, ungrudged praise.
Comes now, to search your manhood
Through all the thankless years
Cold-edged with dear-bought wisdom,
The judgment of your peers![26]

Note how these verses portray imperialists not as barbarians storming the gate but more like kindly neighbors knocking on the door to deliver a casserole. Their burden is taken up not for something as "tawdry" as power (the "rule of kings")—no, not for such low purposes as that! Rather, the colonizer sacrifices the "best" of their people, who suffer in order to "serve" the "need" of the "captives" through the "toil of serf and sweeper." It is the white colonizers, not the oppressed natives, who wear the "heavy harness" to "wait" on the "wild" and "sullen" people who are "half devil and half child." The colonizer acts not out of greed or desire for gain (oh no!) but, on the contrary, to "seek another's profit, and work another's gain." When the colonizers grow weary and long to be free from the work, the poem exhorts them to liken themselves to Moses leading the people out of slavery, to ignore the people's expected grumblings, and to remember that those they conquer will judge not only the colonizers but the colonizer's God. (Those poor, poor colonizers who suffer so!) The multiple layers of xenophobia and racism in the poem are compounded even more by its exaltation of the white colonizers.

This is the one-two punch of the spirit of imperialism. While the imperialism of the nineteenth century was first motivated primarily by the desire for economic profit, it also, Edward Said argues, "allowed decent men and women to accept the notion that distant territories and their native peoples *should* be subjugated."[27] "The White Man's Burden" powerfully expresses the "white savior complex" that has too often characterized both America and the evangelical movement. This phrase describes how even well-intentioned believers who are formed by imperialist ideas tend to try to "rescue" other people rather than empower them. It undergirds the prevailing tendency of evangelicals to confer greater honor on those who evangelize and disciple on foreign soil than on those who do so over backyard fences or neighborhood coffee shops or local homeless shelters and schools. There is something more romantic about bringing the gospel to virgin ears, to those who have never heard it, than sharing it with those who've turned a deaf ear because they grew up within a community or culture that portrayed a distorted or perverted version of the gospel. Evangelists have little honor in their hometown.

The "Burden" of Big Business

Conquering lands and peoples is not the only way to build an empire.

The spirit of empire building permeates modern culture, modern American culture in particular, and that includes American evangelicalism. The connections between empire, evangelicalism, and entrepreneurialism are not by chance. Just as evangelicalism was enmeshed with modern colonialism, so, too, the empire of business colonized evangelicalism.

Success in business is the natural (or at least hoped for) fruit born from the famous Puritan work ethic. Thus, a close relationship between evangelicalism (the child of Puritanism) and the empire of business is not surprising. Indeed, upon setting out to America on their "errand into the wilderness" (the title of a famous 1660 New England Puritan sermon), the Puritans soon turned to "clearing that wilderness."[28] In 1701, Cotton Mather wrote in "A Christian at His Calling" that a Christian has two callings: first, a general calling to serve Christ and, second, a personal calling to a "particular employment." A Christian is therefore, Mather said, "a man in a boat, rowing for Heaven. . . . If he mind but one of his callings, be it which it will, he pulls the oar, but on one side of the boat, and will make but a poor dispatch to the shore of eternal blessedness."[29] This metaphor of two oars, an image that served to "reconcile God and Mammon," would become, arguably, "the essence of the American idea."[30] Despite Mather's insistence that the prosperity that might naturally result from pious living should never take primacy over religion, Mather seems to have fallen prey to the "enchantment" of seeing prosperity as evidence of God's blessings—as did many after him. As American prosperity grew, money and "the desire for money" replaced religion, family, and even class as America's "organizing principle."[31]

Thus, the American enterprise was born. And the prosperity gospel was not far behind.

> Conquering lands and peoples is not the only way to build an empire.

Evangelical Entrepreneurs

The rise of the business empire is connected to improvement, and with that innovation, individualism, and entrepreneurship.

The connection of evangelicalism to entrepreneurship isn't coincidental. Because of their religious beliefs and practices, evangelicals' ancestors within the dissenting movements in England placed them outside not only the established church but often the law itself. This meant they were prohibited from working in government service and many other professions. Exclusion from these positions led many dissenters to turn to a field that was open to them: trade and commerce.[32] Handed the lemons of legal, political, and religious exclusion, our evangelical forebears made lemonade stands.

The open-air preaching pioneered by John Wesley and George Whitefield in the eighteenth century was its own kind of innovation. In fact, it's difficult today to comprehend just how radical the methods of Wesley and Whitefield were during their time. Performed across both England and America, their itinerant preaching not only brought religious revival but revolutionized evangelism itself and the industry that later sprung up around evangelism. Outdoor assemblies allowed many more times the number of people to hear than would have fit inside a church (just as social media today grants a far wider reach to those who have a "message" to share). In the nineteenth century, Charles Grandison Finney's "anxious bench" became one technique among the "New Methods" devised by revivalists of the Second Great Awakening to encourage conversions through emotional appeals. By every account and by every measure—number of conversions, increases in church membership, establishment of new congregations—these revivals birthed new, genuine believers in dramatic numbers.

Thus was born what Martin Marty calls the "evangelical empire,"[33] one in which evangelicals "dominated all cultural institutions, including the public schools and universities."[34] While the United States has been considered by most to be a Protestant empire from early on, evangelicalism in particular became a "kind of national church or national religion."[35] Modern-day rallies, crusades, and megachurches (the entirety of what some today refer to as the "evangelical industrial complex") owe their existence to the innovations of these founders of the evangelical movement.

Today's entrepreneurs and business leaders fill the roles once held by prophets, priests, and poets. Many of these entrepreneurs and business leaders are evangelicals and operate within evangelicalism. It has even become common for pastors today to refer to themselves as "leaders," a trend that became pronounced in the 1980s and '90s when conferences, publications, and websites began aggressively selling the idea of the pastor-leader.[36] This word choice is an odd one for pastors given the association throughout the New Testament of leaders with corruption and worldly authority—not to mention Jesus's words that in his kingdom those who want to be first shall be last (Mark 9:35). In contrast, the words in the Bible often translated as "pastor" (etymologically related to "pasture")—as seen in Ephesians 4:11, or "shepherd," which recurs throughout the Old Testament—are metaphors that connote the caring, nurturing, tending, and feeding that are commanded throughout Scripture of those who hold that office. The word "leader" doesn't preclude these actions, but it markedly shifts the emphasis.

As the lines blur, so do the roles and the callings.

> Today's entrepreneurs and business leaders fill the roles once held by prophets, priests, and poets.

D. L. Moody Is a Whole Mood

One central figure who helped to bring about this emphasis on entrepreneurship in the church is Dwight L. Moody. Along with proclaiming the gospel of Jesus Christ, this famous nineteenth-century revivalist and Bible college founder preached the gospel of hard work. Moody's own life served as proof of his thesis. Born into a poor farming family, Moody ended his formal education at fifth grade. He converted to evangelical Christianity while attending Sunday school as a young man and from that obscurity became one of the most renowned revivalist preachers across England and America. By developing innovative and ecumenical methods of evangelizing and by targeting youth, working-class adults, and immigrants for these evangelistic efforts, Moody changed American Christendom profoundly. One of Moody's most significant impacts on evangelicalism was in marrying business models to Christian ministry. It's a marriage now so common that it's almost impossible to imagine things any other way.

In *Guaranteed Pure: The Moody Bible Institute, Business, and the Making of Modern Evangelicalism*, Timothy Gloege describes how a number of "corporate evangelicals" connected with D. L. Moody transformed American evangelicalism into a religion "that was not only compatible with modern consumer capitalism but also uniquely dependent upon it."[37] Building on evangelicalism's "individualistic religious assumptions," this network of evangelical businessmen applied the "metaphors of industrial work" to Christian life and practice. In true business fashion, this brand of evangelicalism emphasized "empirically measurable outcomes" even in matters of faith.[38] Yet, this corporate support did not necessarily come because these businessmen believed in Moody's message. Rather, they saw in that message their own best hope for domesticating the masses that made up their workforce.[39]

The founding of Moody Bible Institute in Chicago in 1886 was Moody's most lasting material legacy. The school was organized and run by the principles of business that Moody had learned over the years, and the institution targeted and attracted students from the working classes. When Henry Parsons Crowell, the founder of Quaker Oats Company, was appointed in 1904 as chairman of the Board of Trustees of Moody, a position he held for forty years, he brought to the school the same techniques he had used to make Quaker Oats one of the most trusted brands in America: "trademark, package, and promotion."[40] In this way, as Timothy Gloege details, Quaker Oats Company's "guaranteed pure" trademark—one of the most successful in American branding—was transferred to the broad fundamentalist-evangelical spirit that was overtaking working and middle class America.[41] Thus, Moody Bible Institute "pioneered the idea that religion was something to be consumed rather than practiced."[42] Moody brought into the evangelical imagination the paired primacy of theological education and a business mindset, a set of values that has been passed on for generations and virtually defines evangelicalism today. It was Moody who shifted the fashion among pastors from clerical dress to business attire.[43]

This "consumer orientation" that took hold in twentieth-century evangelicalism, focusing on individual choice and minimizing denominational and academic ties,[44] has never lost its influence. It continued evangelicalism's shift away from

> Moody brought into the evangelical imagination the paired primacy of theological education and a business mindset, a set of values that has been passed on for generations and virtually defines evangelicalism today.

the community and authority of the church toward a personal relationship with Jesus—but made even that relationship take on more of the flavor of a business relationship (which is just a hop, skip, and a jump—perhaps not even that—to the prosperity gospel).

The language Gloege uses to describe the evangelical culture carved out by Moody, his supporters, and those who succeeded him is illuminating. He says their approach employed an "interlocking set of metaphors" drawn from the corporate world that "functioned as a set of unexamined first principles"[45]—or in other words, a social imaginary.

The Jesus Nobody Knows

You might begin to wonder whether corporate values have become an idol when Christ himself is cast as "the grandest achievement story of all!"[46] This is how advertising executive Bruce Barton puts it in his 1925 bestselling book, *The Man Nobody Knows*, which portrays Jesus as a business entrepreneur, whom he describes in the book as an "executive,"[47] a "leader" with winning "personal magnetism,"[48] the "founder of modern business,"[49] and "the most popular dinner guest in Jerusalem!"[50] whose parables are "the most powerful advertisements of all time."[51] The book's narrator (a thinly disguised Barton) describes the book's provenance in his exposure as a boy to portrayals of a Jesus who was "pale," "flabby," "sad," and not a "winner" like Daniel, David, and Moses.[52]

Largely forgotten now, *The Man Nobody Knows* was tremendously popular and influential when it appeared. It went through dozens of reprintings and received accolades in sermons, newspapers, and even from President Calvin Coolidge.[53] *The Man Nobody Knows* may be the book nobody knows today, but its enormous influence advanced ideas and values that have lasted a century.

In God We Trust

By the middle of the twentieth century a "generalized religion" informed by evangelicalism and characterized by "the old theocratic and imperial language" linking God and America had been firmly established.[54] During the Eisenhower administration, "In God We Trust" became the official American motto and was stamped on all US currency. (It was only in adulthood that I learned this addition had been made so recently in American history, a realization that was so startling that it was one of the many long-dormant seeds that brought forth the fruit of this book.) It was also during the Eisenhower years that the first National Prayer Breakfast was held, an annual event in Washington, DC, that draws movers, shakers, politicians, and celebrities from across partisan (and religious) lines to offer or hear generic prayers offered up on behalf of the nation. In 1976, a *Newsweek* cover story declared that "the emergence of evangelical Christianity into a position of respect and power" was the "most significant—and overlooked—religious phenomenon" of the decade.[55] Even more recently, one historian claimed that evangelicals "oversee what is arguably the most powerful religious movement in the United States and one of the most powerful around the globe."[56]

This twentieth-century syncretic religion—a mixture of patriotism, business, capitalism, and consumerism—came to be seen as part and parcel of "conservative, traditional 'old-time religion.'"[57] Such mixing of Christianity with the ways of the world was, at least in part, what the fundamentalist movement in the earlier part of the century had been resisting by staking out their claims for the fundamentals of the faith. But by the mid-twentieth century, fundamentalists, too, became divided over whether doctrinal purity or political power was more important.[58] This division, within both the fundamentalist and the evangelical camps, continues to play out today, and the lines between the camps are ever blurred and shifting.

But two prominent figures changed their identities decidedly over the years from fundamentalist to evangelical: Billy Graham and Jerry Falwell Sr.

Billy Graham Rules

As Frances Fitzgerald recounts in *The Evangelicals*, Billy Graham had a conversion experience during a revival in his native North Carolina as a teenager. Later, attending Bob Jones University and then Wheaton College, Graham began to preach while he was still a student, leaning into his natural persona as an earthy, bumbling country preacher. He eventually became a full-time evangelist, and several weeks of tent revivals in Los Angeles in 1949 led to sudden fame and the start of his world-famous crusades held across the globe.[59] Slowly, the rural, southern minister transformed into a more urbane, sophisticated, businesslike one.[60] Eventually, invitations over the years to speak with several US presidents gave him the title "pastor to presidents," and Graham came to be considered one of the most admired men in America.[61]

Graham also helped build some of the most influential evangelical institutions of the twentieth (and twenty-first) century. These include the National Association of Evangelicals, *Christianity Today*, the Billy Graham Evangelistic Association, and Fuller Seminary.

Like Moody, Graham preached a message of "rugged individualism," saying it was "individualism that made America great."[62] (Incidentally, the campaign promise to "Make America Great Again" was first pledged not by Donald Trump but by Graham's friend Ronald Reagan in his speech accepting the Republican Party's nomination as their presidential candidate in 1980.[63]) As Graham and "his neo-evangelical allies" came to reject the fundamentalist label in favor of the evangelical one, they also became concerned not only with evangelism but with the formation of "a coherent social and intellectual framework" for the evangelical mind.[64] For Graham, this framework manifested politically in his vocal opposition to communism, an issue that brought American evangelicals together, rallying them around Reagan, whose famous 1983 "Evil Empire" speech was delivered, not incidentally, to the National Association of Evangelicals.

It was now empire against empire.

The Falwell Empire

Perhaps the biggest evangelical empire to date is one founded by a man born to an obscure, rural family of small-time businessmen (including at least one bootlegger): Jerry Falwell Sr. Falwell grew up in what Susan Friend Harding, a scholar of American culture who studied Falwell close-up and extensively, describes as "a fundamentalist culture that privileged only two types of Christian masculinity: the preacher and the businessman."[65] Falwell, the founder of Liberty University (which long touted itself as the world's largest Christian university[66]), successfully combined both. By applying "worldly means to soul-winning ends,"[67] Falwell eventually amassed a multimillion-dollar enterprise (today worth billions) that took the gospel all over the world and gained the support of generations of evangelicals. It is an empire that is formidable by every worldly measure.[68]

It is also "an immense empire of words," Harding argues in *The Book of Jerry Falwell*, "a factory of words, a veritable Bible-based language industry . . . a hive of workshops, of sites of cultural production, that smelted, shaped, packaged, and distributed myriad fundamentalist rhetorics and narratives." This point is interesting in itself, but even more so because of how it connects to the word-centered nature of the evangelical faith. Of course, such a successful evangelical empire would be driven by words. Yet, ironically, many of Falwell's words were not written by him but by teams of ghostwriters.[69] This is, of course, an all-too-frequent practice among evangelicals, one that is well-documented.

What does it mean that a culture founded on authenticity, subjectivity, and individual authority so readily devours words produced by nameless souls working behind the curtain? This is a question evangelicals must grapple with as long as we say we believe in the necessity of genuine, individual conversion for salvation.

Perhaps it's not so much ironic as it is emblematic. To be a product of a subculture—to inherit unthinkingly, uncritically, and assumingly all its images, metaphors, and stories—is to plagiarize a faith.[70] It brings us back, full circle, to the condition the first evangelicals sought to redress by emphasizing genuine conversion over cultural Christianity, authentic faith over borrowed belief, and honest truth over institutional power.

> To be a product of a subculture—to inherit unthinkingly, uncritically, and assumingly all its images, metaphors, and stories—is to plagiarize a faith.

From televangelism to real estate holdings, to amusement park takeovers, to an educational program that spanned kindergarten through a doctorate, the spirit of entrepreneurialism was infused through all that Falwell established. Televangelists and their "electronic empires" (which were businesses as much as ministries), Harding writes, were "harbingers of an emerging political economic order in which the stakes were collective identities, cultural ideas, and symbols as well as profits, markets, political power, and lost souls."[71] Despite constant appeals to conservative values and tradition, such entrepreneurialism is inherently connected to novelty and to advancing the "new and improved." Strictly speaking, entrepreneurialism occurs in the context of business and financial risk. And Falwell's enterprise was nothing if not risky. Attraction to entrepreneurial risk-takers is as American as apple pie, not only in the realm of business but in the business of religion as well. Thus, Harding argues, the skepticism that surrounded Falwell from the start was actually "part of what made it work so well" because that risk created "the grounds for a leap of faith" by donors and supporters through their sacrificial giving. By participating in the risk, supporters became vicarious entrepreneurs. Any opposition to the effort—whether from national politicians or disgruntled locals—simply leveraged the power of the risk in favor of the risk-takers. As Harding explains, by "harnessing the generative power of his opposition," Falwell turned criticism into donations, and those donations turned his ministries into a multimillion-dollar empire.[72] It's the same culture-wars model that continues to empower many today, although it happens more often now on social media platforms than in pulpits. Opposition farming yields abundant crops.

As the founder of a megachurch, a political organization, a private school, and a university, Falwell was one of modern evangelicalism's greatest entrepreneurs. The satisfied customers are legion. For many years, I was one of them.[73] But, as Abraham Joshua Heschel warns, religion that "survives on the level of activities" rather than genuine faith creates a religion of "institutional loyalty."[74]

To be sure, institutional ministries have done good that only God in his omniscience can fully measure. But I've also seen up close the harm done when people are counted as less important than the institution. It would be impossible to calculate in human terms how much good it takes to offset the damage done when empires built in the name of Jesus put his kingdom second to their own.

Some have come to see the culmination of Falwell's efforts nowhere more starkly than in the overwhelming support by white evangelicals (chief among them Falwell's son, Jerry Falwell Jr.) for an entrepreneur-in-chief, former president Donald Trump.

The Evangelical Elect

In 2016, when Trump announced his intention to run for president, many Americans "saw Trump as a charmingly brash entrepreneur with an unfailing knack for business." However, this persona was largely the making of Tony Schwartz, the ghostwriter of Trump's *The Art of the Deal*, the 1987 bestseller that made Trump a household name.[75]

In a *New Yorker* profile of Schwartz, who attempted to get to know Trump better than anyone did in order to ghostwrite the memoir, Schwartz asserts that Trump showed little if any commitment to any framework of thinking or ideology. Struggling to capture in the book a coherent picture of Trump in his many relationships, negotiations, and deals, Schwartz, writing in Trump's voice, explains, "I play to people's fantasies. . . . People want to believe that something is the biggest and the greatest and the most spectacular. I call it truthful hyperbole. It's an innocent form of exaggeration—and it's a very effective form of promotion."[76]

Not only was the book by Trump not even written by him; it wasn't even his idea. According to Schwartz, as is too often the case in the publishing empire, the book was the idea of the publisher who, seeing rising interest in magazine coverage of the real estate magnate, aggressively pursued the project with Trump.[77] Trump the celebrity, who became Trump the president, was a product made in America's business empire—and bought by the evangelical empire. And as always, we get what we pay for.

Our Empire of Dirt

In 2002, Johnny Cash—who was raised a Baptist and baptized at age thirty-nine in the Jordan River—recorded a cover of "Hurt," a song originally performed by the industrial rock band Nine Inch Nails (a name said by some to be a reference to the nails used to crucify Christ). Cash transformed a song seething with unsettling, quiet rage into one of the most haunting and soulful songs in modern music. His performance deservedly won numerous awards and nominations. Even Trent Reznor of Nine Inch Nails, who wrote the song, admitted, "That song isn't mine anymore."[78]

If you've not heard Cash's rendition of the song or viewed the accompanying video, stop reading now and go do both. I will wait here while you do. Even if you have, go—listen and watch again.

Notice those lines that disavow it all, all that he has done, acquired, and accomplished. You can have all of it, he sings, this "empire of dirt."

Here is one of the most successful, iconic artists of the modern day—who has won so many awards that there's an entire Wikipedia page just to list them[79]—counting it all as dirt, or as the apostle Paul would say, dung (Phil. 3:8). Notably, the Hebrew word *adam*, the name of the first person God created, means "earth" or "ground"—or "dirt."

> All empires of man are empires of dirt in the end.

All empires of man are empires of dirt in the end. That includes whatever it is of evangelicalism that is of man, not of God. The kingdom of heaven is not an empire.

Though his life was tumultuous and often troubled, Cash embraced a devout and genuine, albeit flawed, Christian faith through the end. Poignantly, that end—the end of Cash's earthly empire—took place just months after filming the video for this song. The video spans a bittersweet retrospective of Cash's life, highs and lows alike. If he could do it all over, he sings, he would "keep" himself. One can't help but recall Jesus's piercing question in Matthew 16:26: "What good will it be for someone to gain the whole world, yet forfeit their soul?"

The song closes abruptly with Cash singing regretfully that if he could do it all over again, he would "find a way."

Rather than an empire, Cash sings, he seeks *a way*.

I imagine that the way he seeks is the way of Jesus.[80]

10

Reformation

Pardon Me, Reckoning or Rip Van Winkle?

About a century before the Protestant Reformation, Geoffrey Chaucer wrote *The Canterbury Tales*. This unfinished collection of stories revolves around a group of mostly strangers—who collectively represent the three medieval classes or estates (nobility, clergy, and layperson)—riding horseback on an obligatory pilgrimage to the cathedral at Canterbury. To pass the time along the way, they hold a storytelling contest. Before they begin, we are introduced to each pilgrim in the general prologue.[1] Each pilgrim's physical appearance also reveals his or her moral character, in keeping with the medieval belief in physiognomy, a personality assessment based on one's outer appearance. The pilgrims are also introduced in order of decreasing moral character. The last—and therefore most immoral character on the pilgrimage—is the Pardoner.

In the medieval church, pardoners were laypeople, essentially clerks who carried out the function of raising money for the church by selling indulgences—or pardons—for sins. Pardons were substitutes for penance. While pardons were officially sanctioned by the church, those who trafficked in them often exploited the office for personal gain.

In the prologue to his tale, the Pardoner tells the other pilgrims that his tale will consist of the one sermon he delivers wherever he goes to peddle his wares.[2] He may have only one sermon, but it is so well-practiced that it forms, arguably, the most moral and artistically perfect tale of all in *The Canterbury Tales*.[3] Ironically, given the Pardoner's ignoble character, his tale's lesson exemplifies the moral teaching that the root of evil is greed (based on the common Latin phrase *radix malorum est cupiditas*).

But before he tells his amazing tale, the Pardoner confesses (really, brags) openly and unashamedly to the other pilgrims what he's up to. He tells them that he travels from town to town, delivers this sermon on greed, and uses the guilt it conjures in his listeners to swindle them into buying his indulgences or the alleged magic powers of the fake relics he also carries with him. He openly makes this confession, but it doesn't stop him from trying to swindle the other pilgrims at the conclusion of his tale. The pilgrims don't fall for it. But what's most interesting and revealing is that the Pardoner is seduced and deluded by his own rhetorical powers. He believes he's so good that he can tell his audience what he's up to and still convince them to be swayed by the power of his story. He has fooled countless victims along the way (so perhaps we can't blame him for his confidence). But this is the kind of rampant corruption in the church that Chaucer's tale exposes. A century before the Reformation, Chaucer—a middle-class public servant, clerk, and poet—saw and powerfully illustrated the need for church reform.

The Honeymoon Was Over

The original aim of what came to be called the Protestant Reformation was not to breach but to reform the existing institution. But rather than face the truth about the church's egregious departures from the truths taught in Scripture, the leaders in Rome, Martin Luther complained, "protected themselves by these walls in such a way that no one has been able to reform them." Because of their self-protection, he lamented, "the whole of Christendom has fallen abominably."[4]

(If this is true of our evangelical institutions today as it was then, will another reformation be in order? I believe so.)

Upon refusing to recant some of his key criticisms of the church, Luther was excommunicated by Leo X in 1521. Luther was left no choice but to form a church body that would better reflect the Scriptures that he had long studied and that, he saw, the church had abandoned. Other Reformers across Europe followed suit, and what followed was a range of reforms that attempted to restore and uphold the councils and creeds established in the first centuries of the church and make them manifest.

The Protestant Reformation was centered on truth—the truth of biblical doctrine. Yes, the medieval church's widespread corruption took the form of practices, but these evil deeds—including the sale of pardons and indulgences for sin that expanded the church's wealth and power to obscene levels by taking advantage of the fact that the illiterate masses could not read the Bible for themselves—were made possible by distorting the truth. The church was able to get away with it because few could read the Bible for themselves and thereby see the lies. The people—who had no political power and no ability to read the Bible even if they were able to gain access to one—were made captive by illiteracy to an institution that grew more corrupt as it grew wealthier and more powerful.

What holds evangelicals—who not only can read but have easy access to Bibles of all kinds—captive today? That is an important question.

Why Johnny Can Read

One answer is that we suffer under a different kind of illiteracy today, another kind of "dark age" created by too much information, too much disinformation and misinformation, and an inability (or unwillingness) to do the labor necessary to "read" information, the times, and ourselves better. Perhaps this kind of functional illiteracy is a crisis of the imagination.

The Reformation's emphasis on each person reading the Word of God for themselves rather than receiving that Word mediated through a priest brought widespread literacy to the world. This fact is universally recognized and understood. But Martin Luther emphasized not just the importance of the Bible as it existed then. Luther translated the Bible into his own language and thereby, philosopher Samuel Loncar writes, revolutionized the world's relationship not only to both the Bible and to language but to "the entire system of authority in a culture." By translating the Bible into his own language, Luther "created both the theological rationale and the institutional impetus for a total transformation through the spread of literacy as a means of access to the Bible."[5] This metaphysical revolution created the conditions for the emergence of the modern individual.

In relation to the Protestant Reformation, the evangelical movement clearly is but a coda, an addendum. Yet, three hundred years after inking its postscript to the Reformation,

> What holds evangelicals—who not only can read but have easy access to Bibles of all kinds—captive today? That is an important question.

evangelicalism is in the midst of a reckoning. We will give an account; whether sooner or later is up to us.

If the Reformation was over the Word as written (over who can and should read and interpret it), then this reckoning of evangelicalism concerns the Word as it has been incarnated. If the Reformation was over the truth revealed in Scripture, then this evangelical reckoning is over the way and the life revealed in Jesus—and how the church has failed to follow and embody it.

They—the Word written and the Word incarnated—can't be separated, of course. But the failure of the evangelical imagination is in failing to see and embody this whole.

Instead, we have developed a false division between biblical theology and spiritual formation. Between orthodoxy and orthopraxy. Between religion and politics.[6] Jesus showed us the way to unite these—indeed, he was the union of these things.

The Way, the Truth, and the Life

Jesus said, "I am the Way and the Truth and the Life" (John 14:6).

Consider what it means that Jesus calls himself "the Life." Part of what has always defined the evangelical movement is its focus on the essential gospel message that through Jesus Christ and through him alone one gains eternal life. Evangelicals have tended to focus so much on getting to heaven, however, that the reason for existence in this earthly life is often elusive. Even more often forgotten is that eternal life will be spent here—in a new heaven and a new earth. Eternal life doesn't begin in the future. Eternal life begins *now*.

Jesus also says he is "the Truth." Among the defining characteristics of evangelicalism outlined in chapter 1, the centrality of the Bible is prominent. Evangelicals have always emphasized biblical truth over church tradition (and over personal experience, at least theoretically and until more recently[7]). Even the spirit of activism that David Bebbington identifies as part of what defines evangelicalism manifests in applying beliefs about biblical truth in a proactive way.[8] Eighteenth-century British evangelicals were activists in abolishing the slave trade, promoting animal welfare, and reforming capital punishment and labor laws. In the nineteenth and twentieth centuries, evangelicals became activists in education, voting, and temperance. The concerns may change, but the heart of evangelicalism has always been application of what is understood to be biblical truth to the cultural issues of the day.

Jesus is also "the Way." No Christian—and certainly no evangelical—would deny it. But when evangelicals talk about Jesus being the Way, it is usually imagined in a straightforward, literal manner: Jesus is the way to God, the way to eternal life, the way to heaven. While this is true, there is so much more embedded in that word, in that image, than simply a path or a road (which is what the Greek word *hodos* in John 14:6 means).[9] Evangelicals tend to emphasize how Jesus is the way *to* something. But he is also the way, period. Consider the difference between saying, "This is the road into town" and "This is the road." One is a means to something. The other is something in and of itself. Jesus isn't only a means to something. He is an ultimate end.

When Jesus invites us to follow him, it means more than just walking behind him on the road toward a destination, or the cross serving as a plank placed over a chasm between you and God. Jesus invites us to adopt his way, and his ways. He invites us to be like him. To imitate him. To call his Father "Father," too. To die to self as he did. To participate in his nature. To be grafted onto the true vine in order to bear fruit that tastes like him—divine.

The Word Became Flesh and Dwelt among Us

Some philosophers say that Jesus entered the world at the precise historical moment in which a convergence of Jewish history and Greek thought gave birth to modern consciousness, a time when the I AM who revealed himself in the Old Testament became incarnated within a human culture ready to receive him and spread his message to all people.[10] Indeed, Jesus says "I am" quite a few times.

Some would even say that the birth of the modern individual—whose conscious existence begins with the expression "I am"—took place all the way back when Christ was born.

> Some would even say that the birth of the modern individual—whose conscious existence begins with the expression "I am"–took place all the way back when Christ was born.

For example, it wasn't by mere accident, Marshall McLuhan says, that "Christianity began in the Greco-Roman culture." With the invention of the phonetic alphabet, the Greeks made it possible to have a "sense of private substantial identity—a self" that "is to this day utterly unknown" in other parts of the world. "Christianity was introduced into a matrix of culture in which the individual had enormous significance," claims McLuhan, a concept that was "not characteristic of other world cultures."[11] With literacy, God's people would have the ability to read longer texts of Scripture to "nurture a sense of divine presence that dwelt internally, in the heart and mind."[12]

This interior life is, of course, the site of the imagination.

God, who calls himself I AM, came to earth, united in spirit and flesh, fully human and fully divine, at just the right moment in human history when human language was ready to take a form that would awaken individual consciousness, interior life, and imagination in a way that would forever alter history and humanity. Recall the earlier discussion in chapter 2 on how conscience as we understand it today was introduced by Christianity. Each time we express ourselves beginning with the words, "I am . . ." we express consciousness, the inner life, and imagination in a way that reflects God's image in us.[13]

Reckoning or Reformation?

There is much of evangelicalism that is of man, not God. I say that as an evangelical.

A young person, a disillusioned evangelical, asked me recently how I have managed to keep the faith, stay in church, and remain evangelical in a time when so many evangelicals have betrayed so much of what they taught us. I honestly think, I told him, that it's because I was born before the modern evangelical culture in which so many young people of the last two generations were raised took root. Yes, I had Chick tracts, *A Thief in the Night*, and "I Wish We'd All Been Ready." But I didn't have VeggieTales, *Adventures in Odyssey*, ACE homeschool workbooks, CCM, lock-ins, hell houses, purity pledges, purity rings, or purity balls. I went to secular schools, read what I wanted to read, got to date boys and make mistakes, was encouraged to ask questions, and was never told my life or value would be ruined or lessened by any of those things. But I have taught an entire generation or more of evangelical students whose lives revolve around these things. I am watching some of them walk away from church, from marriages, from families, and from the faith. Yet, I am watching even more of them do the hard, terrible work of extricating Christian culture from Christ—the Christ who transcends human cultures, human time, and human tradition. This work is not without risk. But it is necessary.

As Alan Noble observes, "When we discover error in the church, we return home with good news." That good news is

the opportunity to correct and clarify. In this way, such understanding "does not lead you away from faith but deeper in."[14]
Is the church in a five-hundred-year moment? Will the reckoning lead to a new reformation?

In one of the last essays he wrote before his assassination in 1968, Martin Luther King Jr. reflected on that quintessential American Revolution-era tale of Rip Van Winkle, who climbed up a mountain and slept for twenty years. King observes, "The most striking thing about this story is not that Rip Van Winkle slept twenty years, but that he slept through a revolution that would alter the course of human history."[15]

The church pews are filled with Rip Van Winkles. The pulpits are too.

If the Reformation was a crisis of authority—one that rightly gave highest authority to the Bible rather than the priests—then this reckoning (or perhaps even a new reformation) is one of credibility: Do we who profess to believe in the authority of the Word present ourselves as credible witnesses of that Way, that Truth, and that Life?

> **The church pews are filled with Rip Van Winkles. The pulpits are too.**

The foibles and faults of the church, while always reflecting the fallible and unchanging human condition of the people who comprise it, will inevitably reflect the particular limitations of its particular time and place. Christian leaders of churches in suburban Chicago in the twenty-first century aren't as likely as those criticized by Geoffrey Chaucer in *The Canterbury Tales* to try to sell congregants the magical healing powers of a sheep's bone. Nor would the seventeenth-century Puritans have embraced a view of God that is reflected in today's prosperity gospel or moralistic therapeutic deism.[16] And most of us today aren't going to use the Bible to support chattel slavery.

Like so many other movements, powers, and institutions over the course of human history, the evangelical empire that has reigned in America for so long is, by some measures, undergoing loss—loss of position, privilege, influence, and power. It is easy for those who have benefited from this empire (I count myself among these) to feel a sense of loss. Having something you've always had taken away is—at least by human calculations—a loss.

> A testimony is something you give. A witness is something you *are*.

But imagine what might be gained.

Let's be honest: it's not that hard to tell the difference between those whose longing is for the good of others and those whose longing is for the good of themselves. To paraphrase the famous line by Supreme Court Justice Potter Stewart as he attempted to offer a legal definition of hardcore pornography, you know it when you see it. There are many who display personal bitterness and anger at the losses they perceive to be at stake—their own rightness, superiority, and ownership in the status quo—and show no joy for the gains being made by others. We may not have pardoners in the post-Reformation church, but we still have grifters. Their wares (and even their tweets) are just fake magical sheep bones.

I exult in the words of Mary's Magnificat, spoken while Jesus was still in her womb, that our Savior—hers, yours, mine—has "scattered the proud in the imagination of their hearts" (Luke 1:51 KJV).

The way of Jesus is not in the power, celebrity, and corruption that has borne the fruit of sexual abuse, spiritual abuse, systemic racism, and imperialism.

A recent example of this reckoning within Christendom writ large is the Catholic Church's apology in 2022 to Indigenous peoples for abuses committed by the Canadian government in Catholic schools over the course of 150 years. In a homily following this apology, Pope Francis quoted Charles Taylor's *A Secular Age*, noting the challenge that secularization presents to the "pastoral imagination." Noting that this secularization requires the church to "look for new languages and forms of expression," Francis said that the first challenge in such an age is "to make Jesus known." The second challenge, he said, is to make Jesus known through a witness that is credible.[17]

A testimony, an image so central to the evangelical imagination (see chap. 4), can meet this challenge of making Jesus known. But a testimony is something you give. A witness is something you *are*. While we might be called on from time to time to give our testimony (or one of them, anyway), we must always be a witness.

And a credible one at that.

Reformed Imaginations

Among the most known and repeated words of Jesus are these from the instructions he gives his disciples upon sending them out: "Whoever finds their life will lose it, and whoever loses their life for my sake will find it" (Matt. 10:39).

Perhaps we've heard and read these words so often that they have lost their meaning. Or perhaps we've heard and read these words so often within particular contexts that their meaning has shrunk. We might think it means only that we gain eternal life by surrendering our life to Jesus. It does mean that. We might think it means that we find ultimate meaning and purpose in life when we serve Jesus. It does. But maybe it also means more specific, concrete things in our particular lives and times. Maybe it means that when we lose platform, or position, or privilege, or pay, or authority, or respect, or work, or elections, or jobs, or followers, or friends, or health, or limbs, or ease, we might find more of our life in Christ.[18]

This loss of language, of meaning—whether through overfamiliarity or lack of real familiarity in the first place—is, at heart, what I am hoping to help us recover in this book. What is imagination but an opening of the eyes of our hearts?

Human beings have individual imaginations and shared social imaginaries. Both are filled with the words, images, sayings, stories, narratives, and concepts that surround us. We can't possibly be aware of them all or the way they shape our thinking and motivate our actions from beneath the surface of our conscious thinking. But what we can do—with awareness and intention—is immerse ourselves more deeply in the stories, images, and words that reflect what is good, true, and beautiful: yes, Scripture, but also the human applications of Scripture that express the fullness of its teaching. We must work to reform our imaginations by filling them with stories, images, and metaphors that are true, lest we be counted among those proud ones scattered by deformed imaginations, as Mary declared in the Magnificat.

> **What is imagination but an opening of the eyes of our hearts?**

As Jesus said of many who were exposed to his parables, "Though seeing, they do not see; though hearing, they do not hear or understand" (Matt. 13:13). We must ask Jesus to open our eyes and ears, to renew our imaginations. Indeed, Paul implores the Lord in Ephesians 1:18 to open the eyes of our hearts so that our hearts will be flooded with the light of his truth.

This passage from Ephesians is invoked by John Stott in the Lausanne Covenant, a document drawn up following the First Lausanne Congress held in 1974. The covenant defines evangelicalism within the modern, global context. In the covenant, Stott describes the nature of the authority of the Bible and its role in the life of believers in every culture:

For as the Holy Spirit used the personality and culture of the writers of his Word in order to convey through each something fresh and appropriate, so today *he illumines the minds of God's people in every culture to perceive its truth freshly through their own eyes*. It is he who opens the eyes of our hearts (Eph. 1:17, 18), and these eyes and hearts belong to young and old, Latin and Anglo-Saxon, African, Asian and American, male and female, poetic and prosaic. It is this "magnificent and intricate mosaic of mankind" (to borrow a phrase of Dr. Donald McGavran's) which the Holy Spirit uses to disclose from Scripture *ever more of the many-colored wisdom of God* (a literal translation of Eph. 3:10). Thus *the whole church is* needed to receive God's whole revelation in all its beauty and richness (cf., Eph. 3:18 "with all the saints").[19]

Seeing is hard.

Change is hard.

But change (for us fallible humans in this fallen world) is also inevitable.

Change is good: *semper reformanda* (always reforming).

The complete phrase from which this oft-repeated refrain comes—*ecclesia reformata, semper reformanda* (the church reformed, always reforming)—emerged following the Protestant Reformation. It expressed the idea that while the church had been reformed in light of the grievous errors that had festered for so long in the church, reforming must also be an ongoing process, not only for each individual believer through the process of sanctification, but for the church itself.

The root of *reformation* is *formation*.

Formation speaks of the Way. The way of salvation. The way of living. The way of growing. The way of going (see fig. 15).

The church cannot rest on her laurels. Even the church *reformed* continues to need *reforming*.

Unless, of course, we are raptured instead.

11

Rapture

Or How a Thief Came in the Night but Left My Chick Tracts Behind

I remember the exact moment when I learned that not all Christians believe in the rapture.

I had grown up being taught that the rapture was as straightforward a "biblical" truth as the virgin birth and Christ's resurrection. Then, well into adulthood, a Presbyterian friend told me, first, it's not universally accepted that believers still living on earth will be "caught up" into the sky to meet Christ at some future point, and, second, it's not even a historical teaching within the church.

This rocked my world.

(Imagine when I learned about the creeds!)

At the time, I was a PhD student studying English literature —which is all about interpretation—so it's a little embarrassing to look back and realize not only what I didn't know but also that I didn't even know what I didn't know.

It's an overstatement, but not much of one, to say everything's an interpretation. The problem isn't so much that a great deal of human experience and understanding depends on interpretation but that we don't always recognize that it does.

It's an overstatement, but not much of one, to say everything's an interpretation.

Left Behind on the Late Great Planet Earth after the Thief in the Night

I was five years old in 1970 when Hal Lindsey published *The Late Great Planet Earth*. I can still picture the paperback copy that lay on the coffee table of my family's living room. For the longest time, I thought it was a book about an impending environmental disaster. I suppose, in some ways, it was.

One of the bestselling books of the twentieth century, *The Late Great Planet Earth* popularized "end-times" prophecies from the perspective of a school of biblical interpretation known as "dispensational premillennialism."

A number of different schools of thought exist around the meaning of the thousand-year reign of Christ (the millennium) mentioned in Revelation 20. Premillennialists believe that Christ's second coming will occur at the start of this period; postmillennialists believe Christ will physically return afterward. The rapture is associated with premillennialist views based on what are considered to be more literal interpretations of Scripture.[1] The history of these interpretations and positions is long and complicated. Entire industries have been built around them. A great deal of discussion revolves around what the Bible means by the word translated into English as "rapture."

Some seventeenth-century Puritans taught that a rapture of some sort would take place in the future. But in the nineteenth century, John Nelson Darby, a leader within a non-conformist movement called the Plymouth Brethren (the same denomination Edmund Gosse grew up in), heavily promoted the rapture along with a novel interpretive approach to biblical hermeneutics that divided biblical history into different periods, each calling for different interpretations, a view known as dispensationalism. In some ways, Darby's ideas were a refashioning of existing premillennialist views that had already been circulating as defenses against the skepticism arising first out of the French Revolution and later from the claims of higher criticism.[2] But Darby's dispensational premillennialism drew new connections between biblical history, eschatology, and secular politics.[3] His teachings became much more popular when they formed the basis for the study notes used in the *Scofield Reference Bible*, published in 1909.[4] A revised edition of the *Scofield Reference Bible* published in 1967 made fertile ground for the reception of *The Late Great Planet Earth*, which sold 7.5 million copies in its first decade, over 28 million in two decades,[5] and in 1977 was adapted into a film.

The rapture had taken flight. Modern American evangelicalism would never be the same.

A couple of years later, a low-budget movie about the rapture, *A Thief in the Night*, was released. Its story centers on a group of groovy young people who variously share, receive, or reject the gospel—just before (you guessed it) the rapture takes place. In the aftermath of the sudden disappearance of millions of people around the globe, a new worldwide government is established (another ingredient of Darby's eschatology) that requires all citizens to receive a stamp—the Bible's "mark of the beast" described in Revelation 13—on their forehead or hand. In addition to introducing Darby's ideas to a new generation of Christians, the film made famous its opening song, Larry Norman's haunting ballad, "I Wish

We'd All Been Ready," which quickly became a favorite in my church's living room sing-alongs. (I still have nearly every word memorized all these years later.)

Although it had been decades since I'd seen the film, in rewatching it recently, I felt afresh the visceral fear the film roused in me of waking up one day to a world in which millions had suddenly disappeared and I had been left behind. This is a common experience for many evangelicals who grew up post–Hal Lindsey. Because I was fairly confident in my salvation, the worst fears were what would happen to the rest of the world if all the Christians were suddenly taken out of it. A particularly traumatic memory I have is of sitting on the steps outside church one summer day after VBS, crying to my mother and asking her what would happen to my horses, my cats, and rabbits if the rapture took place. Try as she did to comfort me, I was inconsolable. I couldn't imagine what would happen to my beloved pets if we were raptured and they were left behind.[6]

Speaking of left behind, the famous franchise of that name (composed of sixteen volumes of novels, youth editions, graphic novels, film adaptations, and related merchandise) debuted in 1995, unseating Hal Lindsey as "the most widely read expositor of biblical prophecy."[7] One title in the series, published in 2001, right after 9/11, sold almost one million copies in a week, putting it immediately onto the *New York Times* bestseller list, a groundbreaking feat for evangelical fiction,[8] and topping the bestseller list for fiction that year.[9] Nothing else within the genre has come close to the sales and influence of this series. But perhaps the more significant feat of the *Left Behind* phenomenon was in replacing nonfiction with fiction as "the most successful cultural conduit of dispensational faith," which was "a paradigm shift in popular prophetic consciousness."[10]

The Left Behind series was the creation of Tim LaHaye—who provided the rapture theology—and Jerry Jenkins—who provided the writing talent. Of this partnership an editor at *Publishers Weekly* observed, "Between [LaHaye's] theology and his co-writer Jerry Jenkins' writing ability, the two of them really managed to capture the popular imagination."[11] The effect of this collaboration was as much political and cultural as it was aesthetic.

A Political Imagination

In *Reading Evangelicals*, Daniel Silliman says that LaHaye had hoped that imagining the rapture, "picturing it, and thinking how it could happen at any moment," would motivate evangelicals toward both evangelism and political action.[12] Even before the sales success of the series, LaHaye had good reason for this hope. For example, Bill Bright, founder of Campus Crusade for Christ (now Cru), had been inspired to found his wide-reaching ministry through his study of end-times prophecies in seminary.[13] Billy Graham, despite embodying and modeling a more urbane, nonfundamentalist, postwar evangelicalism, also embraced apocalypticism.[14] And LaHaye himself had earlier succeeded in persuading Jerry Falwell Sr. to mix politics with religion,[15] which resulted in the two of them eventually cofounding the Moral Majority, a cornerstone in the foundation of the religious right.

One might think that belief in an impending rapture of the church—a giant escape hatch for Jesus's faithful followers—would serve as a disincentive for political activism. But the opposite has been largely true. Premillennialists like LaHaye care about political issues—such as religious liberty—because they directly impinge on evangelistic efforts that would result in fewer people being left behind.[16] The "apocalyptic sensibilities" that modern evangelicals inherited from early-twentieth-century fundamentalists cultivated "a sense of determinism that demanded constant action" as well as a sense of responsibility to "occupy" this world until Christ's return.[17] For example, some who worked with Jerry Falwell reported explicitly that those apocalyptic views motivated them toward political activism, instead of those views being "a pretext for this-worldly despair."[18] In his later work, Hal Lindsey likewise "seamlessly blended apocalypticism with potent conservative activism."[19] In fact, end-times prophecy became so popular and so interwoven with evangelical politics that even George W. Bush in 1998 was surprised by the hostility among evangelicals against the United Nations.[20]

> One might think that belief in an impending rapture of the church—a giant escape hatch for Jesus's faithful followers—would serve as a disincentive for political activism. But the opposite has been largely true.

Furthermore, because some end-times interpretations hold that certain political events must take place before Christ's return, it is believed that human actions can help facilitate God's divinely ordered timeline. "Preparing for Jesus's return fostered intense, relentless engagement with the world," explains Matthew Avery Sutton.[21] As Daniel Silliman puts it,

> For these Christians, political activism wasn't a choice. It was a divine mandate. They had to be involved. And since the end could come any day, it was urgent. The theology, just like the fiction LaHaye was imagining, also had a second audience. The rapture, the tribulation, and the antichrist were compelling, LaHaye argued, to non-Christians. Getting people to imagine the apocalypse was an important tool for evangelism. Just provoking the imagination was a powerful first step.[22]

The establishment of the state of Israel and wars over the control of Jerusalem, particularly the Six-Day War of 1967, are among the events many believe need to be fulfilled before the Lord's return. When those events took place, popular interest in the fulfillment of biblical prophecies only increased. Even Ronald Reagan caught end-times fever, casting the Cold War in terms inspired by apocalyptic prophecy novels.[23] This connection between American politics and biblical prophecy demonstrates the role of the evangelical imagination in a broader, more partisan, and worldly "Spirit of Neo-Imperialism."[24]

Apocalypse Now

Before there was *Left Behind*, there was Frank Peretti's novel *This Present Darkness*, which was published in 1986 and followed in 1988 by *Piercing the Darkness*. While not "end-times" books strictly speaking, these works fit squarely within the larger apocalyptic genre because their plots center on revealing what had been unseen—in this case, spiritual warfare. Peretti's novels emerged at a time when evangelical fiction (in particular, the burgeoning genre of Christian romance) had begun to make its mark in the publishing market. Peretti's novels, which sold millions of copies,[25] expanded that market even further, both in terms of dollars and in stretching the category of Christian fiction, thereby paving the way for the success of *Left Behind*.

I was introduced to *This Present Darkness* a few years after its publication by someone who assumed that because I love literature I would love this work of "Christian literature." *This Present Darkness* was my first foray into "Christian fiction." I regret to inform you that I put it down after reading just a few pages. Charles Dickens it was not.[26] I would never have guessed the impact Peretti's work would have on the church in years to come.

It's noteworthy in this cultural moment—one in the midst of a continuing sexual abuse crisis in the church—that one of the plot points of *This Present Darkness* involves a pastor being falsely accused of rape. The influence of this particular narrative—that false accusations of sexual assault stem from evil spirits behind the New Age movement—on the contemporary evangelical imagination cannot be measured, of course. But given the failures of too many evangelical institutions to effectively address sexual abuse and cover-up of abuse in churches, it's reasonable to wonder what role stories like this have played in developing our social

This Present Darkness was my first foray into "Christian fiction." I regret to inform you that I put it down after reading just a few pages.

imaginary around accusations of abuse. Is such a work a mirror of evangelical culture—or a lamp? Most likely, it is both.

More clearly, and more generally, Peretti's use of genre fiction as a weapon in evangelicalism's ongoing culture war made a significant imprint within the evangelical social imaginary. Indeed, its publishers aimed *This Present Darkness* "for the Moral Majority."[27] The spiritual battles in the stories swirl around nearly all major human arenas: political, governmental, educational, ecclesiastical. As one scholar notes, "Such narratives remap the world, rendering its once-familiar landscapes in the blood-red tones of spiritual warfare."[28] They are works of evangelism and apologetics before they are works of art. Conversion narratives feature centrally in them. *This Present Darkness* has been described as a "thinly veiled allegory for the social concerns of the Religious Right," a reflection of conservative Christian concerns "translated into a fantasy of cosmic struggle."[29]

These apocalyptic and end-times novels were never intended primarily as either literary works or mere entertainment, of course. While literary fiction uses language in ways that cause readers to imagine the world differently, these apocalyptic works are intended to help readers think imaginatively about things they already believe—or that their authors want them to believe. Not that there's anything wrong with that (as Jerry Seinfeld and George Costanza would say)—as long as one understands the nature of the work, which is a good principle to apply to all things.

Is This Real Life? Is This Just Fantasy?

Christian apocalyptic fiction began to appear in the early twentieth century, following the publication of the *Scofield Reference Bible*. Prophecy fiction, as it is also called, depicted what evangelicals saw as a decline of culture and their marginalization from it in the form of "a comprehensive mythology for modern American life" expressed in theological terms.[30] It is not coincidental that it was also during these years, the first half of the twentieth century, that myth, symbol, and archetype became intense objects of study in various disciplines—in psychology through Carl Jung, in literary criticism through Northrop Frye, and in literature and language through J. R. R. Tolkien, C. S. Lewis, Owen Barfield, and Joseph Campbell. The works of these writers are part of the mythopoeic literary genre, a category that includes prophecy fiction and fantasy.

Writing on this genre's writers, critics, and theorists—particularly Lewis and Tolkien—one scholar explains that these creators of the mythopoeic believe

> that the imaginative and spiritual impoverishment characteristic of much of contemporary life may be countered by soul-nourishing stories composed in the "poetics of myth"— that is with conscious use of re-imagined mythic materials such as archetypes, plot structures, characters, events, motifs,

and so on, derived from both ancient mythologies and from myths cherished by contemporary culture.

Such beliefs have clearly tapped into a hunger both within evangelicalism and beyond:

> How perceptive Tolkien and Lewis were in their assessment of the liberating potential of mythopoeia can be glimpsed from the proliferation of fantasy literature and movies, from the growing popularity of Role Playing Games, and from the plethora of scholarly publications of the last four decades, many of which expand certain claims made by Tolkien and Lewis.[31]

I have often asked myself why fantasy is so popular today, particularly among evangelicals. Certainly, Lewis and Tolkien have a leg up among evangelical readers by virtue of being respected Christian thinkers known for other works too. Then along came the Harry Potter series—whose timing coincided with the internet technology that made the spread of fan culture possible—and suddenly the mythopoeic was everywhere.[32] Scads of grown men these days discuss superheroes and medieval fantasy series the way my grandfather once talked about milking the cows, planting string beans, and keeping the aphids off the tomato plants, and the way my father talks about makes and models of cars (all of which actually exist and affect our everyday lives). It's a little disorienting, in some respects.

As someone who is not a fan of fantasy, I want to say, on the one hand, that fantasy is kind of like training wheels for a people who have labored too long under an impoverished social imaginary. As Flannery O'Connor puts it, "To the hard of hearing you shout, and for the almost-blind you draw large and startling pictures."[33]

I think, for example, of the first time I read *Pride and Preju-dice*. I was in tenth grade and had been a voracious reader since I was five years old, but this novel was the most boring thing I'd ever read. Now that I've grown up, I adore Austen. I understand that the drama in *Pride and Prejudice*, as in all great literature, isn't in what happens but in how it's told. It isn't in soap-opera-worthy plot points but in the ordinary details of everyday life. When Elizabeth Bennet is scorned by her social superiors because her petticoats have been stained by mud from walking miles to come to her sister's aid, a mac-rocosm of human nature and human drama is revealed in this minuscule event. It may be harder to see the transcendence in the mundane, but believe me, eternity is in Lizzie's scandal-ously dirty ankles. Her stained petticoat isn't a symbol for anything, of course. Rather, it functions in the story simply as a sign, a sign of the ways in which people value different things, disdain others far too easily, or care little about what others think. If only we were more attuned to seeing and reading the world of the real in this way. But centuries of immersion in literalism, as opposed to literariness, makes such layered and nuanced readings of the world more elusive.

> **Believe me, eternity is in Lizzie's scandalously dirty ankles.**

The works we read today and understand to be epic or myth—*The Iliad*, *The Odyssey*, *Beowulf*, for example—were not understood by their contemporary audiences to be "fantasy." These works expressed what their first readers saw as the reality of the enchanted world they lived in.[34] Today's fantasy (not only literature but films, games, cosplay, and even the growing popularity of Halloween celebrations) reflects an awareness that we live in a disenchanted world, as well as our desire to return to that sense of transcendence in the imminent.[35]

A lion, a ring, and Sauron are symbols writ large. They are billboards on the highway of a disenchanted world, pointing us, with bold letters and bright lights, to the forgotten places on the side roads of the modern soul. It is always tempting, and sometimes helpful, to see the world and to interpret stories (whether the true ones of history or the Bible or the fictional ones of novels and films) along broad sweeps and grand archetypes: good versus evil, cowboy with the white hat versus cowboy with the black hat, angel versus demon. Myth, symbol, and archetypes—along with dreams and visions— are universal signs of the timeless and eternal aspects of reality. They point to a divine order of creation and remind us that we are made in the image of the Creator. The mythopoeic externalizes the transcendent truths of the inner, spiritual life, making them manifest. Such stories meet a hunger caused by the general absence of myth and mystery in the modern world—that much-discussed disenchantment—and that modern world includes evangelicals, whether we realize it or not. This hunger helps explain why a Jungian psychologist like Jordan Peterson—whose ideas are rooted in symbols and archetypes—is so popular, even among evangelicals.

Samuel Coleridge explains in his 1816 commentary on the Bible how the nature of the symbol is connected to the eternal, writing,

> A symbol is characterized by a translucence of the Special in the Individual, or of the General in the Special, or of the Universal in the general: above all by the translucence of the Eternal through and in the Temporal. It always partakes of the Reality which it renders intelligible; and while it enunciates the whole, abides itself as a living part in that Unity of which it is the representative.[36]

We are a symbol-starved people. We need enchanted worlds to help us see the enchantment in our own. This famine results from our modern inattention to aesthetic experi-

> We are a symbol-starved people. We need enchanted worlds to help us see the enchantment in our own.

ence generally. In exploring Coleridge's ideas about the relationship between symbols and the imagination, Peter Cheyne explains that symbols are inherently aesthetic because they are first perceived by the bodily senses and then connected through both reason and imagination to some idea or meaning, to an "enlightened understanding."[37] To be moved by something, to have an aesthetic experience, is to "intuit, however dimly," that thing's "ultimate" purpose.[38] Imagination is an expression of the human desire for meaning beyond the literal surface of our lives.

Loosely Literal

Prophecy novels embody an approach to interpretation that is more literal than literary. The long history of seeing signs that turn out not to be signs, of interpreting biblical prophecies (then reinterpreting them as history unfolds), of predicting dates for Christ's return (then making new predictions when those dates come and go), surely has played no small part in the popularity of conspiracy theories. These novels embed a certain hermeneutical approach into the evangelical social imaginary.[39] They reinforce among those who ascribe to these interpretive practices "a confidence that they alone understand the world in which they are living, and a hope for a future in which they will reign supreme."[40] Apocalypticism has been so ingrained within the evangelical imagination over the past century or more (as numerous polls and surveys show) that the premillennial teaching that Jesus's imminent second coming to earth "has become such a standard part of evangelical rhetoric that few believers ever question it."[41]

In the nineteenth and twentieth centuries, largely in response to Darwinism, higher criticism, and theological liberalism, dispensationalists and fundamentalists argued for more literal interpretations of Scripture. However, language being what it is (subject to translation from one to another and composed of words that often have multiple meanings that change over time), literalism is tricky business—as anyone who has read the delightful *Amelia Bedelia* children's books knows.

The problem with taking the Bible literally absent literary understanding isn't as much a theological problem as it is an interpretive one. It's also a problem of imagination.

Serious theologians know that there is room, to varying degrees, for differing interpretations and applications of scriptural texts. An understanding of language that fails to recognize that words have different, layered, sometimes changing meanings cannot by its very nature account for the meaning of "literal" itself. For to speak of the "literal" meaning of a word, phrase, or passage is to acknowledge implicitly that there are nonliteral meanings (or at least possibilities of such meanings). This is why, for example, the Chicago Statement on Biblical Inerrancy rightly explains that "the text of Scripture is to be interpreted by grammatico-historical exegesis, taking

> Even to read "literally" requires interpretation.

account of its literary forms and devices, and that Scripture is to interpret Scripture."[42] In other words, even to read "literally" requires interpretation. Interpretation is a theological commitment. Rightly interpreting God's Word is how we rightly know him.

Furthermore, the insistence on literalism is a particularly modern problem, one that arose, as already mentioned, in reaction against nineteenth-century liberalism. Recall from an earlier chapter how even the division between fiction and nonfiction is also a modern categorization. But the literalist fetish goes back even further, really. It is the outgrowth of a Cartesian dualism that separates things that cannot be separated: mind and body, spiritual and physical, rational and emotional, immaterial and material. One might as well try to sever the Word from flesh as to separate these. It can't be done.

In his 1907 memoir, *Father and Son,* Edmund Gosse (whom we met in an earlier chapter as a friend of Thomas Hardy and one of many notable second-generation Victorians who rejected the evangelical faith of their parents) describes the ultraliteral approach to Scripture taken by his parents, who were members, like John Nelson Darby, of the Plymouth Brethren sect:

> For [my Mother], and for my Father, nothing was symbolic, nothing allegorical or allusive in any part of Scripture, except what was, in so many words, proffered as a parable or a picture. . . . Hence, although their faith was so strenuous that many persons might have called it fanatical, there was no mysticism about them. They went rather to the opposite extreme, to the cultivation of a rigid and iconoclastic literalness.[43]

As Gosse goes on to describe it, this extreme literalness led to misreading the highly symbolic book of Revelation:

> When they read of seals broken and of vials poured forth, of the star which was called Wormwood that fell from Heaven, and of men whose hair was as the hair of women and their teeth as the teeth of lions, they did not admit for a moment that these vivid mental pictures were of a poetic character, but they regarded them as positive statements, in guarded language, describing events which were to happen, and could be recognized when they did happen.[44]

Now, it is clear that Gosse's portrayal is at times tongue-in-cheek and perhaps favors colorfulness more than objective reporting. Even so, Gosse's felt sense of his parents' discouraging him from pursuing the imaginative life, whether through reading novels or creating stories of his own, shaped the course of his life. He yearned to delight in the Scriptures but could not do so with the same enthusiasm he had for imaginative literature. His father continued to hound the son about reading the Scriptures as he, the father, saw fit.[45] Here he describes his rejection of his father's appeals and his father's evangelical Christianity (using the third person to describe himself):

> No compromise, it is seen, was offered; no proposal of a truce would have been acceptable. It was a case of "Everything or Nothing"; and thus desperately challenged, the young man's conscience threw off once for all the yoke of his "dedication," and, as respectfully as he could, without parade or remonstrance, he took a human being's privilege to fashion his inner life for himself.[46]

If there was only one way to read the Bible, Gosse decided he would not read it at all.[47]

A Good Metaphor Is Hard to Find

All language is metaphorical. All words point to the thing; they are not the thing. But words can point in different directions. Some words point to a thing that points to the thing. Some employ indirection or have layers of metaphor. A word that points most directly is understood to be "literal" (such as when "cat" signifies a cat). A word that points to something that is understood to represent something else is a symbol (such as when, in a certain context, "a dark wood" symbolizes evil, fear, or confusion). A word that points to something that is like something else is a metaphor (such as "thy word is a lamp unto my feet"). The ability to see and draw true comparisons is so essential to critical thinking—to our sheer humanity—that in the novel *1984*, George Orwell observes that the first step in creating a loyal Party member of Big Brother's totalitarian rule is to impede that person's instinctive human ability of "grasping analogies."[48]

All language is metaphorical. All words point to the thing; they are not the thing.

It's easy to mix metaphors. (Ask any writer!) Sometimes the results are amusing, but they always reveal muddled thinking. One example that went viral on the internet revealed such confusion poignantly. The clip featured a woman being interviewed about why she wouldn't receive a newly developed vaccination. Pointing to her trust in God over government agencies, the woman said that the vaccination was separating the sheep from the goats. (During the COVID pandemic, "sheep" became a derogatory term for those who adhered to government recommendations.) When the interviewer asked which one she was, sheep or goat, she hesitated, as if remembering that the Bible refers to Christians metaphorically as sheep and unbelievers as goats. But then, stepping into the trap her metaphors had set for her, she proudly replied, "I'm a goat."[49]

Metaphors show likeness; symbols express sameness. Getting the difference is crucial to understanding reality. Consider the profound difference, for example, between the human beings in the Bible who try to be *like* God and the one human being who actually *is* God. As Peter Leithart explains, "Symbols are more than mere signs or indications of reality; they actually lead to other forms of reality."[50] Getting symbols right is more than a mere literary exercise, because symbols (as well as metaphors and all language, ultimately) shape our understanding—or misunderstanding—of reality. Getting it right can be a matter of life and death.

Conspiracy theories, for example, are misguided attempts to re-enchant the world through fantasy. Conspiracy theories employ symbols, see symbols everywhere, and encourage symbolic interpretations of reality. Isolated facts are put together in ways that click with the satisfaction of puzzle pieces that fit—while leaving out the vast majority of the pieces so that the picture created is distorted and incomplete.

When surveillance tape caught an election worker passing something under the table to another worker (the woman's daughter) on election night in 2020, a narrative was constructed and repeated by the then-president that the item passed was a USB port that was being used to tamper with the ballots. The story spread like wildfire, bringing threats, harassment, and life-changing chaos to the innocent family before the truth came out—what the mother had passed to her daughter under the table while they volunteered to serve their community was a ginger mint.[51] The fact that something was passed was indisputable. But what exactly was passed between the two women led to a very loose interpretation that ruined people's lives.

> **Conspiracy theories are misguided attempts to re-enchant the world through fantasy.**

So, what does all this have to do with the rapture?

The question of the rapture centers on whether the rapture mentioned in the Bible is to be understood literally (see fig. 16), or metaphorically, or even in both ways.

Ironically, some literalist interpretations of the Bible, although presented as conservative, were actually novel teachings, thus more modern than traditional.[52] In fact, they can even be understood as a rejection of history and tradition,[53] an attempt to be like God by positioning believers or the church outside of human history.

Wrong interpretation is dangerous, and we must strive to avoid it. But lack of awareness that one is interpreting and that one interprets in community, within a tradition, is more dangerous. It is a danger to which evangelicals—with all their innovations and individualism—are particularly prone.

For example, throughout the Bible we are told that we will be held to account some day for all we say and do (Rom. 14:10–12; Rev. 20:11–15). Because I grew up reading Chick tracts, I assumed such an accounting would take the form of my entire life being played back as a movie on a large screen in a heavenly theater before God. Such scenes recur throughout the series of tracts, but one notable interpretation portrayed in one depicts the main character standing in heaven next to an angel of the Lord, watching a scene from her infancy playing on the giant screen. The verse accompanying the illustration is Mark 4:22: "For there is nothing hid, which shall not be manifested" (KJV).[54] The faithful from among the great cloud of witnesses who lived on earth before the twentieth century certainly didn't imagine this verse being fulfilled in heaven via a big screen since such a thing hadn't been invented.

To be manifested means to be shown or revealed. While the hidden things that will be made known certainly include things about ourselves and our lives for which God will hold us to account (including our sin), the meaning of this verse in context is much wider and more profound. Earlier in this chapter of Mark, Jesus speaks to the disciples about the secrets or mysteries of the kingdom of God being given to them but that those mysteries will not be understood by all. Quoting from Isaiah, Jesus speaks of those who do not understand: "They may be ever seeing but never perceiving, and ever hearing but never understanding; otherwise they might turn and be forgiven!" (Mark 4:12). Then, using the metaphor of a lamp, Jesus suggests that the kingdom of God, which includes those who follow him, by its very nature reveals all things. Creation reveals the Creator. We shall be known by our fruit. Out of the heart, the mouth speaks. The world will know us by our love for one another. We who are called by him are becoming conformed to his image.

Caught Up in Christ

Belief in the rapture derives from, among other things, a literal (albeit selectively literal) reading of key Scriptures. N. T. Wright explains that it is based on a literal reading of 1 Thessalonians 4:16–17: "For the Lord himself will come down from heaven, with a loud command, with the voice of the archangel and with the trumpet call of God, and the dead in Christ will rise first. After that, we who are still alive and are left will be caught up together with them in the clouds to meet the Lord in the air. And so we will be with the Lord forever." Wright explains that the "rich metaphors" Paul uses in this passage allude to Moses's descent from the mountain with the Torah and a passage in Daniel 7 that describes God's people being lifted up to sit with him in glory. What Paul is saying here, according to Wright, is not that believers will be taken up into the sky but that those still living when Christ returns "will be 'changed' or 'transformed' so that their mortal bodies will become incorruptible, deathless."[55]

Our House Is a Very, Very, Very Fine House[56]

Jesus tells us, "In my Father's house are many rooms" (John 14:2 ESV). Jesus is preparing this house for us. This eternal home and its many rooms will be perfect. He is preparing it now. He is also preparing *us* now. We do not honor this work of Jesus when we are content to live in earthly edifices built on unexamined assumptions.

In these pages, I've examined just a few of the often-unseen foundational elements—the driving stories, images, and metaphors—of the evangelical house. There are, of course, many more. The work of looking, testing, and repairing these foundations must be ongoing until Jesus establishes our new home in the new heaven and the new earth—whenever that might be.

Truth be told, I've never really cared about end-times prophecies. That stuff makes my eyes glaze over the same way action scenes in movies do. (I usually take advantage of those parts to get a refill on snacks.) Just tell me who wins the fight or the chase, and let's get back to the story—and the storytelling. There's a reason Aristotle counted "spectacle" as the least important element of drama in his *Poetics*. And there's a reason that the prophet Nahum declares that God will make a "spectacle" of those who continue in their wicked ways (Nahum 3:6).

The best stories aren't about the ending. The best stories are about how we get there.

That's why Jesus says he is "the Way."

Indeed, the earliest Christians were called followers of the Way. This is what they are called throughout the book of Acts. This name indicates that believers in Christ are defined by "a manner of ongoing Christian living as part of a restoration journey."[57]

Those who are in Christ are defined by our manner—or way—of going. (Just as those who are not in Christ are likewise revealed by their way of going.) The mystery, as short story writer Flannery O'Connor says, is revealed in the manners.[58] Whatever form the rapture takes, it will simply—and surely—manifest the truth about those who are in Christ.

> Those who are in Christ are defined by our manner—or way—of going.

The Greek word translated into English as "rapture" means "caught up" or "carried away"—whether bodily or spiritually or both.[59] The phrase "caught up" is interesting. We use it in a lot of ways. Sometimes the context for its use is negative. We might say someone is "caught up" in the drug trade or in an illicit affair. People get "caught up" in controversies. (Those of us on social media can easily identify certain ones who are constantly "caught up" in some controversy.) Using it in a different sense, we might say we "caught up" with an old friend.

> To be caught up with Christ, in Christ, is to be filled with a love not only powerful enough to move the sun and stars but powerful enough to love that person we would otherwise despise.

The rapture is assuredly this: we who are in Christ will be caught up with him, caught up *in* him. To be caught up with Christ, in Christ, is to be filled with a love not only powerful enough to move the sun and stars (see fig. 17) but powerful enough to love that person we would otherwise despise. It is to love the kingdom of God more than the kingdoms of this world. It is to count all human empires as dirt, all our petty platforms and performances as dung.

To be caught up in Christ is to be enraptured by him, to be beholden to him, to be taken by him, to be—as seventeenth-century poet John Donne puts it—ravished by him.[60]

Not just in the sky and on some future day.

But here.

And now.

Just imagine it.

ACKNOWLEDGMENTS

I'm grateful to Southeastern Baptist Theological Seminary for providing me time and resources with which to research and write this book. Thank you to president Danny Akin, provost Keith Whitfield, to the SEBTS library, and to my research assistants Meridith Berson, Meagan Dickerson, and Becky Barnes for their diligent and cheerful help.

Without the resources and suggestions offered throughout this process by Brian Auten, Sarah Pulliam Bailey, Nathan Cartagena, Josh Chatraw, Joey Cochran, Kristin Kobes Du Mez, Eileen Lass, Henry Reichman, Joshua Swamidass, and Bethany Williamson, this would be a lesser work. Thank you all for your insights and expertise. I'm grateful for your generous insights and collegiality.

I am especially thankful to Nick Olson, not only for all the helpful feedback along the way but for sending countless book and article recommendations that are woven throughout this book, and my life too. My library and my mind have grown immeasurably through our friendship.

Thank you to the brilliant team at Brazos, especially Bob Hosack, Jeremy Wells, Eric Salo, Paula Gibson, and Janelle Mahlmann. Not only are you the best at what you do, but you are a joy to work with. Writers dream of partnering with such committed and talented publishing professionals. I will never take for granted getting to do so.

I owe a special gratitude to so many of my students who over the years have taught me more than I could ever imagine about growing up evangelical—the good, the bad, and the heartbreaking. In many ways, this book is because of you and for you.

Finally, to my steadfast husband, family, and friends: I can't imagine life without your unwavering love and support.

NOTES

Introduction

1. Timothy Larsen, interview by Albert Mohler, "A Closer Look at Victorian Christianity: A Conversation with Historian Timothy Larsen," *Thinking in Public*, November 11, 2011, https://albertmohler.com/2011/11/21/a-closer-look-at-victorian-christianity-a-conversation-with-historian-timothy-larsen.

2. Augustine, *Confessions* 1.6, trans. Sarah Ruden (New York: Modern Library, 2018), 7.

3. As Psalm 11:5 tells us, God shows his love for the righteous by examining them.

4. Dante Alighieri, *Divine Comedy, Paradiso*, canto 33, trans. Henry Wadsworth Longfellow, available at https://standardebooks.org/ebooks/dante-alighieri/the-divine-comedy/henry-wadsworth-longfellow/text/paradiso.

Chapter 1 Made in His Image

1. Owen Barfield, *Saving the Appearances: A Study in Idolatry*, 2nd ed. (Middletown, CT: Wesleyan University Press, 1988), 23.

2. Barfield, *Saving the Appearances*, 20.

3. Samuel Taylor Coleridge, *Biographia Literaria*, in *The Major Works* (Oxford: Oxford University Press, 2009), 313.

4. The year 1776 is when the appearance of the word "imagination" peaked in published works, according to the Google Ngram Viewer, and it is also, of course, the year in which so many of the ideas that characterized the Age of Reason resulted in the start of the American experiment, the fruit of reason and imagination. Google Books Ngram Viewer, "Imagination," accessed October 4, 2022, https://books.google.com/ngrams

/graph?content=imagination&year_start=1600&year_end=2018&corpus
=15&smoothing=3#.

5. David Morgan, *The Embodied Eye: Religious Visual Culture and the Social Life of Feeling* (Berkeley: University of California Press, 2012), 147.

6. James K. A. Smith, *Imagining the Kingdom: How Worship Works*, Cultural Liturgies 2 (Grand Rapids: Baker Academic, 2013), 19.

7. Smith, *Imagining the Kingdom*, 31–32.

8. Smith, *Imagining the Kingdom*, 34.

9. This is why it's important that the verses and passages we emphasize in the Bible reflect the weight that the Bible itself puts on these ideas within the scope of the entirety of Scripture.

10. Coleridge, *Biographia Literaria*, 313.

11. C. S. Lewis, *The Weight of Glory and Other Addresses* (New York: Harper-Collins, 2001), 26.

12. Janine Langan, "The Christian Imagination," in *The Christian Imagination: The Practice of Faith in Literature and Writing*, ed. Leland Ryken (Colorado Springs: Shaw Books, 2002), 64.

13. Kieran Egan, *Imagination in Teaching and Learning: The Middle School Years* (Chicago: University of Chicago Press, 1992), 924.

14. Douglas Hedley, *The Iconic Imagination* (New York: Bloomsbury, 2016), 10.

15. Hedley, *Iconic Imagination*, xii.

16. Percy Bysshe Shelley, *A Defence of Poetry*, ed. Mary Wollstonecraft Shelley (Indianapolis: Bobbs-Merrill, 1904), 90.

17. Charles Taylor, *Modern Social Imaginaries* (Durham, NC: Duke University Press, 2004), 23.

18. Taylor, *Modern Social Imaginaries*, 24.

19. Taylor, *Modern Social Imaginaries*, 25.

20. Taylor, *Modern Social Imaginaries*, 31.

21. Virginia Woolf, "A Sketch of the Past," in *Moments of Being* (New York: Houghton Mifflin Harcourt, 1985), 80.

22. David Foster Wallace, quoted in Jenna Krajeski, "This Is Water," *New Yorker*, September 19, 2008, https://www.newyorker.com/books/page-turner/this-is-water.

23. George Lakoff and Mark Johnson, *Metaphors We Live By* (Chicago: University of Chicago Press, 1980), 3.

24. Lakoff and Johnson, *Metaphors We Live By*, 3.

25. Lakoff and Johnson, *Metaphors We Live By*, 4.

26. Lakoff and Johnson, *Metaphors We Live By*, 5.

27. Mark Johnson, *Moral Imagination: Implications of Cognitive Science for Ethics* (Chicago: University of Chicago Press, 1993), 3.

28. Lakoff and Johnson, *Metaphors We Live By*, 15.

29. A version of this paragraph appears in *Technē: Christian Visions of Technology*, ed. Gerald Hiestand and Todd A. Wilson, The Center for Pastor Theologians Series (Eugene, OR: Cascade, 2022), 199, which itself draws on material from an earlier lecture of mine.

30. Mary Midgley, *The Myths We Live By* (Oxford: Routledge, 2011), 1–3.

31. Amy Julia Becker (@amyjuliabecker), "Please don't call anyone low-functioning," Twitter, November 14, 2022, 10:50 a.m., https://twitter.com/amyjuliabecker/status/1592183077526175747.

32. Abraham Joshua Heschel, *The Insecurity of Freedom: Essays on Human Existence* (New York: Farrar, Straus & Giroux, 1966), 12.

33. Kaidi Wu and David Dunning, "Unknown Unknowns: The Problem of Hypocognition," *Scientific American*, August 9, 2018, https://blogs.scientific american.com/observations/unknown-unknowns-the-problem-of-hypocognition.

34. Todd M. Brenneman, *Homespun Gospel: The Triumph of Sentimentality in Contemporary American Evangelicalism* (Oxford: Oxford University Press, 2014), 4.

35. Cornel West, *Prophesy Deliverance!* (Louisville: Westminster John Knox, 2002), 50.

36. West, *Prophesy Deliverance!*, 47.

37. Sébastien Fath, cited in "660 Million Evangelicals in the World?," *Evangelical Focus Europe*, February 18, 2020, https://evangelicalfocus.com/print/5119/660-million-evangelicals-in-the-world.

38. The word "evangelical" and its Greek counterpart are much older, of course. I speak here of the uninterrupted movement referred to by those during its time (or not long after) as "evangelical."

39. National Association of Evangelicals, "What Is an Evangelical?," NAE, accessed July 28, 2022, https://www.nae.net/what-is-an-evangelical.

40. National Association of Evangelicals, "What Is an Evangelical?"

41. Timothy Larsen, "Defining and Locating Evangelicalism," in *The Cambridge Companion to Evangelical Theology*, ed. Timothy Larsen and Daniel Treier (New York: Cambridge University Press, 2007), 1.

42. John G. Stackhouse Jr., *Evangelicalism: A Very Short Introduction* (Oxford: Oxford University Press, 2022), 24.

43. Kristin Kobes Du Mez, "There Are No Real Evangelicals, Only Imagined Ones," *Religion News Service*, February 6, 2019, https://religionnews.com/2019/02/06/there-are-no-real-evangelicals-only-imagined-ones.

44. Willie James Jennings, *The Christian Imagination: Theology and the Origins of Race* (New Haven: Yale University Press, 2010), 6.

45. Google Books Ngram Viewer, "evangelical," accessed January 5, 2023, https://books.google.com/ngrams/graph?content=evangelical&

year_start=1600&year_end=2019&case_insensitive=on&corpus=15&smo thing=3.

46. Frances FitzGerald, *The Evangelicals: The Struggle to Shape America* (New York: Simon & Schuster, 2017), 5.

47. Molly Worthen, *Apostles of Reason: The Crisis of Authority in American Evangelicalism* (New York: Oxford University Press, 2014), 7.

48. Worthen, *Apostles of Reason*, 2.

49. Worthen, *Apostles of Reason*, 11.

50. Worthen, *Apostles of Reason*, 264–65.

51. Jennings, *Christian Imagination*, 6.

52. Smith, *Imagining the Kingdom*, 124–25.

Chapter 2 Awakening

1. Coolness is totally subjective, of course.

2. Augustine, *Confessions* 10.27.38, trans. Sarah Ruden (New York: Modern Library, 2018), 312–13.

3. Alexander Moseley, "Philosophy of Love," Internet Encyclopedia of Philosophy, accessed July 5, 2022, https://iep.utm.edu/love/#SH1a.

4. Zora Neale Hurston, *Their Eyes Were Watching God* (1937; repr., New York: HarperPerennial Modern Classics, 2006), 10.

5. Hurston, *Their Eyes Were Watching God*, 10.

6. Hurston, *Their Eyes Were Watching God*, 10.

7. Hurston, *Their Eyes Were Watching God*, 11.

8. Another famous example of the awakening metaphor's place in modern literature is Kate Chopin's 1899 novel, *The Awakening*. While the story centers on sexual awakening, it is laden with the imagery of birth and death so tightly intertwined that one of these ideas can hardly be untangled from the other.

9. William Shakespeare, Sonnet 55, in *The Oxford Shakespeare: The Complete Sonnets and Poems* (Oxford: Oxford University Press, 2008), 527.

10. William Shakespeare, *Hamlet*, act 3, scene 1, in *A New Variorum Edition of Shakespeare*, ed. Horace Furness (Philadelphia: J. B. Lippincott, 1877), 3:209–11.

11. John Donne, "Death, Be Not Proud," sonnet 10, available at https:// poets.org/poem/death-be-not-proud-holy-sonnet-10.

12. Augustine, *Confessions* 1.1.1, trans. Sarah Ruden (New York: Modern Library, 2018), 3.

13. John Bunyan, *The Pilgrim's Progress: From This World to That Which Is to Come; Delivered under the Similitude of a Dream* (Peabody, MA: Hendrickson, 2004), 11.

14. J. O. Peck, *The Probationer's Companion: With Studies in "The Pilgrim's Progress"* (New York: Hunt and Eaton, 1893), 52.

15. Northrop Frye, *Words with Power: The Bible and Literature* (San Diego: Harcourt, Brace, Jovanovich, 1990), 261.

16. David Bebbington, *Victorian Religious Revivals: Culture and Piety in Local and Global Contexts* (Oxford: Oxford University Press, 2012), 1.

17. Google Books Ngram Viewer, "Awakening," accessed October 4, 2022, https://books.google.com/ngrams/graph?content=awakening&year _start=1800&year_end=2018&corpus=15&smoothing=3.

18. Samuel Torrey, *An Exhortation unto Reformation* (Cambridge, MA, 1674), 5, available at https://quod.lib.umich.edu/e/eebo2/A62960.0001 .001. I am indebted to Thomas S. Kidd for pointing me to this source.

19. Thomas S. Kidd, *George Whitefield: America's Spiritual Founding Father* (New Haven: Yale University Press, 2014), 48.

20. Karen Burns, "The Awakening Conscience: Christian Sentiment, Salvation, and Spectatorship in Mid-Victorian Britain," *19: Interdisciplinary Studies in the Long Nineteenth Century* 23 (2016), https://doi.org/10.16995/ntn.769.

21. Terry Riggs, "William Holman Hunt: The Awakening Conscience," Tate Museum, accessed July 6, 2022, https://www.tate.org.uk/art/artworks /hunt-the-awakening-conscience-t02075.

22. Julia Thomas, *Victorian Narrative Painting* (London: Tate, 2000), 30–31.

23. Paul Strohm, *Conscience: A Very Short Introduction* (Oxford: Oxford University Press, 2011), 6–8.

24. Frances FitzGerald, *The Evangelicals: The Struggle to Shape America* (New York: Simon & Schuster, 2017), 14.

25. Aja Romano, "A History of Wokeness," Vox.com, October 9, 2020, https://www.vox.com/culture/21437879/stay-woke-wokeness-history -origin-evolution-controversy.

26. W. E. B. Du Bois, *The Souls of Black Folk* (Kingston, RI: Millennium, 2014), 5.

27. Romano, "History of Wokeness."

28. Dante Stewart, *Shoutin' in the Fire: An American Epistle* (New York: Convergent, 2021), 115.

29. Stewart, *Shoutin' in the Fire*, 114.

30. C. S. Lewis, *The Weight of Glory: And Other Addresses*, rev. ed., C. S. Lewis Signature Classics (New York: HarperCollins, 2001), 139–40.

31. Langston Hughes, "Harlem," in *Hughes: Poems*, ed. David Roessel, Everyman's Library Pocket Poets Series (New York: Knopf, 1999), 238.

Chapter 3 Conversion

1. Bob Smietana, "Lifeway Research: Many Who Call Themselves Evangelicals Don't Actually Hold Evangelical Beliefs," *Lifeway Newsroom*, December 6,

2017, https://news.lifeway.com/2017/12/06/lifeway-research-many-who
-call-themselves-evangelical-dont-actually-hold-evangelical-beliefs.

2. A. D. Nock, *Conversion: The Old and the New in Religion from Alexander the Great to Augustine of Hippo* (Baltimore: Johns Hopkins University Press, 1993), 7.

3. Douglas Harper, "Conversion," Online Etymology Dictionary, updated April 7, 2018, https://www.etymonline.com/word/conversion.

4. Matt. 23:15; Acts 2:11; 6:5; 13:43.

5. Susan Friend Harding, *The Book of Jerry Falwell: Fundamentalist Language and Politics* (Princeton: Princeton University Press, 2000), 19.

6. Google Books Ngram Viewer, "born again," accessed November 30, 2022, https://books.google.com/ngrams/graph?content=%22born+again%22&year_start=1600&year_end=2018&corpus=26&smoothing=3.

7. Jeremy Weber, "Evangelicals vs. Born Again: A Survey of What Americans Say and Believe beyond Politics," *Christianity Today*, December 6, 2017, https://www.christianitytoday.com/news/2017/december/you-must-be
-born-again-evangelical-beliefs-politics-survey.html.

8. Harding, *Book of Jerry Falwell*, 34.

9. Valerie Hobbs, *An Introduction to Religious Language: Exploring Theolinguistics in Contemporary Contexts* (London: Bloomsbury Academic, 2021), 51–52, 168–70.

10. Karen Swallow Prior, "Doing Authentic Ministry with My Smokin' Hot Bride," *Christianity Today*, July 19, 2011, https://www.christianitytoday
.com/ct/2011/julyweb-only/doing-authentic-ministry-with-my-smokin
-hot-bride.html.

11. Jonathan Swift, *Letter to a Young Clergyman*, January 9, 1719, in *The Prose Works of Jonathan Swift*, vol. 3, *Writings on Religion and the Church*, vol. 1, ed. Temple Scott (1898), http://www.online-literature.com/swift
/religion-church-vol-one/7.

12. Charles Marsh describes his experience of psychoanalysis as an "incarnational ordering of language" in *Evangelical Anxiety: A Memoir* (New York: HarperOne, 2022), 132.

13. Douglas Harper, "Logos," Online Etymology Dictionary, updated August 3, 2022, https://www.etymonline.com/word/logos.

14. Marsh, *Evangelical Anxiety*, 132.

15. Mark Noll, *The Work We Have to Do: A History of Protestants in America* (Oxford: Oxford University Press, 2000), 22.

16. Edmund S. Morgan, *Visible Saints: The History of a Puritan Idea* (New York: New York University Press, 1963), 33.

17. Thomas Goodwin and Philip Nye, *The Application of Redemption by the Effectual Work of the Word, and Spirit of Christ, for the Bringing Home of*

Lost Sinners to God, quoted in Bruce Hindmarsh, *The Evangelical Conversion Narrative: Spiritual Autobiography in Early Modern England* (Oxford: Oxford University Press, 2005), 33.

18. David W. Bebbington, *Evangelicalism in Modern Britain: A History from the 1730s to the 1980s* (London: Taylor & Francis, 2003), 17–18.

19. Hindmarsh, *Evangelical Conversion Narrative*, 38–39.

20. Bebbington, *Evangelicalism in Modern Britain*, 6.

21. John D. Clayton, *The Curious Conversion of Thomas Chalmers* (New York: Peter Lang, 2021).

22. Ian Bradley, *The Call to Seriousness: The Evangelical Impact on the Victorians* (London: Cox & Wyman, 1976), 59.

23. Jonathan Edwards, "Personal Narrative," quoted in Mark A. Noll, *The Rise of Evangelicalism: The Age of Edwards, Whitefield, and the Wesleys* (Downers Grove, IL: InterVarsity, 2003), 75.

24. The Wesleys were Arminian while Whitefield was Calvinist. The Wesleys opposed slavery, and Whitefield owned slaves in America.

25. John Wesley, *The Journal of John Wesley*, ed. Percy Livingstone Parker (Chicago: Moody Press, 1951), chap. 2, under "I felt my heart strangely warmed," available at https://www.ccel.org/ccel/wesley/journal.vi.ii.xvi .html.

26. Thomas S. Kidd, *George Whitefield: America's Spiritual Founding Father* (New Haven: Yale University Press, 2014), 47.

27. Bebbington, *Evangelicalism in Modern Britain*, 8.

28. Bebbington, *Evangelicalism in Modern Britain*, 8.

29. Frances FitzGerald, *The Evangelicals: The Struggle to Shape America* (New York: Simon & Schuster, 2017), 14, 25.

30. FitzGerald, *Evangelicals*, 39.

31. Elisabeth Jay, *The Religion of the Heart: Anglican Evangelicalism and the Nineteenth-Century Novel* (Oxford: Oxford University Press, 1979).

32. Bradley, *Call to Seriousness*, 22.

33. FitzGerald, *Evangelicals*, 13.

34. Emily Heady, *Victorian Conversion Narratives and Reading Communities* (London: Taylor & Francis, 2016), 11.

35. Bradley, *Call to Seriousness*, 51.

36. Nock, *Conversion*, 14.

37. Nock, *Conversion*, 8.

38. Bradley, *Call to Seriousness*, 30–34.

39. Alan D. McKillop, "Wedding Bells for Pamela," *Philological Quarterly* 28 (January 1, 1949): 323.

40. Sheridan W. Baker Jr., introduction to *Samuel Richardson's Introduction to "Pamela,"* ed. Sheridan W. Baker Jr. (Los Angeles: William Andrews Clark

Memorial Library, University of California, 1954), 3n6, available at https://www.gutenberg.org/files/24860/24860-h/24860-h.htm.

41. Pamela Regis, "The First Best Seller: On Samuel Richardson's *Pamela* and the Prehistory of the Romance Novel," *Lapham's Quarterly*, July 24, 2020, https://www.laphamsquarterly.org/roundtable/first-best-seller.

42. Matthew Wills, "Why the First Novel Created Such a Stir," JSTOR Daily, January 11, 2018, https://daily.jstor.org/why-the-first-novel-created-such-a-stir; Regis, "First Best Seller."

43. William James, *The Varieties of Religious Experience* (New York: Penguin, 1982), 189.

44. Thomas Hardy, *Tess of the D'Urbervilles*, ed. Margaret Randolph Higonnet and Tim Dolin (New York: Penguin, 2003), 305.

45. Hardy, *Tess of the D'Urbervilles*, 305.

46. Hardy, *Tess of the D'Urbervilles*, 302.

47. In his edited anthology *Christian Literature* (Malden, MA: Blackwell, 2001), Alister McGrath includes some of the work of Thomas Hardy not because Hardy was a professing Christian but because his work is so drawn from (and critical of) the Christian ethos of his age.

48. Edmund Gosse, *Father and Son* (Oxford: Oxford University Press, 2009), 19.

49. Gosse, *Father and Son*, 102.

50. Gosse, *Father and Son*, 106.

51. Henri J. M. Nouwen, *The Wounded Healer* (New York: Image Doubleday, 2010), 23.

52. FitzGerald, *Evangelicals*, 625.

Chapter 4 Testimony

1. Northrop Frye, *The Educated Imagination* (Bloomington: Indiana University Press, 1964), 64.

2. C. S. Lewis, "Letter 172—The Kilns, Oct. 18th, 1931," in *They Stand Together: The Letters of C. S. Lewis to Arthur Greeves (1914–1963)*, ed. Walter Hooper (London: William Collins, 1979), 427.

3. Charles Dickens, *Hard Times*, ed. Kate Flint (1854; repr., London: Penguin, 2003), 9.

4. Dickens, *Hard Times*, 12.

5. Richard Baxter, *Reliquiae Baxterianae, or, Mr. Richard Baxters narrative of the most memorable passages of his life and times faithfully publish'd from his own original manuscript by Matthew Sylvester* (London: Printed for T. Parkhurst, J. Robinson, F. Lawrence and F. Dunton, 1696), under p. 3, sec. 3, https://quod.lib.umich.edu/e/eebo/A27006.0001.001/1:8?rgn=div1;view=fulltext.

6. Baxter, *Reliquiae Baxterianae*, p. 3, sec. 3.

7. Jonathan Edwards, *The Collected Works of Jonathan Edwards*, vol. 1, ed. Edward Hickman (Carlisle, PA: Banner of Truth Trust, 1995), 355, https:// ccel.org/ccel/edwards/works1/works1.viii.iii.html.

8. David W. Bebbington, *Evangelicalism in Modern Britain: A History from the 1730s to the 1980s* (London: Taylor & Francis, 2003), 7.

9. Bebbington, *Evangelicalism in Modern Britain*, 8.

10. Valerie Hobbs, *An Introduction to Religious Language: Exploring Theolinguistics in Contemporary Contexts* (London: Bloomsbury Academic, 2021), 45.

11. Hobbs, *Introduction to Religious Language*, 169.

12. Emily Heady, *Victorian Conversion Narratives and Reading Communities* (New York: Routledge, 2016), 8.

13. Miranda Klaver, Johan Roeland, Peter Versteeg, Hijme Stoffels, and Remco van Mulligen, "God Changes People: Modes of Authentication in Evangelical Conversion Narratives," *Journal of Contemporary Religion* 32, no. 2 (2017): 237–51, under "introduction," https://doi.org/10.1080/13537903 .2017.1298905.

14. John Bunyan, *The Pilgrim's Progress*, in *A Library of Famous Fiction Embracing the Nine Standard Masterpieces of Imaginative Literature (Unabridged)*, introduction by Harriet Beecher Stowe (New York: Ford, 1873), 16.

15. Bunyan, *Pilgrim's Progress*, 16.

16. John Bunyan, *Grace Abounding: With Other Spiritual Autobiographies*, Oxford World Classics (Oxford: Oxford University Press, 1998), 37–38.

17. Bunyan, *Grace Abounding*, 38.

18. Bunyan, *Grace Abounding*, 65–66.

19. Anne Hawkins, "The Double-Conversion in Bunyan's *Grace Abounding*," *Philological Quarterly* 61, no. 3 (Summer 1982): 259.

20. Edmund Sears Morgan, *Visible Saints: The History of a Puritan Idea* (New York: New York University Press, 1963), quoted in Bruce Hindmarsh, *The Evangelical Conversion Narrative: Spiritual Autobiography in Early Modern England* (Oxford: Oxford University Press, 2005), 37.

21. Hindmarsh, *Evangelical Conversion Narrative*, 50–59.

22. Bunyan, *Grace Abounding*, 53.

23. Bunyan, *Grace Abounding*, 7.

24. Bunyan, *Grace Abounding*, 18–19.

25. David Parry, "Playing the Fool: The Subversive Literary Apologetics of John Bunyan and Blaise Pascal," *Etudes Epistémè* 35 (2019): 57, https:// journals.openedition.org/episteme/4474?lang=en.

26. Parry, "Playing the Fool," 61.

27. Charles Dickens, *A Christmas Carol: A Ghost Story of Christmas* (1843; repr., Waiheke Island, New Zealand: Floating Press, 2009), 141.

28. See, e.g., Herbert Schlossberg, *The Silent Revolution and the Making of Victorian England* (Columbus: Ohio State University Press, 2000).

29. Hindmarsh, *Evangelical Conversion Narrative*, 38.

30. Hindmarsh, *Evangelical Conversion Narrative*, 49.

31. Neil Postman, *Amusing Ourselves to Death: Public Discourse in the Age of Show Business*, 20th anniv. ed. (New York: Penguin, 2006).

32. Hindmarsh, *Evangelical Conversion Narrative*, 15.

33. Heady, *Victorian Conversion Narratives*, 17.

34. Louisa May Alcott, *Little Women* (New York: Signet Classics, 1983), 15.

35. Alcott, *Little Women*, 15–16.

36. Alcott, *Little Women*, 16.

37. Alcott, *Little Women*, 16.

38. Bunyan, *Pilgrim's Progress*, 16.

39. Christianity Today Editorial, "Bearing True Witness," *Christianity Today*, June 28, 2010, https://www.christianitytoday.com/ct/2010/july/4.45.html.

40. Hindmarsh, *Evangelical Conversion Narrative*, 289.

41. *Pray Away*, directed by Kristine Stolakis (Artemis Rising Foundation, 2021), distributed by Netflix. See also Michelle Boorstein, "She Believed in Conversion Therapy. Now She Regrets It. Julie Rodgers Explains Why in 'Pray Away,'" *Washington Post*, August 6, 2021, https://www.washington post.com/religion/2021/08/06/pray-away-exgay-ex-gay-lgbtq-christian -evangelical-conversion.

42. Robert Kellemen and Karole A. Edwards, *Beyond the Suffering: Embracing the Legacy of African American Soul Care and Spiritual Direction* (Grand Rapids: Baker Books, 2007), 106.

43. Charles Taylor, *Sources of the Self* (Cambridge: Cambridge University Press, 1992), 47.

44. Taylor, *Sources of the Self*, 48.

45. Klaver et al., "God Changes People."

46. Klaver et al., "God Changes People."

Chapter 5 Improvement

1. "Home Improvement Market Size in the United States from 2008 to 2025," Statista, January 2022, https://www.statista.com/statistics/239753 /total-sales-of-home-improvement-retailers-in-the-us.

2. Porter Anderson, "NPD: 'A Decade of Personal Exploration' Ahead in US Self-Help Books," *Publishing Perspectives*, January 17, 2020, https:// publishingperspectives.com/2020/01/npd-sees-decade-of-personal-explor ation-opening-usa-self-help-books.

3. Paul Slack, *The Invention of Improvement: Information and Material Progress in Seventeenth-Century England* (Oxford: Oxford University Press, 2015), 1.

4. Slack, *Invention of Improvement*, 3–6.

5. Slack, *Invention of Improvement*, vii.

6. Slack, *Invention of Improvement*, 7–8.

7. Slack, *Invention of Improvement*, 1.

8. Slack, *Invention of Improvement*, 1–6.

9. Slack, *Invention of Improvement*, 15.

10. William Shakespeare, Sonnet 55, in *The Oxford Shakespeare: The Complete Sonnets and Poems* (Oxford: Oxford University Press, 2008), 491.

11. Slack, *Invention of Improvement*, 2.

12. Neil Postman, *Building a Bridge to the Eighteenth Century* (New York: Knopf, 2000), 26.

13. Postman, *Building a Bridge to the Eighteenth Century*, 28.

14. Samuel Johnson et al., *Johnson's English Dictionary—As Improved by Todd and Abridged by Chalmers* . . . (Boston: Charles Ewer and T. Harrington Carter, 1828), 342.

15. Stefan Kanfer, "Horatio Alger: The Moral of the Story," *City Journal* (Autumn 2000), https://www.city-journal.org/html/horatio-alger-moral -story-11933.html.

16. Martin Luther King Jr., interview by Sander Vanocur, NBC News, May 8, 1967, video, 26:43 (at 16:42 mark), https://www.nbcnews.com/video /martin-luther-king-jr-speaks-with-nbc-news-11-months-before-assassina tion-1202163779741.

17. Michael Moon, "'The Gentle Boy from the Dangerous Classes': Pederasty, Domesticity, and Capitalism in Horatio Alger," *Representations* 19 (Summer 1987): 88.

18. Martin Luther King Jr., *Where Do We Go from Here: Chaos or Community?* (Boston: Beacon, 1968), 181–82.

19. Slack, *Invention of Improvement*, 1.

20. Daniel Nayeri, *Everything Sad Is Untrue (A True Story)* (Montclair, NJ: Levine Querido, 2020), 6.

21. US Environmental Protection Agency, "National Overview: Facts and Figures on Materials, Wastes, and Recycling," EPA, last updated July 31, 2022, https://www.epa.gov/facts-and-figures-about-materials-waste-and -recycling/national-overview-facts-and-figures-materials.

22. Su Kyong Park, "Developing Countries Don't Want Your Clothes," *The Stern Opportunity*, November 22, 2018, https://sternoppy.com/2018 /11/developing-countries-dont-want-your-clothes.

23. Australian Broadcasting Corporation (ABC), "The Environmental Disaster That Is Fueled by Used Clothes and Fast Fashion," *Foreign Correspondent*, August 12, 2021, YouTube, 30:02, https://youtu.be/bB3kuu BPVys.

24. Charles Taylor, *A Secular Age* (Cambridge, MA: Harvard University Press, 2007), 111.

25. Taylor, *Secular Age*, 112.

26. Taylor, *Secular Age*, 159.

27. Taylor, *Secular Age*, 107.

28. Slack, *Invention of Improvement*, 13.

29. Max Weber, *The Protestant Ethic and the "Spirit" of Capitalism and Other Writings*, ed. and trans. Peter Baehr and Gordon C. Wells (New York: Penguin, 2002), 79.

30. Weber, *Protestant Ethic*, 72–85.

31. Weber, *Protestant Ethic*, 34.

32. John Henry Newman, "Discourse 6: God's Will the End of Life," in *Discourses Addressed to Mixed Congregations* (London: Longmans, Green, 1913), 105–23.

33. Thomas Gisborne, *An Enquiry into the Duties of the Female Sex*, 9th ed. (London: Cadell and Davies, 1813), 116.

34. Weber, *Protestant Ethic*, 80.

35. Robert Wilberforce and Samuel Wilberforce, *The Life of William Wilberforce in Five Volumes* (London: John Murray, 1838), 1:149.

36. Samuel Smiles, *Self Help; With Illustrations of Character, Conduct and Perseverance—A New Edition* (London: Albemarle Street, 1866), 2.

37. Smiles, *Self Help*, iv.

38. Smiles, *Self Help*, 1.

39. Smiles, *Self Help*, 7.

40. Walter E. Houghton, *The Victorian Frame of Mind, 1830–1870* (New Haven: Yale University Press, 1957), 184–89.

41. Benjamin Franklin, "Advice to a Young Tradesman: 21 July 1748," in George Fisher, *The American Instructor: or Young Man's Best Companion . . .*, 9th ed. (Philadelphia: B. Franklin and D. Hall, at the New-Printing-Office, in Market-Street, 1748), 375–77, available at https://founders.archives.gov/documents/Franklin/01-03-02-0130.

42. Benjamin Franklin, letter to Benjamin Franklin Bache, September 25, 1780, available at https://founders.archives.gov/documents/Franklin/01-33-02-0270.

43. Ian Bradley, *The Call to Seriousness: The Evangelical Impact on the Victorians* (London: Cox & Wyman, 1976), 153–54.

44. John Henry Newman, *The Idea of a University: Defined and Illustrated: New Edition* (London: Longmans, Green, 1891), 193.

45. Elizabeth Cleghorn Gaskell, *North and South* (New York: Penguin, 1996), 85.

46. Daniel Vaca, *Evangelicals Incorporated: Books and the Business of Religion in America* (Cambridge, MA: Harvard University Press, 2019), 233–34.

47. Bradley, *Call to Seriousness*, 155.

48. Houghton, *Victorian Frame of Mind*, 187–89.

49. John Ruskin in preface to the second edition (1865) of *Sesame and Lilies*, ed. Deborah Epstein Nord (New Haven: Yale University Press, 2002), 14.

50. Todd M. Brenneman, *Homespun Gospel: The Triumph of Sentimentality in Contemporary American Evangelicalism* (Oxford: Oxford University Press, 2014), 22–24.

51. Brenneman, *Homespun Gospel*, 24–25. Peale's influence reached its logical outcome in the election of one of his congregants to the office of US president, whose first marriage Peale presided over: Donald Trump. James Barron, "Overlooked Influences on Donald Trump: A Famous Minister and His Church," *New York Times*, September 5, 2016, https://www.nytimes.com /2016/09/06/nyregion/donald-trump-marble-collegiate-church-norman -vincent-peale.html.

52. Brenneman, *Homespun Gospel*, 25.

53. Brenneman, *Homespun Gospel*, 31.

54. Brenneman, *Homespun Gospel*, 46.

55. Flannery O'Connor, *Wise Blood*, in *Three by Flannery O'Connor* (New York: Signet, 1983), 58.

56. "Not that there's anything wrong with that," as Jerry Seinfeld would say.

Chapter 6 Sentimentality

1. Leslie Stephen, *History of English Thought in the Eighteenth Century* (London: Smith, Elder, 1876), 2:436.

2. "Behind the Artist: Thomas Kinkade," Park West Gallery, January 24, 2018, https://www.parkwestgallery.com/behind-the-artist-thomas-kinkade.

3. Randall Balmer, "The Kinkade Crusade," *Christianity Today*, December 4, 2000, https://www.christianitytoday.com/ct/2000/december4/6.48.html.

4. Joe Carter, "Thomas Kinkade's Cottage Fantasy," *First Things*, June 16, 2010, https://www.firstthings.com/web-exclusives/2010/06/thomas -kinkades-cottage-fantasy.

5. Oliver Burkeman, "Dark Clouds Gather over 'Painter of Light,'" *Guardian*, March 25, 2006, https://www.theguardian.com/world/2006/mar/25 /arts.artsnews; Mike Swift, "Details of Artist Thomas Kinkade's Tumultuous Final Years Surface," *Mercury News*, April 7, 2012, https://www.mercury news.com/2012/04/07/details-of-artist-thomas-kinkades-tumultuous-final -years-surface.

6. Balmer, "Kinkade Crusade."

7. Burkeman, "Dark Clouds Gather"; Swift, "Details of Artist Thomas Kinkade's Final Years."

8. Aaron Meskin, Mark Phelan, Margaret Moore, and Matthew Kieran, "Mere Exposure to Bad Art," *British Journal of Aesthetics* 53, no. 2 (April 2013): 139–64, here 155.

9. Antti Kauppinen, "Moral Sentimentalism," *Stanford Encyclopedia of Philosophy,* updated November 11, 2021, https://plato.stanford.edu/archives/spr2022/entries/moral-sentimentalism.

10. John Locke, *An Essay Concerning Human Understanding,* ed. Alexander Campbell Fraser (Oxford: Clarendon, 1894), 141.

11. Todd M. Brenneman, *Homespun Gospel: The Triumph of Sentimentality in Contemporary American Evangelicalism* (Oxford: Oxford University Press, 2014), 54.

12. See a brief but detailed history in Brenneman, *Homespun Gospel,* 53–65.

13. Frances FitzGerald, *The Evangelicals: The Struggle to Shape America* (New York: Simon & Schuster, 2017), 75–77. On Luther and beauty, see Mark C. Mattes, *Martin Luther's Theology of Beauty: A Reappraisal* (Grand Rapids: Baker Academic, 2017).

14. Janet Todd, *Sensibility: An Introduction* (London: Methuen, 1986), 22–23.

15. Brenneman, *Homespun Gospel,* 11.

16. Brenneman, *Homespun Gospel,* 12.

17. See Robert Bellah, Richard Madsen, William Sullivan, Ann Swidler, and Steven Tipton, *Habits of the Heart: Individualism and Commitment in American Life* (Berkeley: University of California Press, 1985); Charles Taylor, *The Ethics of Authenticity* (Cambridge, MA: Harvard University Press, 1992); Charles Taylor, *Sources of the Self: The Making of the Modern Identity* (Cambridge, MA: Harvard University Press, 1989); Carl R. Trueman, *The Rise and Triumph of the Modern Self: Cultural Amnesia, Expressive Individualism, and the Road to Sexual Revolution* (Wheaton: Crossway, 2020).

18. Brenneman, *Homespun Gospel,* 9.

19. Daniel Wickberg, "What Is the History of Sensibilities? On Cultural Histories, Old and New," *The American Historical Review* 112, no. 3 (June 2007): 661–84, https://doi.org/10.1086/ahr.112.3.661.

20. Wickberg, "What Is the History of Sensibilities?"

21. Wickberg, "What Is the History of Sensibilities?"

22. Wickberg, "What Is the History of Sensibilities?"

23. For a consideration of the relationship between beauty and justice, see Elaine Scarry, *On Beauty and Being Just* (Princeton: Princeton University Press, 1999).

24. C-SPAN, "Clinton's I Feel Your Pain Moment," 1992 Presidential Town Hall Debate, National Cable Satellite Corp, October 15, 1992, https://www.c-span.org/video/?c4842764/user-clip-clintons-feel-pain-moment.

25. A reference to the title character in the 1774 novel *The Sorrows of Young Werther* by Johann Wolfgang von Goethe, the story of a passionate young man who commits suicide as a result of unrequited love.

26. Hannah More, "Sensibility," in *The Works of Hannah More* (London: Henry G. Bohn, 1853), 5:336, 337.

27. For more background on this, see my book *Fierce Convictions: The Extraordinary Life of Hannah More—Poet, Reformer, Abolitionist* (Nashville: Thomas Nelson, 2014).

28. Walter E. Houghton, *The Victorian Frame of Mind, 1830–1870* (New Haven: Yale University Press, 1957), 278.

29. Houghton, *Victorian Frame of Mind*, 277.

30. Houghton, *Victorian Frame of Mind*, 277.

31. Susan Lanzoni, "A Short History of Empathy," *The Atlantic*, October 15, 2015, https://www.theatlantic.com/health/archive/2015/10/a-short-history-of-empathy/409912.

32. Kimberly J. Largent, "Harriet Beecher Stowe: The Little Woman Who Wrote the Book That Started This Great War," eHistory, Ohio State University, accessed October 20, 2022, https://ehistory.osu.edu/articles/harriet-beecher-stowe-little-woman-who-wrote-book-started-great-war.

33. Houghton, *Victorian Frame of Mind*, 278.

34. Lauren Berlant, *The Female Complaint: The Unfinished Business of Sentimentality in American Culture* (Durham, NC: Duke University Press, 2008), 41.

35. Houghton, *Victorian Frame of Mind*, 277.

36. Edward J. Blum and Paul Harvey, *The Color of Christ: The Son of God and the Saga of Race in America* (Chapel Hill: University of North Carolina Press, 2012), 211.

37. Erika Doss, "Making a 'Virile, Manly Christ': The Cultural Origins and Meanings of Warner Sallman's Religious Imagery," in *Icons of American Protestantism: The Art of Warner Sallman*, ed. David Morgan (New Haven: Yale University Press, 1996), 65–66.

38. David Morgan, "Warner Sallman and the Visual Culture of American Protestantism," in Morgan, *Icons of American Protestantism*, 30–31.

39. Morgan, "Warner Sallman and the Visual Culture," 31–33.

40. Doss, "Making a 'Virile, Manly Christ,'" 91.

41. Neil Harris, foreword to Morgan, *Icons of American Protestantism*, x–xii.

42. Morgan, "Warner Sallman and the Visual Culture," 60.

43. Doss, "Making a 'Virile, Manly Christ,'" 69.

44. David Morgan, introduction to Morgan, *Icons of American Protestantism*, 3.

45. David Morgan, introduction to Morgan, *Icons of American Protestantism*, 3.

46. Morgan, "Warner Sallman and the Visual Culture," 28–29.

47. James K. A. Smith, *You Are What You Love: The Spiritual Power of Habit* (Grand Rapids: Brazos, 2016), 59.

48. Sally M. Promey, "Interchangeable Art: Warner Sallman and the Critics of Mass Culture," in Morgan, *Icons of American Protestantism*, 178–80.

49. Doss, "Making a 'Virile, Manly Christ,'" 62.

50. Harris, foreword to Morgan, *Icons of American Protestantism*, viii.

51. Morgan, "Warner Sallman and the Visual Culture," 60.

52. Robert Paul Roth, "Christ and the Muses," *Christianity Today*, March 3, 1958, https://www.christianitytoday.com/ct/1958/march-3/christ-and-muses.html, quoted in Colleen McDannell, *Material Christianity: Religion and Popular Culture in America* (New Haven: Yale University Press, 1995), 189.

53. Marion Junkin, "Truth in Art," *Motive* 10, no. 1 (October 1949): 22, quoted in Promey, "Interchangeable Art," 163.

54. Betty A. Deberg, "The Ministry of Christian Art: Evangelicals and the Art of Warner Sallman, 1942–1960," in Morgan, *Icons of American Protestantism*, 99.

55. Morgan, "Warner Sallman and the Visual Culture," 28–29.

56. Morgan, "Warner Sallman and the Visual Culture," 54–55.

57. Morgan, "Warner Sallman and the Visual Culture," 35.

58. Milan Kundera, *The Unbearable Lightness of Being*, trans. Michael Henry Heim (London: Faber & Faber, 2020), 251.

59. Flannery O'Connor, "The Church and the Fiction Writer," in *Mystery and Manners: Occasional Prose*, ed. Robert Fitzgerald and Sally Fitzgerald (New York: Farrar, Straus & Giroux, 1970), 148.

60. Brenneman, *Homespun Gospel*, 13.

61. Frank Burch Brown, *Good Taste, Bad Taste, and Christian Taste: Aesthetics in Religious Life* (Oxford: Oxford University Press, 2000), 23.

62. True, we have free, easy access to God. But it is only because of the sacrifice made by Christ that we have this access. Even the clean water we have in most communities—although seemingly free and easy to access—is available only through the sacrifices made to create and sustain the infrastructure and governing authorities that make it possible.

63. Brenneman, *Homespun Gospel*, 111–12.

64. Brenneman, *Homespun Gospel*, 4.

65. Brenneman, *Homespun Gospel*, 12.

66. Todd, *Sensibility*, 23–24.

Chapter 7 Materiality

1. Evangelicalism is frequently described as a "subculture," particularly within the context of the broader American culture. However, the breadth

and depth of its history and influence do, I would argue (and am arguing here), qualify it as a culture in and of itself even as it readily participates in the larger cultures that surround it.

2. Lauren Winner, *A Cheerful and Comfortable Faith: Anglican Religious Practice in the Elite Households of Eighteenth-Century Virginia* (New Haven: Yale University Press, 2010), 26.

3. David Morgan, *The Embodied Eye: Religious Visual Culture and the Social Life of Feeling* (Berkeley: University of California Press, 2012), 179.

4. Morgan, *Embodied Eye*, 178.

5. Morgan, *Embodied Eye*, 147.

6. Do read Gregory Thornbury's *Why Should the Devil Have All the Good Music? Larry Norman and the Perils of Christian Rock* (New York: Convergent, 2018).

7. Colleen McDannell, *Material Christianity: Religion and Popular Culture in America* (New Haven: Yale University Press, 1995), 13.

8. David Morgan, "Warner Sallman and the Visual Culture of American Protestantism," in *Icons of American Protestantism: The Art of Warner Sallman*, ed. David Morgan (New Haven: Yale University Press, 1996), 54.

9. McDannell, *Material Christianity*, 26.

10. David Morgan, introduction to Morgan, *Icons of American Protestantism*, 10–18.

11. Morgan, *Embodied Eye*, 31.

12. Morgan, *Embodied Eye*, 6.

13. Morgan, *Embodied Eye*, 168–69.

14. Morgan, *Embodied Eye*, 180.

15. Morgan, *Embodied Eye*, 178.

16. Morgan, *Embodied Eye*, 173.

17. Julia Thomas, *Victorian Narrative Painting* (London: Tate, 2000), 30.

18. Thomas, *Victorian Narrative Painting*, 9.

19. Thomas, *Victorian Narrative Painting*, 19, 33.

20. Thomas, *Victorian Narrative Painting*, 35.

21. Thomas, *Victorian Narrative Painting*, 55.

22. Thomas, *Victorian Narrative Painting*, 9–10.

23. Thomas, *Victorian Narrative Painting*, 95–96.

24. Karen Burns, "The Awakening Conscience: Christian Sentiment, Salvation, and Spectatorship in Mid-Victorian Britain," *19: Interdisciplinary Studies in the Long Nineteenth Century* 23 (2016), https://doi.org/10.16995/ntn.769.

25. Morgan, "Warner Sallman and the Visual Culture," 29.

26. Neil Harris, foreword to Morgan, *Icons of American Protestantism*, xi.

27. Morgan, "Warner Sallman and the Visual Culture," 26.

28. Morgan, "Warner Sallman and the Visual Culture," 44–45.

29. Morgan, "Warner Sallman and the Visual Culture," 52–53.

30. McDannell, *Material Christianity*, 12.

31. Erika Doss, "Making a 'Virile, Manly Christ': The Cultural Origins and Meanings of Warner Sallman's Religious Imagery," in Morgan, *Icons of American Protestantism*, 64, 75–77.

32. Morgan, *Embodied Eye*, 105.

33. McDannell, *Material Christianity*, 15.

34. Colleen McDannell, "Marketing Jesus: Warner Press and the Art of Warner Sallman," in Morgan, *Icons of American Protestantism*, 100.

35. McDannell, *Material Christianity*, 228.

36. McDannell, "Marketing Jesus," 100–102.

37. Oliver Burkeman, "Dark Cloud Gathers over 'Painter of Light,'" *Guardian*, March 25, 2006, https://www.theguardian.com/world/2006/mar/25/arts.artsnews.

38. Randall Balmer, "The Kinkade Crusade," *Christianity Today*, December 4, 2000, https://www.christianitytoday.com/ct/2000/december4/6.48.html.

39. McDannell, *Material Christianity*, 1–2.

40. McDannell, *Material Christianity*, 6.

41. McDannell, *Material Christianity*, 8.

42. McDannell, *Material Christianity*, 6.

43. Mircea Eliade, *The Sacred and the Profane: The Nature of Religion*, trans. Willard Trask (New York: Harcourt, 1959), 28.

44. Eliade, *The Sacred and the Profane*, 28.

45. McDannell, *Material Christianity*, 5, 8.

46. David L. Jeffrey, *People of the Book: Christian Identity and Literary Culture* (Grand Rapids: Eerdmans, 1996), 209–64.

47. Philip Kosloski, "How 'Theotokos' Became the Perfect Title of the Virgin Mary," Aleteia, October 11, 2017, https://aleteia.org/2017/10/11/how-theotokos-became-the-perfect-title-of-the-virgin-mary.

This and the preceding three paragraphs appear in similar form in *Technē: Christian Visions of Technology*, ed. Gerald Hiestand and Todd A. Wilson, The Center for Pastor Theologians Series (Eugene, OR: Cascade, 2022), 192, which itself draws on material from an earlier lecture of mine.

48. McDannell, *Material Christianity*, 14.

49. Morgan, *Embodied Eye*, 147.

Chapter 8 Domesticity

1. Library of Nottingham, "Property Ownership," Manuscripts and Special Collections, University of Nottingham, accessed July 26, 2022, https://www

.nottingham.ac.uk/manuscriptsandspecialcollections/learning/medieval women/theme3/propertyownership.aspx.

2. Judith Flanders, *Inside the Victorian Home: A Portrait of Domestic Life in Victorian England* (New York: Norton, 2003), 20.

3. Flanders, *Inside the Victorian Home*, 4–5.

4. Colleen McDannell, *The Christian Home in Victorian America, 1840–1900* (Bloomington: Indiana University Press, 1986), 7.

5. Ian Bradley, *The Call to Seriousness: The Evangelical Impact on the Victorians* (London: Cox & Wyman, 1976), 152.

6. John Stuart Mill, *On Liberty and The Subjection of Women* (London: Penguin, 2006), 236.

7. Flanders, *Inside the Victorian Home*, 8.

8. Walter E. Houghton, *The Victorian Frame of Mind, 1830–1870* (New Haven: Yale University Press, 1957), 343.

9. Houghton, *Victorian Frame of Mind*, 342.

10. McDannell, *Christian Home in Victorian America*, 8.

11. McDannell, *Christian Home in Victorian America*, xiii.

12. McDannell, *Christian Home in Victorian America*, 50–51.

13. McDannell, *Christian Home in Victorian America*, 20–28, 45–51.

14. George Graham, *Parliamentary Papers 1852/53*, vol. 85, quoted in Flanders, *Inside the Victorian Home*, 21.

15. George Graham, cited by Flanders, *Inside the Victorian Home*, 22.

16. Hippolyte Taine, *Notes on England*, trans. W. F. A. Rae (London: Strahan, 1872), cited in Flanders, *Inside the Victorian Home*, 21.

17. Charles Dickens, *Great Expectations in Two Volumes* (Leipzig: Bernhard Tauchnitz, 1861), 1:273.

18. Dickens, *Great Expectations*, 1:275.

19. Lawrence Stone, *The Family, Sex and Marriage: In England 1500–1800* (New York: Harper & Row, 1977), 141.

20. Charles Taylor, *A Secular Age* (Cambridge, MA: Harvard University Press, 2007), 25–218.

21. Of course, as Taylor also argues, when everything is sacred (or enchanted), then nothing is, resulting in what he describes as the disenchantment of the world that characterizes the secular age.

22. Nancy Armstrong, *Desire and Domestic Fiction: A Political History of the Novel* (Oxford: Oxford University Press, 1987), 18.

23. Armstrong, *Desire and Domestic Fiction*, 18–19.

24. John Ruskin, "Of Queens' Gardens," in *Sesame and Lilies, Selected Works* (Oxford: Oxford University Press, 2004), 158–59.

25. G. K. Chesterton, *The Autobiography of G. K. Chesterton* (San Francisco: Ignatius, 2006), 36.

26. Charles Kingsley, *His Letters and Memories of His Life* (London: Macmillan, 1890), 101.

27. Flanders, *Inside the Victorian Home*, 6.

28. Todd M. Brenneman, *Homespun Gospel: The Triumph of Sentimentality in Contemporary American Evangelicalism* (Oxford: Oxford University Press, 2014), 7, 36.

29. Taylor, *Secular Age*, 3.

30. Marianne Farningham, *Home Life* (London: James Clarke, 1869), 10–11.

31. Sarah Stickney Ellis, *The Wives of England, Their Relative Duties, Domestic Influence, and Social Obligations* (New York, 1843), 10.

32. L. H. Sigourney, *Whisper to a Bride* (Hartford, 1851), 44, quoted in Barbara Welter, "The Cult of True Womanhood: 1820–1860," *American Quarterly* 18, no. 2 (Summer 1966): 158n34.

33. Quotes from *The Angel in the House*, taken from https://www.gutenberg.org/files/4099/4099-h/4099-h.htm.

34. Mill, *On Liberty and The Subjection of Women*, 216.

35. Ruskin, "Of Queens' Gardens," 158.

36. Virginia Woolf, "Professions for Women," in *Selected Essays*, ed. David Bradshaw (New York: Oxford University Press, 2009), 142.

37. Welter, "Cult of True Womanhood," 152.

38. Armstrong, *Desire and Domestic Fiction*, 3.

39. Flanders, *Inside the Victorian Home*, 13.

40. Houghton, *Victorian Frame of Mind*, 266.

41. Edward Cheshire, "The Results of the Census of Great Britain in 1851, with a Description of the Machinery and Processes Employed to Obtain the Returns; also an Appendix of Tables of Reference," *Journal of the Statistical Society of London* 17, no. 1 (March 1854): 55, https://archive.org/details/jstor-2338356.

42. Bradley, *Call to Seriousness*, 151.

43. Jerry Falwell Sr., *Listen, America!* (New York: Bantam, 1980), 104.

44. McDannell, *Christian Home in Victorian America*, xvi.

45. Colleen McDannell, "Marketing Jesus: Warner Press and the Art of Warner Sallman," in *Icons of American Protestantism: The Art of Warner Sallman*, ed. David Morgan (New Haven: Yale University Press, 1996), 97–98; Flanders, *Inside the Victorian Home*, 18–19.

46. Mark Noll describes the vain effort of James Marsh, a New England Congregationalist minister, to counter the overwhelming influence of Baconian science and "common sense" philosophy on the church with the work of Samuel T. Coleridge, whose work Marsh published in 1829. For Marsh, writes Noll, "direct intuition of the true and the beautiful, rather than the

Baconian intuition of commonsense facts, was the natural complement to divine revelation." Had Marsh succeeded, how different the evangelical imagination might be today. Noll, *America's God: From Jonathan Edwards to Abraham Lincoln* (Oxford: Oxford University Press, 2005), 247–49.

47. McDannell, *Christian Home in Victorian America*, 39.

48. McDannell, "Marketing Jesus," 99.

49. McDannell, *Christian Home in Victorian America*, 49–50.

50. Houghton, *Victorian Frame of Mind*, 348.

51. McDannell, "Marketing Jesus," 100.

52. McDannell, *Christian Home in Victorian America*, 20–51.

53. Julia Thomas, *Victorian Narrative Painting* (London: Tate, 2000), 39.

54. Thomas, *Victorian Narrative Painting*, 58.

55. Armstrong, *Desire and Domestic Fiction*, 8.

56. Armstrong, *Desire and Domestic Fiction*, 25.

57. Armstrong, *Desire and Domestic Fiction*, 4.

58. Armstrong, *Desire and Domestic Fiction*, 14.

59. Armstrong, *Desire and Domestic Fiction*, 4–5.

60. Armstrong, *Desire and Domestic Fiction*, 23.

61. Armstrong, *Desire and Domestic Fiction*, 21.

62. Armstrong, *Desire and Domestic Fiction*, 19–20.

63. Armstrong, *Desire and Domestic Fiction*, 3.

Chapter 9 Empire

1. Edward Said, *Culture and Imperialism* (New York: Vintage, 1994), 7.

2. Said, *Culture and Imperialism*, 9.

3. Said, *Culture and Imperialism*, 7.

4. Cornel West, *Prophesy Deliverance!* (Louisville: Westminster John Knox, 2002), 29.

5. "The Size of the British Empire," Royal Museums Greenwich, accessed July 26, 2022, https://www.rmg.co.uk/stories/topics/size-british-empire.

6. Martin E. Marty, *Righteous Empire: The Protestant Experience in America* (New York: Dial Press, 1970), 9.

7. Joash Thomas, personal email, July 20, 2022. See also Robert Eric Frykenberg, "Christian History Timeline: Christianity in India," *Christian History*, issue 87 (2005), available at https://christianhistoryinstitute.org/magazine/article/christianity-in-india; and Paul Zacharia, "The Surprisingly Early History of Christianity in India," *Smithsonian Magazine*, February 19, 2016, https://www.smithsonianmag.com/travel/how-christianity-came-to-india-kerala-180958117.

8. Said, *Culture and Imperialism*, xxiii.

9. Said, *Culture and Imperialism*, 12.

10. Willie James Jennings, *The Christian Imagination: Theology and the Origins of Race* (New Haven: Yale University Press, 2010), 2–4 (emphasis added).

11. Said, *Culture and Imperialism*, 59.

12. Said, *Culture and Imperialism*, xiii–xiv.

13. Said, *Culture and Imperialism*, 11.

14. *The Complete Poetry and Prose of William Blake*, ed. David V. Erdman (Berkeley: University of California Press, 1982), 636.

15. Daniel Defoe, *Robinson Crusoe*, ed. Thomas Keymer and James Kelly, Oxford World Classics (New York: Oxford University Press, 2007), 85.

16. Defoe, *Robinson Crusoe*, 203.

17. Lance Morrow, *God and Mammon: Chronicles of American Money* (New York: Encounter, 2020), 57.

18. Charles Boyle, "Robinson Crusoe at 300: Why It's Time to Let Go of This Toxic Colonial Fairytale," *Guardian*, April 19, 2019, https://www.theguardian.com/books/2019/apr/19/robinson-crusoe-at-300-its-time-to-let-go-of-this-toxic-colonial-fairytale.

19. James Joyce, quoted in Morrow, *God and Mammon*, 44.

20. Morrow, *God and Mammon*, 44.

21. Morrow, *God and Mammon*, 47.

22. C. S. Lewis, *The Magician's Nephew* (New York: HarperCollins, 1955), 4.

23. Said, *Culture and Imperialism*, xvi–xvii.

24. Catherine Robson, *The Norton Anthology of English Literature: The Victorian Age*, 10th ed. (New York: Norton, 2018), 941–42.

25. Robson, *Norton Anthology of English Literature*, 970n.

26. Rudyard Kipling, "The White Man's Burden," available at The Kipling Society, https://www.kiplingsociety.co.uk/poem/poems_burden.htm.

27. Said, *Culture and Imperialism*, 10.

28. Morrow, *God and Mammon*, 2.

29. Cotton Mather, "A Christian at His Calling," quoted in Robert S. Michaelsen, "Changes in the Puritan Concept of Calling or Vocation," *New England Quarterly* 26, no. 3 (September 1953).

30. Morrow, *God and Mammon*, 5–7.

31. Morrow, *God and Mammon*, 1–2.

32. Donald Davie, *A Gathered Church: The Literature of the English Dissenting Interest, 1700–1930* (Oxford: Routledge & Kegan Paul, 1978), 13.

33. Marty, *Righteous Empire*, 101.

34. Frances FitzGerald, *The Evangelicals: The Struggle to Shape America* (New York: Simon & Schuster, 2017), 4.

35. Marty, *Righteous Empire*, 15, 67, 89–90.

36. I am indebted to Scot McKnight for making this observation during a talk he gave at the Restore conference held at Judson University on May 21, 2022.

37. Timothy Gloege, *Guaranteed Pure: The Moody Bible Institute, Business, and the Making of Modern Evangelicalism* (Chapel Hill: University of North Carolina Press, 2015), 2.

38. Gloege, *Guaranteed Pure*, 6–7.

39. Gloege, *Guaranteed Pure*, 41–65; Myron Raymond Chartier, "The Social Views of Dwight L. Moody and Their Relation to the Workingman of 1860–1900," *Fort Hays Studies Series*, no. 6 (August 1969), https://scholars.fhsu.edu/cgi/viewcontent.cgi?article=1039&context=fort_hays_studies_series.

40. Gloege, *Guaranteed Pure*, 117.

41. Gloege, *Guaranteed Pure*, 225.

42. Gloege, *Guaranteed Pure*, 233.

43. Sarah Pulliam Bailey, "Preachers and Their $5,000 Sneakers: Why One Man Started an Instagram Account Showing Churches' Wealth," *Washington Post*, March 22, 2021, https://www.washingtonpost.com/religion/2021/03/22/preachers-sneakers-instagram-wealth.

44. Gloege, *Guaranteed Pure*, 4–5.

45. Gloege, *Guaranteed Pure*, 2–3.

46. Bruce Barton, *The Man Nobody Knows* (repr., Chicago: Ivan R. Dee, 2000), 9.

47. Barton, *Man Nobody Knows*, 6.

48. Barton, *Man Nobody Knows*, 13.

49. Barton, *Man Nobody Knows*, 75.

50. Barton, *Man Nobody Knows*, 4.

51. Barton, *Man Nobody Knows*, 52.

52. Barton, *Man Nobody Knows*, 3.

53. Richard M. Fried, introduction to Barton, *Man Nobody Knows*, vii–ix. It does not seem insignificant that Barton, who became a US congressman in 1938, praised the fascist leader Benito Mussolini. "Rival Says Barton Advocated Fascism," *New York Times*, October 22, 1937, p. 14.

54. Marty, *Righteous Empire*, 259.

55. Kenneth L. Woodward, John Barnes, and Laurie Lisle, "Born Again! The Year of the Evangelicals," *Newsweek*, October 26, 1976, p. 68, quoted in FitzGerald, *Evangelicals*, 289.

56. Matthew Avery Sutton, *American Apocalypse: A History of Modern Evangelicalism* (Cambridge, MA: Belknap, 2014), 368.

57. Gloege, *Guaranteed Pure*, 14.

58. FitzGerald, *Evangelicals*, 147.

59. When my own city hosted a Billy Graham crusade in the late 1980s, my church participated in the event. We were a small, independent, conservative congregation, and the event, as well as our participation, was controversial within our larger community of like-minded believers: Graham was

viewed as too liberal and too ecumenical. It is strange within the context of the political, cultural, and evangelical developments that have taken place over the past few years to realize that I come from a time and place in which Billy Graham was viewed as liberal, one of many unsettling points for me throughout the process of thinking about and writing this book.

60. FitzGerald, *Evangelicals*, 17–78.

61. Marty, *Righteous Empire*, 257.

62. Cited in Kevin Kruse, *One Nation under God: How Corporate America Invented Christian America* (New York: Basic Books, 2015), 51.

63. Ronald Reagan, "Acceptance of the Republican Nomination," PBS Primary Source Documents, July 17, 1980, http://www.shoppbs.pbs.org /wgbh/amex/reagan/filmmore/reference/primary/acceptance.html.

64. FitzGerald, *Evangelicals*, 209.

65. Susan Friend Harding, *The Book of Jerry Falwell: Fundamentalist Language and Politics* (Princeton: Princeton University Press, 2000), 15–16.

66. Jack Jenkins, "Liberty University Is No Longer the Largest Christian University," *Religion News*, April 27, 2018, https://religionnews.com/2018 /04/27/liberty-university-is-no-longer-the-largest-christian-university.

67. Harding, *Book of Jerry Falwell*, 15–16.

68. Harding, *Book of Jerry Falwell*, 15.

69. Harding, *Book of Jerry Falwell*, 15.

70. As an English professor, I deal with plagiarism. A lot. Plagiarism can occur both purposefully and unintentionally. While intentional plagiarism is more immoral, unintentional plagiarism also wrongs others and oneself. It is still plagiarism.

71. Harding, *Book of Jerry Falwell*, 258.

72. Harding, *Book of Jerry Falwell*, 122–24.

73. I was an English professor at Liberty University from 1999 to 2020. My time there was overwhelmingly rewarding and joyful. After announcing my departure, a vice president who I hadn't seen in some time, saw me and said, with smiling lips and serious eyes, "Traitor!" I must have looked taken aback for he quickly added he was "just kidding." I can't help but think upon this exchange when I read the quote from Rabbi Heschel that comes next.

74. Abraham Joshua Heschel, *The Insecurity of Freedom: Essays on Human Existence* (New York: Farrar, Straus & Giroux, 1966), 12.

75. Jane Mayer, "Donald Trump's Ghostwriter Tells All," *New Yorker*, July 18, 2016, https://www.newyorker.com/magazine/2016/07/25/donald -trumps-ghostwriter-tells-all.

76. Mayer, "Donald Trump's Ghostwriter Tells All."

77. Mayer, "Donald Trump's Ghostwriter Tells All."

78. Trent Reznor, interview by Geoff Rickly, *Alternative Press*, June 26, 2004, https://web.archive.org/web/20171015203101/http://www.then inhotline.net/archives/articles/manager/display_article.php?id=11.

79. Wikipedia, s.v. "List of Awards and Nominations Received by Johnny Cash," last modified March 11, 2022, https://en.wikipedia.org/wiki/List_of_awards_and_nominations_received_by_Johnny_Cash.

80. On this note, I commend this essay on Cash: Hannah Anderson, "The Masculinity Debate Needs Johnny Cash," *Christianity Today*, July 12, 2022, https://www.christianitytoday.com/ct/2022/july-web-only/masculinity-manhood-debate-needs-johnny-cash.html.

Chapter 10 Reformation

1. Geoffrey Chaucer, "General Prologue," in *The Canterbury Tales*, in *The Riverside Chaucer* (Boston: Houghton Mifflin, 1987), 23–36.

2. Chaucer, "Pardoner's Prologue," in *Canterbury Tales*, 194–96.

3. Chaucer, "Pardoner's Tale," in *Canterbury Tales*, 196–202.

4. Martin Luther, "To the Christian Nobility of the German Nation, Concerning the Reform of the Christian Estate 1520," in *The Christian in Society 1*, ed. James Atkinson, trans. Charles M. Jacobs, Vol. 44 of *Luther's Works*, ed. Helmut Lehmann (Philadelphia: Fortress, 1966), 126.

5. Samuel Loncar, "The Protestant Reformation as a Metaphysical Revolution," *Marginalia Review of Books*, October 26, 2017, https://themarginalia review.com/protestant-reformation-metaphysical-revolution.

6. For a reading that reintegrates religion and politics, see N. T. Wright, "Paul and Caesar: A New Reading of Romans," in *A Royal Priesthood? The Use of the Bible Ethically and Politically: A Dialogue with Oliver O'Donovan*, ed. Craig Bartholomew, Jonathan Chaplin, Robert Song, and Al Wolters (Grand Rapids: Zondervan Academic, 2002), 173–93.

7. See Carl R. Trueman, *The Rise and Triumph of the Modern Self: Cultural Amnesia, Expressive Individualism, and the Road to Sexual Revolution* (Wheaton: Crossway, 2020).

8. David W. Bebbington, *Evangelicalism in Modern Britain: A History from the 1730s to the 1980s* (London: Taylor & Francis, 2003), 10–12.

9. "John 14:6," NASB Lexicon, Bible Hub, accessed August 5, 2022, https://biblehub.com/lexicon/john/14-6.htm.

10. Mark Vernon, *A Secret History of Christianity: Jesus, the Last Inkling, and the Evolution of Consciousness* (Winchester, UK: Christian Alternative, 2019), 28–41.

11. Marshall McLuhan, "Electric Consciousness and the Church," in *The Medium and the Light: Reflections on Religion and Media*, ed. Eric McLuhan and Jacek Szklarek (Eugene, OR: Wipf & Stock, 2010), 81.

12. Vernon, *Secret History of Christianity*, 27.

13. Mark Vernon and Malcolm Guite have done a lot of work exploring these ideas in detail. See, e.g., Vernon and Guite, interview by Justin Brierley, "The Faith of the Inklings, with Malcolm Guite," *Unbelievable*, August 9, 2019, available at https://www.markvernon.com/the-faith-of-the-inklings -with-malcolm-guite; Malcolm Guite, panel discussion at "Evolving Consciousness: Spiritual Experience in a Secular Age," Scientific and Medical Network with the Fetzer Institute, London, November 30, 2019, available at https://youtu.be/zRFNM6mqLg4; Mark Vernon, "The Mossy Face of Christ," *Mark Vernon—Talks and Thoughts* (podcast), June 14, 2022, https:// www.buzzsprout.com/1574515/10791825-the-mossy-face-of-christ-martin -shaw-talks-w-mark-vernon-about-an-unexpected-return-to-christianity.

14. Alan Noble, "Your Education Is Not Your Own," lecture, Lamppost Conference, Oklahoma Baptist University, September 2, 2022.

15. Martin Luther King Jr., *Where Do We Go from Here: Chaos or Community?* (Boston: Beacon, 1968), 181.

16. Christian Smith and Melinda Lundquist Denton, *Soul Searching: The Religious and Spiritual Lives of American Teenagers* (New York: Oxford University Press, 2005).

17. Pope Francis, "Homily of His Holiness Pope Francis," Notre-Dame de Québec Basilica Cathedral, July 28, 2022, https://slmedia.org/blog/pope -francis-homily-at-vespers-in-notre-dame-de-quebec-cathedral.

18. I confess that when I first wrote this sentence, I was thinking about other people. By the time I was making my final revisions to the manuscript, I realized that I needed these words—and needed to heed them too.

19. John Stott, "The Lausanne Covenant: An Exposition and Commentary," Lausanne Occasional Paper 3 (Lausanne Committee for World Evangelization, 1975), https://lausanne.org/content/lop/lop-3.

Chapter 11 Rapture

1. Robert G. Couse, Robert N. Hosack, and Richard V. Pierard, *The New Millennium Manual: A Once and Future Guide* (Grand Rapids: Baker, 1999), 46–70.

2. Susan Friend Harding, *The Book of Jerry Falwell: Fundamentalist Language and Politics* (Princeton: Princeton University Press, 2000), 236.

3. Matthew Avery Sutton, *American Apocalypse: A History of Modern Evangelicalism* (Cambridge, MA: Belknap, 2014), 16.

4. Crawford Gribben, *Writing the Rapture: Prophecy Fiction in Evangelical America* (New York: Oxford University Press, 2009), 5–6; Daniel Silliman, *Reading Evangelicals: How Christian Fiction Shaped a Culture and a Faith* (Grand Rapids: Eerdmans, 2021), 92–93.

5. Gribben, *Writing the Rapture*, 8.

6. A longer version of this story appears in my memoir, *Booked: Literature in the Soul of Me* (Ossining, NY: T. S. Poetry Press, 2012), 84–85.

7. Gribben, *Writing the Rapture*, 16.

8. Silliman, *Reading Evangelicals*, 127.

9. Sutton, *American Apocalypse*, 369.

10. Gribben, *Writing the Rapture*, 16.

11. Ken Camp, "Tim LaHaye: Religious Right Wing Leader and 'Left Behind' Author, Dead at 90," *Baptist Standard*, July 26, 2016, https://www.baptiststandard.com/news/baptists/tim-lahaye-religious-right-leader-and-left-behind-co-author-dead-at-90.

12. Silliman, *Reading Evangelicals*, 94.

13. Silliman, *Reading Evangelicals*, 95.

14. Sutton, *American Apocalypse*, 326–31.

15. Robert Dreyfuss, "Reverend Doomsday," *Rolling Stone*, January 28, 2004.

16. Silliman, *Reading Evangelicals*, 96.

17. Sutton, *American Apocalypse*, 5.

18. Sutton, *American Apocalypse*, 359.

19. Sutton, *American Apocalypse*, 353.

20. Paul Boyer, "Give Me That End-Time Religion: The Politization of Prophetic Belief in Contemporary America," *Reflections*, Spring 2005, https://reflections.yale.edu/article/end-times-and-end-gamesis-scripture-being-left-behind/give-me-end-time-religion.

21. Sutton, *American Apocalypse*, 9.

22. Silliman, *Reading Evangelicals*, 98.

23. Gribben, *Writing the Rapture*, 10.

24. Silliman, *Reading Evangelicals*, 108.

25. Silliman, *Reading Evangelicals*, 55–56.

26. Commercial fiction is not literary fiction, and it is perfectly fine for it not to be. The problem arises when a culture (or subculture) does not even know that there is such a thing as literary art and how it differs from other kinds of works.

27. "Singer's Plug Puts 'This Present Darkness' in Spotlight: Fundamentalist Novel Finds Wide Appeal," *LA Times*, September 23, 1989, quoted in Silliman, *Reading Evangelicals*, 58.

28. Jason C. Bivins, *Religion of Fear: The Politics of Horror in Conservative Evangelicalism* (Oxford: Oxford University Press, 2008), 178.

29. Silliman, *Reading Evangelicals*, 71.

30. Gribben, *Writing the Rapture*, 3–4.

31. Marek Oziewicz, "Joseph Campbell's 'New Mythology' and the Rise of Mythopoeic Fantasy," *The Free Library*, January 1, 2007, https://www

.thefreelibrary.com/Joseph+Campbell%27s+%22new+mythology%22+and
+the+rise+of+mythopoeic+fantasy.-a0225938526.

32. See Tara Isabella Burton, *Strange Rites: New Religions for a Godless World* (New York: PublicAffairs, 2020).

33. Flannery O'Connor, "The Fiction Writer and His Country," in *Mystery and Manners: Occasional Prose*, ed. Robert Fitzgerald and Sally Fitzgerald (New York: Farrar, Straus & Giroux, 1970), 34.

34. In *A Secular Age* (Cambridge, MA: Harvard University Press, 2007), Charles Taylor describes the centuries-long process of the secularization of the world as one that becomes disenchanted. Before the secular age, belief in God (or gods) and the supernatural was the default. In this way, the world was "enchanted," whereas in the modern world, as Taylor shows, such belief is no longer assumed. Even when it is held, it is chosen from among other possibilities.

35. I am indebted to a fantastic thread in the *Close Reads* podcast discussion group on Facebook for helping me flesh out this idea.

36. Samuel Coleridge, *The Statesman's Manual: or, The Bible the best guide to political skill and foresight: a lay sermon, addressed to the higher classes of society, with an appendix, containing comments and essays connected with the study of the inspired writings* (London: Gale and Fenner, 1816), 37.

37. Peter Cheyne, *Coleridge's Contemplative Philosophy* (Oxford: Oxford University Press, 2020), 113.

38. Cheyne, *Coleridge's Contemplative Philosophy*, 118.

39. Gribben, *Writing the Rapture*, 7.

40. Sutton, *American Apocalypse*, 373.

41. Sutton, *American Apocalypse*, 372.

42. "The Chicago Statement on Biblical Inerrancy," 1978, https://www
.etsjets.org/files/documents/Chicago_Statement.pdf.

43. Edmund Gosse, *Father and Son* (1907; repr., Oxford: Oxford University Press, 2009), 41.

44. Gosse, *Father and Son*, 42.

45. Edmund Gosse's father, Philip Henry Gosse, was a naturalist who is most remembered for his 1857 book, *Omphalos: An Attempt to Untie the Geological Knot*, which proposed the novel young-earth theory that God created the world with fossils that only appeared to be millions of years old, a theory that was widely scorned by his contemporaries.

46. Gosse, *Father and Son*, 186.

47. This passage is adapted from my journal article, "The Importance of Being Earnest: The Aesthetics of Evangelical Sincerity," *Southeastern Theological Review* 12, no. 2 (Fall 2021): 85–98.

48. George Orwell, *1984* (New York: Signet, 1961), 212.

49. "'I Don't Trust the CDC': Trump Rally Attendee on Why She Is Unvaccinated," *Anderson Cooper 360*, August 24, 2021, https://www.cnn .com/videos/business/2021/08/24/donie-osullivan-trump-supporters -ac360-biz-vpx.cnn.

50. Peter Leithart, "Image of God: What Does It Really Mean?," Anselm Society: Why We Create Series, March 27, 2022, https://www.anselmsociety .org/blog/2021/10/12/greatstory-d754l-c35t3-72t5a-wj82l-dm9la.

51. Calvin Woodward and Eric Tucker, "January 6th Hearings Traced an Arc of Carnage Wrought by Trump," *Washington Post*, July 23, 2022, https:// www.washingtonpost.com/politics/jan-6-hearings-traced-an-arc-of-carnage -wrought-by-trump/2022/07/23/f6437782-0a3c-11ed-80b6-43f2bfcc6662 _story.html.

52. Sutton, *American Apocalypse*, 16.

53. Roger Lundin, "Offspring of an Odd Union: Evangelical Attitudes toward the Arts," in *Evangelicalism and Modern America*, ed. George Marsden (Grand Rapids: Eerdmans, 1984), 135–49.

54. Jack T. Chick, *You Have a Date* (US: Chick Publications, 2011), 11.

55. N. T. Wright, "Farewell to the Rapture," *Bible Review*, August 2001, https://ntwrightpage.com/2016/07/12/farewell-to-the-rapture.

56. Shout-out to Crosby, Stills, Nash, and Young.

57. G. K. Beale, *A New Testament Biblical Theology: The Unfolding of the Old Testament in the New* (Grand Rapids: Baker Academic, 2011), 856–58.

58. O'Connor, "The Teaching of Literature," in *Mystery and Manners*, 124.

59. "Where Did the Term 'Rapture' Come From?," Bible.org, January 1, 2001, https://bible.org/question/where-did-term-8216rapture%E2%80 %99-come.

60. John Donne, "Batter My Heart, Three-Person'd God," holy sonnet 10, available at https://www.poetryfoundation.org/poems/44106/holy -sonnets-batter-my-heart-three-persond-god.